The Millionaire Castaway

The Incredible Story Of How I Lost My Fortune But Found New Riches Living On A Deserted Island.

David Glasheen
With Neil Bramwell

16pt

Read How You Want
LARGE PRINT BOOKS, BRAILLE & DAISY

Copyright Page from the Original Book

Affirmpress
books that leave an impression

Published by Affirm Press in 2019
28 Thistlethwaite Street, South Melbourne, VIC 3205.
www.affirmpress.com.au

Text and copyright © Dave Glasheen and Neil Bramwell
All rights reserved. No part of this publication may be reproduced
without prior permission of the publisher.

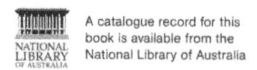

A catalogue record for this book is available from the National Library of Australia

Title: The Millionaire Castaway/ Dave Glasheen and Neil Bramwell, authors

Cover design by Christabell Designs.
Image of Dave Glasheen on back cover by Brian Cassey Photographer.
Typeset in Granjon 12.5/18 pt
Proudly printed in Australia by Griffin Press

Every effort has been made to acknowledge and contact the owners of copyright for permission to reproduce material. Any copyright owners who have inadvertently been omitted from acknowledgements and credits should contact the publisher and omissions will be rectified in subsequent editions.

TABLE OF CONTENTS

Introduction	viii
Chapter 1: Down and out	1
Chapter 2: Restoration	26
Chapter 3: Go home	56
Chapter 4: Nature's bounty	89
Chapter 5: Father time	123
Chapter 6: Boxhead	153
Chapter 7: Quassi	181
Chapter 8: Miranda	214
Chapter 9: Sink or swim	242
Chapter 10: Visiting time	267
Chapter 11: Ricky	291
Chapter 12: Kinship	321
Chapter 13: The slap	343
Chapter 14: The battle of Resto	361
Chapter 15: Sorrow	388
Chapter 16: Survival	404
Chapter 17: Solo	425
Epilogue	451
Acknowledgements	470
Back Cover Material	496

Neil Bramwell is a Melbourne-based award-winning journalist and author of numerous books, including *Foggy,* the number one bestselling autobiography of motorcycle racer, Carl Fogarty. He first saw Dave on *Martin Clunes: Islands of Australia* and was spellbound. He still is.

David Glasheen is the former chairman of a publicly-listed company, who has lived alone on the deserted Restoration Island off the coast of Far North Queensland since 1997. His incredible life has been the subject of several international television documentaries. This is his first book.

'Dave Glasheen is a 21st-century Robinson Crusoe. A man marooned from 21st-century financial woes on his very own desert island in the Coral Sea close to Papua New Guinea. His story, as you will soon discover, is wild, eccentric, romantic and sad. His life is as extraordinary as the man himself. I don't use that word lightly. I have been fortunate to travel the world meeting amazing people but Dave transcends the term. He is a whirlwind of energy, conversation, debate, theory, ideas and plans.

I first met Dave nearly seven years ago when I visited him as part of my series *Where the Wildmen Are.* I spent ten days living with him on Restoration Island. Dave probably doesn't realise it but he had a profound impact on my own life. His story was the catalyst that has since taken me to more than fifty other people who have abandoned their urban lives for new lives in the wild. His story blends romance, eccentricity, loss, and a man principled enough to take on the state for the right to stay on his beloved island, Resto.

I have been lucky enough to revisit Dave since. He made me question my own principles, hopes and dreams. Once you meet Dave, you never forget him. Dave is a man of principle and conviction. Non-conformist and fiercely opinionated, he is kind and funny. I often find myself thinking about Dave, living alone on that remote island. I find myself worrying and marvelling in equal measure. Dave changed my life and maybe, just maybe, his story will also change yours.'

– Ben Fogle, TV presenter, bestselling author and United Nations Patron of the Wilderness.

For Erika Ruby Glasheen.

Aboriginal and Torres Strait Islander readers are warned that this book contains the names and dialogue of deceased persons. All care has been taken to preserve and respect the original meaning of these words.

The authors are also mindful that much of the book is set on Restoration Island and we thank the Traditional Owners of this land, the Kuuku Ya'u and pay our respects to Elders past and present.

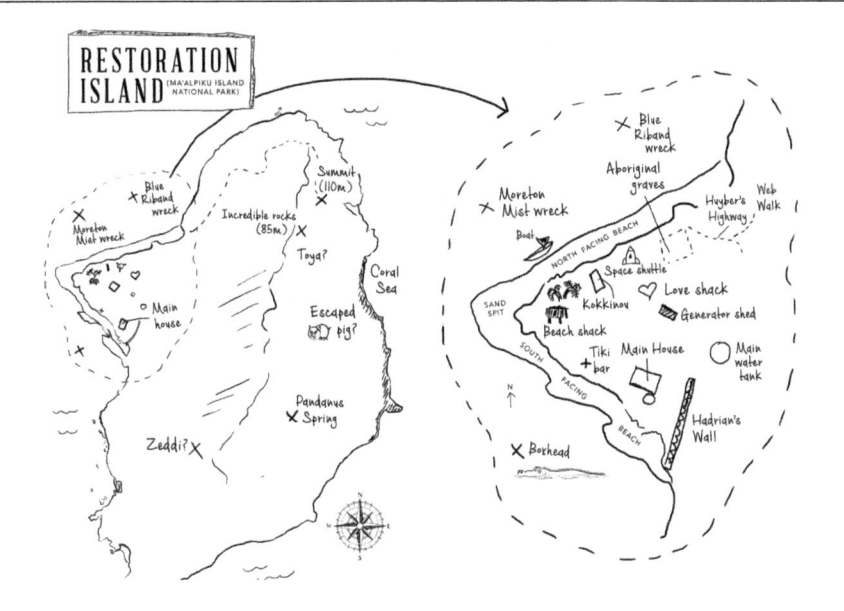

Introduction

'For once, will you just listen to me, please,' Dave Nissen barked through the phone. 'The bureau has got this all wrong. This cyclone's not hitting Cooktown, it's heading right towards Resto. I reckon you have twenty-four hours to get yourself out of there. Oh, and before you leave, make sure my boat's safe.'

Shit, I thought. *This doesn't sound good.* When Dave Nissen said jump, you asked how high. He was a big Viking of a man who had seen it all – a real bushie, who made his money building power stations. Dave had been a regular visitor to the island since my mate Hippy Richard first brought him up here for some fishing. Some of his values were a bit rough around the edges – I didn't agree with a few of his opinions on Aboriginal issues – but at heart he was a gentle giant and a humanist, who would do anything for anyone. He also knew practically everyone on the Cape York Peninsula and had the ear of all the key people in Cairns.

This fact was made clear to me on the day I received a phone call minutes after I'd returned from a trip to Restoration Rock, a small island of granite about one kilometre east of Restoration Island, to load some coral into the boat. There's one particular spot on the rock where it's hard to land, and the coral is pushed up to form gleaming white ledges. I crush up this coral and use it for the floor of the kitchen. It makes it look homey, especially when it's been freshly raked, but it also absorbs any spills before the ants can get to them. Most visitors complain that it's impossible to walk on without thongs, but the soles of my feet are like elephant hide from years of walking barefoot everywhere, so I don't feel a thing. Taking the coral is not strictly legit, but I figure that I wasn't actually removing it from the reef.

'Is that Mr Glasheen? The guy who lives on his own on Restoration Island?' asked a muffled voice on the phone.

'Yes, who's this?' I replied.

'Never mind who this is. I have reason to believe that you have just relocated a quantity of protected coral from an area of national parkland. That is a serious offence. What do you have to say for yourself?' What the hell? How could anyone know that? Was this God calling?

'I've no idea what you're talking about, sir,' I spluttered. Dave couldn't contain himself any longer and burst out laughing.

'It's Nissen, you prick. I'm in the customs office and they are trying out some new drones. These things are amazing. We saw you head over to the rock in the boat. I could tell you weren't fishing, so I reckoned there was only one other reason you'd be at that spot. You'd better watch your step from now on, eh? And put some clothes on, will ya?'

The bastard had done me up like a kipper. But drones – really? That was worse than having CCTV outside your house. I thought I'd escaped Big Brother when I came to live here, and I didn't like the idea of being spied on one little bit. So I later had a word with the bosses at the customs office, and promised them that they would be the first to know if I saw anything dodgy.

And plenty of smuggling goes on in these remote parts – drugs, of course, but also rare species of birds and snakes. From then on, I have been their eyes and ears, their man on the ground.

When Dave Nissen said something in earnest, he wasn't bullshitting. And there was more than a hint of alarm in his voice when he called to warn me about Cyclone Ingrid. According to all the news bulletins, she was heading well south of Lockhart River, closer to Cooktown, several hundred kilometres away. But television stations use weather reports from the Bureau of Meteorology, which bases its weather predictions on air pressure. Everyone I know around here uses Buoy Weather, which uses satellite technology to monitor sea levels and marine conditions. And, according to Buoy, Ingrid was making a beeline for Resto. Plus, Dave would not have called me if he wasn't genuinely worried for my safety.

'I've seen some tasty storms here already,' I said. 'I reckon I'll be fine, but I promise I won't take any chances.'

'Look, it's up to you. But don't say I didn't warn you,' he said, frustrated, and hung up.

It was true – there had been some wild weather since I had been living on the island. Winds speeds of 100 kilometres per hour were not uncommon in the wet season, but they were forecasting wind speeds of around 250 kilometres per hour for Ingrid. It's generally thought to be impossible to stand up at speeds of around 200 kilometres per hour. Maybe I did need to rethink this. I had no doubt that what Dave said was true, I just had to figure out the best course of action. And it wasn't just me and Quassi, my fearless four-legged friend, I had to worry about. As I put down the phone, I looked out the window at my two Japanese wwoofers, Nanako and Asami, weeding the pumpkin patch and jabbering happily away, oblivious to the imminent danger.

WWOOFers – World Wide Opportunities on Organic Farms – is a scheme to promote non-monetary cultural experiences for travellers. Most of my wwoofers were backpackers who wanted a unique remote island experience on their travels around Australia. After months on the road, most were ready and willing to roll up their sleeves and get their hands dirty doing various jobs around the island in exchange for a free stay and food for a couple of weeks. Not these two. The Japanese wwoofers were willing to work; they just weren't willing to get dirty in the process. They arrived with two brand-new suitcases on wheels, which had to be carried everywhere because, strangely enough, the wheels didn't work on sand or rough ground. Then, on their first morning, dressed in perfectly ironed white cotton shirts, they both pulled on pristine white silk gloves. 'For garden,' Nanako beamed. 'Clean.'

'No, no, no,' I said. 'No good. You wear these.' I pulled out two pairs of stinky, heavy-duty rubber gloves and their jaws dropped. Nanako shook her head and pointed to my gloves.

'No! Very dirty,' she said, grimacing. Within twenty minutes, their gloves had disintegrated into strips of cloth, so they went back to their suitcases and dug out another pair each. There was a pair for every day of their stay. And a new clean shirt. There was no way that these two would survive a storm, let alone a full-blown cyclone. Even if I was going to stay here with Quassi, I had to move the wwoofers from the island. By now, the sky was overcast and the wind had picked up. There was no time to lose, although the sea was already very choppy and I didn't really want to risk a trip to the mainland, especially if I wasn't sure I would be able to make it back. When in doubt, call the fishos.

The numerous local trawler captains and their crews were regular visitors to Resto. The bay was a beaut of a natural harbour for them to drop anchor for the night, and we often traded company, yarns, fish and grog around the camp fire. That day, the nearest fisho was a Vietnamese bloke called Wye Ng. Ironically, most of the boats had headed north on the basis of the bureau report, before Buoy produced the more accurate update. There was no time to head back south and many were effectively stranded in the area. Their only option was to sail up Lockhart River, drop anchor and lash themselves together to increase their critical mass. No cyclone was going to lift twenty boats out of the water, and the trees on the banks would provide shelter. Once secured, there was little else for them all to do except drink grog – a good old-fashioned hurricane party. Wye was heading for the river when I called him, and we agreed that I would meet him with the girls in the tinny. Now I had to try to explain to them what the hell was going on.

'See boat. You go boat. Big *whooooosh*,' I said, pointing to the trees, which were now starting to bend in the wind, and doing my best hurricane impression. The girls looked at me blankly. I staggered around, pretending to fight my way against the wind. I thought it was a pretty good performance, but the girls stared wide-eyed, clearly thinking that their trusted host had lost his marbles. So I hustled them over to their sleeping area, grabbed their bags and led them down to the beach. It had finally dawned on them that something significant was happening. Asami started to sob and was comforted by Nanako, the more confident of the two.

'Look after them, mate,' I said to Wye, as the girls climbed nervously onto his boat. 'Maybe ask the deckies to sleep on one of the other boats. They'll feel safer without so many blokes around.'

'You come too, Davo. This look very bad,' said Wye.

'I'll be okay, don't worry about me and Quassi. I'll see you tomorrow,' I said. I'm not sure I even convinced myself. But I had to keep up the pretence, and so I waved cheerily as the dinghy disappeared with the girls, terror in their eyes as the lively sea tossed them around. It was early afternoon, and Dave Nissen had predicted that Ingrid would be calling by early the next morning. The heaviest storms always tend to coincide with high tides, so I had around four hours of daylight left in which to make all the preparations. My first priority was to secure my prized possessions. And that proved to be a mistake.

The aim was to pile up everything in the middle of the house and cover it with a tarpaulin, which I would then secure to the walls. If worst came to worst, and the roof was blown off the house, these items would stay safe and dry. I had collected plenty of washed-up tarpaulins from around the island in just a few years, but when I'd told myself I was saving them for a rainy day, I wasn't expecting quite this much rain. Outside, the wind had reached a gentle howl and the rain was already relentless. Travelling the sixty metres to and from the storage shed was no fun, so I loaded anything of use – rope, nets, wires – into my wheelbarrow to take back to the house in one trip. Quassi never left my side. This was one smart dog – he sensed my anxiety and stayed close for his own protection, and to reassure me.

At the bottom of the pile, I placed waterproof boxes filled with pictures, books and important documents. If any water did come into the house, those items would remain dry no matter what. Then I stacked tables and chairs on top of the boxes and jammed into the spaces any loose objects that might fly away, like pots and pans and bric-a-brac. Finally, I threw my mattress on the top for extra weight. I covered everything with a huge fishing net and tied that to the walls, just in case the tarpaulin didn't hold, and then added the tarpaulin and secured it in the same way. It looked like a big bonfire, but it was rock-steady; Ingrid would have to be one feisty lady to shift this. I left one chair free to rest in after I finished my preparations, and to take to the old generator shed, where I would sit out the cyclone. The shed door faced the hill, out of the wind, and the trees around the hut provided more cover than the house. My final job was to check for any loose pieces of roofing that might catch the wind and tie them down securely. I worked calmly and efficiently, but hurriedly.

Then the phone stopped me in my tracks. 'Dave, it's Gary from the police station. Someone just told me you're still on the island. We need you and your visitors off there now, mate. The cyclone's heading right for Lockhart River and the whole town has been evacuated and everyone is spending the night in the station, hospital, church or the town hall. We can't be responsible for your safety if you stay there,' he said.

'I'm responsible for my own safety, not you,' I replied, quite tetchily. Didn't they realise that now it would be more dangerous to try and take the boat across to the mainland than to stay put? 'Anyway, I reckon my shed is the safest place around here. But maybe just check on me when it's all over, okay?' I knew the cyclone would likely knock out the phones, and I didn't want to be stranded here if anything did go awry.

'Righto! And good luck,' he said. Did I hear him mutter 'You're going to need it' as he put the phone down?

Stage two of my preparation was to secure the boats. Why the hell had I not done that first? The palm trees were already protesting at the bullying wind, and dead branches were being propelled into the gathering gloom. The older coconuts were loosening in their trees, too, and I had to keep my wits about me to make sure one of these missiles didn't take me out. I was always careful about standing under trees, even on the calmest of days, for that very reason. Even without the added propulsion of the wind, you would be lucky to survive if one of these bastards dropped on your head from a great height.

There were two boats to secure. The priority was my fibreglass boat – not only was it the heaviest, but it was also my lifeline. Dragging it to shore was not much of a problem, although lifting the anchor was no easy task as, even in the heart of the sheltered bay, the waves were making it hard to stand in the water. Using a few pipes as rollers, I heaved her up to the high-tide mark, though it was likely the water would rise during the night. First, I secured the prow around one of the biggest trees with a length of good, heavy rope that I had found on one of my scouting missions around the island. Finding rope was always a treat. One time out in the boat, I spotted some of that really strong tiger rope used by fishos, and thought Christmas had come early. I leaned over the side to scoop it out of the water, then had the fright of my life when a beautiful yellow and brown snake darted away.

Even tying my boat to the tree was not enough insurance in these winds, and I spent the best part of an hour frantically filling her with sand to make sure that she didn't flip. It was back-breaking work and, despite the rain, the air was still humid so I lost lots of water through sweat. Exhausted, I was tempted to leave Dave's tinny, which he had left up here for his next fishing trip, and hope for the best. But he was a good mate and had asked me specifically to take care of his boat. The light was fading quickly. I probably had another hour, tops, before total darkness, and I wanted to be back in the house before that. Wading to the boat now was a real struggle, because the tide was coming in and it was almost up to my waist. There was no way I would be able to drag her out of the water and secure her in the time I had. But I *could* remove the motor, which was worth way more than the boat itself.

I climbed aboard just as a big wave crashed in from the side, flicking me back into the water and flipping the boat upside down like a tossed coin. *That was stupid,* I told myself. If the boat had landed on my head, I would have been Ingrid's first fatality. I staggered out of the water, composed myself on the beach for a second and caught my breath, and then braced to battle the headwind back to the house. It must have taken me five minutes to complete that one-hundred-metre stretch, bent into the wind at a forty-five-degree angle to avoid being batted back to the beach, and pausing at each sturdy tree for a breather. The constant sheet of rain was almost blinding, and the screech of the wind through the trees was ear-splitting. In the chaos, I managed to pick out a dark blur as it whizzed by my head. If that coconut had made contact, it would have been like a cannon ball hitting a watermelon. Another close call – and the cyclone front would not even be here for another few hours. Back at the house, I needed rest and slumped into the one remaining chair, with Quassi curled up beneath it.

xxiii

It must have been a couple of hours before I woke to the sound of the house groaning under the constant pummelling. *Great: everything's still in place as I planned,* I thought, as I turned on the torch. Everything except me and Quassi. We were supposed to be over at the shed, and the short trip was going to be hairy. Quassi wondered what the hell I was doing when I put a makeshift lead around his neck, but I wanted to make sure he wasn't picked up along with the rest of the debris when we ventured outside, and he was too scared to object. Just from the noise, I reckoned the wind speed had picked up another fifty kilometres per hour, but I thought we could stay on our feet for the fifty metres to the shed. I tied Quassi's rope to my arm so I could pick up the chair. Another stupid mistake. Why hadn't I taken it to the shed earlier? Now, if I held the chair upright, it was going to act like a sail, so with one arm I had to almost wrap it around my stomach and edge along, the back of the chair pointing towards the wind. With my spare arm, I grabbed a bag of sandwiches I'd made earlier, a few bottles of beer and the book I was reading, *For the Term of His Natural Life* – an Aussie classic, but perhaps not the best title if I was looking for good omens.

Those fifty metres were nothing short of terrifying. It felt like, at any moment, I might lose the battle to keep my balance and we would be lifted up and dashed into the first object that obstructed our path. The torch was uncontrollable, so I could barely see where I was going. Then, only about ten metres from the safety of the shed, I completely lost my footing and the chair vanished in an instant. As I carefully picked myself up onto my knees, Quassi, happy to be joined at ground level, vigorously licked my face. Not helpful, mate. Together we half-stumbled, half-dragged ourselves the remaining few metres around the edge of the shed and into safety. The shed complained in a constant, violent rattle, but there was nothing I could do now but sit back and hope. I slumped down onto the concrete floor in the corner and put my arm around Quassi, who whimpered softly. This was going to be a very long, very scary and very uncomfortable night. On the safe side of the shed's stone wall, I tried to take stock of the ferocity we had just survived. My life had been in very real danger three times within the space of a few hours. But I wasn't wondering whether the shed would hold firm, what devastation I might find in the morning or even if we would survive the night. Instead, I was asking myself one very simple question.

David Gilronan Glasheen, how the hell did you end up here?

Chapter 1

Down and out

It was a beautiful, sunny spring afternoon in Sydney. Sitting on the balcony of the Royal Prince Alfred Yacht Club, which overlooks Pittwater's picturesque bay in the Northern Beaches, a cold beer in hand and a good friend for company: it's a snapshot of success that most people can only dream of. Hundreds of luxury boats bobbed on the glistening waters, and the only sound came from impertinent gulls, demanding to be fed. It was a setting that should have lifted the soul, but John Reynolds and I were tense and pensive. This was Saturday 17 October 1987, and the financial world was preparing for meltdown.

'Glash, spend that sixpence in your pocket wisely. You won't be earning many more over the next five years,' warned John, a big-hitter on the Sydney stock market scene and a major shareholder in my publicly listed gold-mining company, Carpenters

Investment Trading. John was a risk-taker, but he knew the markets inside out and if he was worried, I knew that I should be worried, too. The market had been jittery the whole previous week, after hostilities between Iran and Iraq created uncertainty about short-term oil supplies. The Dow Jones Index had fallen sharply in the United States and, to make matters worse, London's Great Storm had caused their stock exchange to close on the Friday, which made American share prices drop further. By then, it was Saturday morning in Australia and our hearts were in our mouths.

'Should I be selling my shares?' I asked. Over the past few years, I had built up a holding of several million company shares, which had rocketed in value from twenty-five cents each when we launched on the Australian Securities Exchange (ASX) to $1.40. These shares alone were worth around $10 million, and I also owned a 2.5-acre property in Church Point, not far from the yacht club in the Northern Beaches, plus another terraced house in McMahons Point, overlooking the harbour. I was sitting pretty, as long as my shares retained their value.

'Glash, you're the chairman and major shareholder of a publicly listed company. If you sell all your shares, the market's going to lose confidence in us and the price is going to plummet anyway. There's nothing you can do but ride it out. Right now, the best thing you can do is to go back to the bar and buy us a couple more beers,' John said, smiling. The worrying thing for me was, unlike John and most of our other directors and large shareholders, practically all my eggs were in that one basket. I had used our Church Point home – where I lived with my wife, Sylvi, and our two daughters, Samantha and Erika – as security to borrow heavily from the bank, in order to build my stock in the company. If Carpenters wobbled, my whole house of cards could come tumbling down.

Sunday and Monday were pure torment. How would the markets react when London opened for trading on Monday morning? We didn't need to wait too long to find out because late in the afternoon in Australia, after a day of feverish selling on the ASX, the financial markets in Asia began to collapse, with Hong Kong leading the way. London followed, and then two US warships shelled an Iranian oil platform. Great timing, Mr Reagan! It felt like the world was imploding. Around US$500 billion of capital disappeared in one day as Wall Street crashed and Black Monday was complete. And we knew that, in Australia, the worst was yet to come. Our country braced itself for Black Tuesday.

I prepared to go to the office as usual that morning, hoping that somehow we might be thrown a lifeline. Sylvi stopped me at the front door to give me an unexpected hug. 'Look, you know I don't ask about business stuff,' she whispered, so the girls couldn't hear. 'But I know this is serious. I can see it in your face. I just want you to know that I – we – have every faith in you. Keep a clear head, and your instincts will pull us through.'

Jeez, no pressure! With a peck on the cheek, my wife proudly sent her warrior off into battle. I just couldn't bring myself to warn her about what the next couple of days might mean for us.

At the office, I was no use to anyone; powerless to prevent everything from spiralling out of control, I was infecting everyone with my agitation. I felt that I needed to be doing something, I just didn't know what. The logical place to head to was the ASX on Bridge Street. As the head of a listed company, I was a familiar face there. I used to love watching the chalkies at work, feverishly noting down the latest prices on the huge boards. The brokers always wanted to chat to me to try and find out what our company was up to, but loose lips sink ships, as they say, and this was one of the few times in my life when I had to be very careful what I said, when I said it, and to whom. Nobody wanted to chat on this particular day. Some of the regular operators were slumped against the wall, their heads in their hands. I couldn't even enjoy the distraction of the chalkies, because a new automated system had been introduced just the previous day. So, right before my eyes, I could see the price of Carpenters shares plunge like the timer on a ticking bomb. The board was a sea of red, as the lifeblood drained out of the Australian economy. I had to get out of there and the pub seemed like the only place for sanctuary. The whole of Sydney had the same idea and the pubs were heaving as us suits drowned our collective sorrows deep into the night. It had the atmosphere of a wake. That last sixpence had been spent.

Over the two days, Australian shares were stripped of more than two-fifths of their value. Few companies were hit as hard as Carpenters was in the herd-mentality scramble to sell, sell, sell. High-risk shares are always the first to be off-loaded, and there was no doubt that Carpenters was a high-risk investment. After all, the whole company was only based on a tatty old treasure map, with an 'X' literally marking the spot where gold and platinum *might* be found in remote Papua New Guinea. The map still has pride of place on the wall of my home on Resto, a throwback to an exciting time of exploration and speculation –

the beginning of my downfall but also, indirectly, the trigger of my salvation.

The map had fallen into the hands of one of my long-standing friends, serial entrepreneur Jake Gray, when his grandfather died. It charted an area in the interior highlands of New Guinea, now known as Enga Province, and looked genuine enough. It identified swampland, sandstone cliffs and waterfalls – as well as areas where 'unfriendly natives' might be found – and could have dated back to the 1930s, when Aussie prospectors stealthily scoured the wilderness. Jake knew that I had a couple of connections in the world of mining, so I was the first person he called for advice, bubbling over with excitement. The timing was perfect for me: I was still licking my wounds from a failed business venture with my brother, Mick, called Tetra Toys and I knew from dabbling in uranium shares that it was an exciting time for the mining industry in Australia. The price of gold continued to rise considerably, but I needed an expert's second opinion before taking this giant leap of faith.

My connections led me to the door of Peter Howe Associates, part of a successful Toronto-based mining consultancy group run by John Felderhof. At the time, Felderhof was a superstar in the field who made his name when he discovered a massive gold and copper deposit called Ok Tedi in the mountains of Papua New Guinea. At one point, that mine was responsible for a quarter of all of Papua New Guinea's exports. John seemed like a good guy to have on our side, although his reputation was damaged when, more than a decade later, he was caught up in the Bre-X affair, the biggest scandal in mining history that inspired the recent Hollywood film *Gold.* John, one of the straightest guys you could meet, was charged with insider trading, and it took eight years to fully clear his name.

John's eyes lit up when I showed him the map and, rather than sell him the rights, I found myself funding an exploratory expedition to Papua New Guinea. Back in Sydney, I waited nervously for the initial geological report, which was glowing. There was a very good chance of finding substantial amounts of gold in that region. But to find the gold, we would have to drill for the gold. And to drill for the gold, we would have to buy the rights to drill on the land. And that meant paying rent to the Papua New Guinean government per square kilometre. Our map covered an area of 2500 square kilometres – about one per cent of the size of Victoria. It was vast. We were going to have to raise some serious dough. Fortunately, my little black book was full of wealthy and influential contacts who were more than willing to take a punt on our shelf company, called Brisa.

Jake was our man on the ground in Papua New Guinea and, instead of pegging the 200 square kilometres that he and our geologist described as the sweet spot, we pegged a total 25,000 square kilometres – more than one-third of the size of Tasmania. The Papua New Guinea mines department was very excited by this ambitious new exploration company from Sydney, and provided lots of support, and we turned down offers of capital from the professional investment community in Australia. People were ringing me up offering half a million dollars for a slice of the action. But that would have meant diluting our own shareholdings. We didn't want that much – and didn't *need* that much until we started drilling. However, whenever we did need a capital raise, as company chairman I had to lead by example and put my hand in my pocket. For instance, when our Brisa consortium bought control of a dormant existing listed company, Carpenters, in order to go public in April 1987, we raised $2 million, which dragged me into serious debt. The bank was happy to continue to loan money to me against the security of our home because we planned to subdivide the land, which would increase its value considerably.

I always had a nagging doubt that the company's risk, and therefore my own, was spread too thinly. So I tried to convince our board to diversify into insurance and a US frozen yoghurt company; but we were like magpies, distracted by the glitter of gold. The prospects of finding gold looked good, though, and Carpenters was one of the darlings of the stock exchange. I ate, drank and slept business, often at the expense of our family life. I started work early and came home late, fuelled by the cut and thrust of high-end finance. Sydney was a financial playground and I was suddenly a big player, backed by some very clever business brains. The future of Carpenters – not to mention that of Dave Glasheen – looked very bright.

That was before Black Tuesday. Within six months of listing at twenty-five cents, and peaking at $1.40, shares in the company slumped to just two cents. My assets had vanished overnight. It would have been enough to push some people over the edge, but my response was to dig deep and work harder. I scoured the world for a solution, and we came close. An Australian company called Crestwin almost baled us out before going bust themselves. Then Adolf Lundin – who was the man behind a powerful Swedish oil and mining company and sponsored Ronald Reagan's election campaign – showed serious interest.

All the while, our efforts to strike gold in Papua New Guinea continued, but now on a tight budget because we no longer had the capacity to raise more capital. However, we managed to peg a new, nearly one-hundred-square-kilometre plot near the Hawain River, including some ocean, and flew out a rig that we had built in Australia. At the time it felt like everything was riding on this last throw of the dice. Imagine my relief when Jake rang me shortly after drilling started.

'Glash, are you sitting down?' he asked. 'I think we've found gold. I'll call you back when it's official.'

'Don't you dare hang up,' I told him. 'Stay on the line, even if it takes all week.'

'Okay ... what's that ... hang on a second, Glash, someone wants me ... *no,* you're kidding ... righto. Sorry, Glash, false alarm. A bit of brass from the drilling equipment sheared off. It looked like gold in the sunlight.' *Jeez,* I thought. *Someone, somewhere give me a break, please!*

All along, I tried to run the company on a shoestring and do everything by the book. My company car was a modest Peugeot 604, which cost $6000 at most. I was paid a modest wage at an hourly rate, and I always undercharged. I kept a tight rein on expenses and, at this time of crisis, frugality was even more crucial. Still, every Friday afternoon I allowed a carton of beer and a box of salted peanuts for the staff. Somebody once moaned that we should have cashews for a change. 'You can have cashews when we strike gold,' I said. 'Until then, you're literally working for peanuts.' But being in charge was becoming too challenging. I was tired of the stress and the constant infighting, and was happy to eventually step down as chairman.

Through all this trauma, the plan to subdivide our property at Church Point was our financial safety net. This was prime Sydney real estate, with sumptuous views over Pittwater, and people would pay a premium to live there. The plan was for the developer to build six new properties. One would go to each of our daughters and be held in trust funds. Our house, which was definitely in need of a lick of paint, would be totally renovated. The developer was then free to sell the remaining four new houses. I wasn't keen on subdividing, but I was paying a crippling $25,000 a year in land tax on the 2.5 acres, and it was a way to provide a more secure future for the girls.

Once again, I tried to do everything by the book. Our plans created minimal disruption to the landscape, and not one bulldozer would enter the site. The homes were to be built on poles because the land sloped steeply, but I didn't want lots of driveways crisscrossing the property; they would have ruined the aesthetics. My idea was to have a central communal parking area at the bottom of the development and an inclinator, a type of lift that runs on a rail up steep inclines, for residents to reach their homes.

Everything was looking good when the architect's drawings were approved by the council planners, as we expected. The next step was public consultation before the plans were put to a council vote. That's when the problems started.

Nine or ten neighbours, led by a local councillor, objected to the plans on the basis that the site contained a culturally significant midden, an Aboriginal waste site for old shells. I argued that the midden would be perfectly preserved under our plans. The battle made front-page news in the local paper, and the group took me to the Land and Environment Court of New South Wales. I was caught slap-bang in the middle of a populist movement to prevent 'rich arseholes' – like me – from running roughshod through the suburbs. It would have gone ahead without a second thought today. It was the first time that this David felt like he was taking on the Goliath that is the legal system.

The whole drawn-out affair proved to be another drain on our resources, and the $100,000 I had received from the sale of my childhood home was gobbled straight up by lawyers and planning consultants. It's not a good feeling to see your inheritance disappear in an instant, but I was determined to fight my corner, even though I didn't have the funds for a lengthy legal battle. And a lengthy battle is what it turned out to be. This time, as is so often the case in real life, Goliath won hands down.

It was a huge blow: the straw that broke the camel's back. Advance Bank, now part of St George, was keen to recover bad debts after the crash, and was on my back as soon as the verdict came through. We sold our other house at McMahons Point for around $400,000 to ease the pressure but, again, it was soul-destroying to see it vanish straight into the bank's grabbing, grubby hands. It felt like everything I'd worked so hard for throughout my life was going up in smoke. And the bank wasn't finished. With debt still outstanding, my shares were their next target.

In the meantime, Carpenters had struck it lucky. Shortly after the crash, gold was discovered at Mount Kare, about 600 kilometres west of Port Moresby, the Papua New Guinea capital, and not far from our early exploration. The site was snapped up by Rio Tinto, who then fell out with the Papua New Guinea government, and our great early relationship with the mines department paid off when Carpenters was invited to take over exploration. On the back of this invitation, our share price started to climb again. One new offer of investment valued our shares at sixty cents. The bank had already made a move on my shares and sold millions at twenty-eight cents, practically halving their value. I pleaded with them to wait to see if the investment materialised, but they wanted an immediate sale and it wasn't enough to clear my debt. Our only remaining asset – our family home – was firmly in their sights.

***

I will never forget 11am on Friday 4 October 1991. That point in time is seared into my soul. The setting: the plush Sydney offices of Advance Bank. I had spent the morning pleading for a stay of financial execution, but this axeman was hungry for his pound of flesh. The bank could see no way that I could pay back what I still owed and was going through the formalities of transferring the ownership of the Church Point property to their name.

18

'The sheriff will turn up at noon precisely and secure the premises. Make sure you have removed everything you need, because you will not be able to return to the house after this,' he calmly stated.

'This all seems a bit severe,' I said, forlorn. 'I haven't committed any crime here. I've made a few mistakes – I accept that. But this isn't the best outcome for your bank, or your shareholders. Why can't you work with me to resolve this? Why can't I pay you rent for a while? I'm talking to you man to man here. What you are doing is hurting my wife and children – and it's killing me. You have my word that the bank will receive all of what's owed, and more, if you just show some understanding and patience. Take my passport as security – I'm not about to leave the country. Just please, *please* don't take the house,' I begged. The assassin just sighed and twiddled his thumbs. He had heard it all before.

I had never felt so desperate. My one role had been to feed my family and keep a roof over their heads. And now that roof was about to disappear.

In hindsight, I shouldn't have been so hard on myself. Even though my early corporate career in the food industry provided the financial stability that Sylvi craved, I couldn't have remained a paid employee for a minute longer. I needed to be in control of my own destiny and to break free of those corporate shackles. That meant going it alone and taking risks, like the failed toy company and the gold exploration, but risks that could and should have rewarded my family handsomely in the long run. Perhaps I risked too much, too soon, although I was never reckless. My risks were always calculated, and shared with friends and associates who had proven track records in business and investment. Maybe I relied too much on good fortune while chasing *my* fortune. Almost certainly, I wasn't prepared for the rigours of going it alone. It's a hard slog, and I salute anyone who pulls it off.

This wasn't the time to lick my wounds, though. The sheriff was turning up in an hour and I had to warn Sylvi. I somehow managed to remain composed, shook the bastard's hand

and then dashed out of the bank's office to find the nearest public phone. 'It's happening. There was nothing I could do or say to him. You need to grab everything you can lay your hands on and get the kids away from there within the hour,' I told her. 'Please don't let them see this.'

This outcome had been almost inevitable for some weeks. As was the end of our marriage. Ever since I started to pursue my entrepreneurial dreams, Sylvi and I had struggled to see eye to eye on many things. Sylvi much preferred the shelter of the corporate umbrella, although she didn't enjoy the role of corporate wife. If she thought one of my bosses was being an idiot, she was not afraid to let him or her know, although I did tell her that I was perfectly capable of doing that on my own!

When I first met her, on a blind date at a fancy black-tie ball, she looked quite familiar – an absolute knockout with luscious long blonde hair and an hourglass figure. It was easy to see why she was a part-time model and the face of a major billboard campaign right across Australia for French oil company Total. I instantly knew I wanted to marry her, although perhaps we were never a good match. Sylvi had grown up in cosmopolitan Budapest until the Russian tanks rolled in to quell the Hungarian Uprising against the Soviets, forcing her wealthy parents to flee the city. She was used to going to fancy restaurants and the opera, not camping out in the wild.

Sylvi had raised the girls well, though. Samantha, who was sixteen, and Erika, thirteen, had enjoyed a privileged but sheltered upbringing. They were good, sociable, caring girls. I tried to protect all three from the turmoil, but Sylvi wasn't stupid. I was drinking more, I was irritable and I was distant. Not the symptoms of good mental or financial health. The girls were still young enough that they possibly didn't pick up on my problems, or the growing tension in their parents' marriage.

My biggest regret from that period of my life is that I was never there for the kids. Before my financial demise, we'd enjoyed some lovely family holidays, like our annual ski trip to

Charlotte Pass and a one-off three-week skiing holiday in the United States. But, even on holiday, Sylvi and I were poles apart. I was up at the crack of dawn with Erika to catch the first lift up the mountain, while Sylvi and Samantha would spend all morning making sure their outfits were colour coordinated. Erika and I would still be on the slopes for the final run of the day, while Sylvi and Sam were already in the shops. During our trips to Fraser Island, Sylvi preferred to stay in a fancy resort, while I went bush and slept under the stars. These were rare and precious times together – even if we'd often do our own things – because I was hardly ever around. I was married to the job, and the job was a demanding partner. When I was home, I was on the phone, ranting and raving, or buried under the latest batch of legal documents. My weekends, when not travelling for work, were spent at the yacht club. I was much more concerned with providing financial security for the girls than building their emotional security. I know now, from having seen the cost firsthand, which one really matters.

By the time I returned home from the bank, Sylvi had been and gone with the kids and some possessions, and the sheriff turned up on the stroke of midday – our high noon.

'Look, mate,' I pleaded, as he started to drill holes to secure the doors. 'You don't look like a bad bloke. I'm in a mess here. But I can't clear out all our stuff right now. There's nowhere for it to go. Can you at least give me twenty-four hours?'

'Sorry, Mr Glasheen, I have to follow my instructions,' he said. Then he looked over his shoulder to check that nobody was listening.

'See this nail? It's pretty loose, isn't it?' he whispered. 'I reckon anyone could just tug it out and open the front door. Someone who did that could almost come and go as they pleased.' At last, a glimpse of humanity. There was only one way to show my appreciation: to buy him a beer. Or, more accurately, to let him buy me several beers. So we spent the afternoon in the local, where I put the world to rights and the sheriff's eyes glazed over.

Sylvi had already made plans to take the girls to her best friend, a Russian lady called Natalie. But Natalie insisted that we came as a full family or not at all. That wasn't a practical option, given the tension between Sylvi and me. So our next-door neighbour stepped in to offer beds to Sylvi and the girls. It must have been a traumatic time for Samantha and Erika. Instead of arriving home from school and running freely in the gardens at Church Point with their daft Dalmatian, Claude, the girls were now squabbling over who had to sleep on the couch.

There was another problem. Where could I go? I didn't want to stay with any of my mates. I'd been too proud to let anyone know the full extent of our troubles. Besides, I was a wreck. I didn't want to lose my last remaining shred of dignity by showing up in this state. Considering the circumstances, I couldn't justify spending money on a hotel. I tried the back seat of my car – the bank had at least allowed me to keep that. But I have always hated being cooped up in confined spaces, especially at night. Fortunately, it was a warm Sydney evening, so I drove down to Palm Beach with a blanket and a bottle of plonk and lay down for the night on the grass next to the beach.

Four years earlier, I had been the chairman of a successful publicly listed company. Now, I was effectively homeless, penniless and my marriage was over. I'm not normally one for showing my emotions but, with just the lapping of the waves to sooth my mind, and a few inquisitive possums for company, I allowed the tears to flow.

Chapter 2

Restoration

There was no doubt my health was in serious trouble. I realised this in the bathroom, as I furtively tried to insert a needle into my dick before having sex with my new girlfriend. Denise was a ball of fire; she had a tanned, athletic figure and a rich, seductive Zimbabwean accent that made me drool. I knew her from the kids' school, and she had split up with her husband at around the same time that we lost the house. Denise had a spare room and had offered to let me stay there for a few weeks while I found my feet. The first time I squeezed past her in the narrow corridor, I realised that the arrangement was going to be torture. I also realised that it was way too soon for a rebound relationship. It wouldn't have been fair on Sylvi and the girls, or Denise, so I packed my bags before I did anything I'd regret.

It was a period of constant upheaval. For weeks, I had slept on the couch in the office of a mate's factory, until a short-term rental house became available in Palm Beach. It was far too big for me and the dog, but the only person to answer my ad for a flatmate was an American woman called Justa, who taught fire-walking and Native American drumming. One evening, I came home to find a full-blown powwow in the backyard, where guests were banging tom-toms and dancing round a totem pole in the shape of a wolf. This girl was clearly bonkers. A few nights later, Justa opened the door dressed in a revealing silk dress. The house was filled with candles and incense burners, martinis were already poured, Barry White was playing on the cassette player and Justa had prepared a bubble bath for me. All of a sudden we were supposed to be soulmates, not flatmates. 'You're a Leo and I'm a Virgo. We're so compatible,' she purred. *There's no bloody way* you're *a Virgo,* I thought. I wanted none of it.

Next, I moved in with two girls who shared a flat in Whale Beach. One worked for the *Manly Daily,* the other worked for men nightly. While the journalist kept regular office hours, her friend left for work in the evening and didn't return until the early hours of the morning. She told me she was a model – and she *was* stunning – but no photography studio kept those business hours. And when I was invited to one of their friends' parties, one of my mates recognised the 'model' from an upmarket knocking shop in Roseville. Time to move on again!

Ian Curtis, a friend from school we called 'Bluey' because of the unusual combination of his red hair and piercing blue eyes, was also going through a marriage breakdown, so we moved in together in another rental house in Palm Beach, just down the road from Denise. Over the course of a couple of years, Denise and I had finally become an item, despite Sylvi telling her that I was 'as romantic as an amputated leg'. There was electricity with Denise. But, like a power switch, we were constantly on or off. One minute, we would be at each other's throats, the next we would be kissing and making up. Or, to be more accurate, we kissed and I tried to make up.

Then, all of a sudden, I wasn't firing on all cylinders. It was like trying to push start a ute with a tow rope. This had never been a problem before. I had had a couple of other girlfriends since my marriage break-up, and everything had seemed to be working fine – and I didn't even find those women particularly attractive. Denise was different; I fancied the pants off her! So why couldn't I get a hard-on? *I must have some kind of disease,* I thought. I didn't fancy going to a doctor, so I called my old mate Peter Ryan, whose family owned some of the most iconic pubs in Sydney. Peter – or 'Itchy' as his schoolmates called him – was a handsome bloke who had been brought up in the country, surrounded by animals rooting everywhere. This stuff was second nature to him. He was just about the most worldly-wise bloke that I knew. 'Itchy, I need to talk to you about something very personal,' I said. We agreed to meet at one of his hotels and, after way too many beers, Itchy eventually asked, 'Well, what did you want to talk about?'

'I need another beer first,' I said, then finally plucked up the courage. 'Do you know anyone whose ... thing ... doesn't work?' I asked, pointing to the guilty party.

'What, your soldier won't salute?' he roared. 'That's priceless.'

'Shut up, will ya? Keep your voice down. It's not with everyone, it's just Denise. I think I must be dying.'

Itchy said I needed to go to a urologist or, as he called it, a cock doc. I looked in the phone book and called the number, but hung up immediately when a woman answered. Perhaps that was the issue – I thought I might still have hang-ups from my strict Catholic upbringing. But the problem wouldn't go away, despite Denise's best efforts. There was no option but to see the doctor.

'Let me guess – you're Catholic, you feel guilty about starting a new relationship and you're severely stressed,' said the doctor when I finally swallowed my pride enough to see him. 'Don't worry, we can fix this with a simple injection.'

Righto, I thought, *I'm not scared of needles.* So I hopped off the bed, dropped my duds and presented my bare bum. 'Not there, Mr Glasheen, in the penis,' he said. I was still pulling up my pants as I sprinted through the packed waiting room. 'You'll be back!' I could hear the doctor shouting. And back I went, because Denise was pissed off and running out of ideas.

The injection didn't actually hurt, but the next hour did. I couldn't make this monster go away. Women were sniggering and pointing at the bulge in my pants as I passed them on the street after my appointment. I had to go and find a park bench, cover myself with a newspaper and sit it out. It was like that episode of *The Simpsons,* where Homer has to tell himself to 'think unsexy thoughts, think unsexy thoughts', which only makes him think more about sex. I couldn't wait to get home and try it out, although I hadn't quite ironed out the logistics of how to use my syringe kit without Denise knowing that I was on weapons-grade Viagra.

So, when the opportunity arose that night and, as per usual, nothing else arose, I made the excuse that I needed the bathroom and frantically got to work. It was very fiddly, and I must have been gone a good few minutes before Denise knocked on the bathroom door. 'Are you okay in there? I'm waiting,' she said. I didn't really want to tell her that I was sticking a needle into my dick, because there was a fair chance that might kill the moment. So I flushed the dunny and limped back to the bedroom. Except I was no longer limp. Her eyes nearly popped out of their sockets.

Obviously, this was not a practical long-term solution. When the blood tests came back all clear, the doctor told me it was psychosomatic – all in my head. It was an indication that I was leading a very unhealthy life: working too hard, eating badly, drinking too much and putting myself under too much stress. Ever since the stock market crash, and especially since our eviction, I'd been like a hamster on a wheel. I was working as hard as ever but getting nowhere. Not only was I trying to get myself back on my feet, but I also had Sylvi and the girls to think about. My relationship with Sylvi was cordial, but Sam had wrongly accused Denise of breaking up our marriage and Erika, or 'Ricky' as we called her, had clearly taken the break-up badly. Her act of rebellion was to leave school, and then home, at the age of fifteen to find a job as an apprentice chef. She was a lot like me in terms of motivation and work ethic, always on the go and never one to lounge around or stay late in bed. But she moved in with a group of other young people – the wrong crowd, in hindsight – and was introduced to alcohol and marijuana. The hospitality industry is notorious for problem drinking.

Friends tried to help me out whenever they could, finding projects for me to sink my teeth into. An old advertising colleague, Roger Richmond-Smith, or 'Smithy' to his mates, wanted me to look at the commercial production of shark cartilage as a cure for prostate cancer and a whole heap of other conditions. Then, he asked me to look into building a vineyard on his 300-acre property near Avoca. Nothing came of either idea, but the help was appreciated. And I hadn't lost my own entrepreneurial drive. I tried to set up a furniture production business with my flatmate, Bluey. Our flat-packed benches looked like church pews, but were not as comfy as church pews, and Cathedral Furniture Productions was doomed to fail. Occasionally, I also received small commissions for making profitable introductions in the mining sector, so I was just managing to keep my head above water.

Denise and I also tried a couple of ventures, including selling biltong – a dried, cured meat – from her home. That's when my food marketing experience kicked in again. 'You need a brand name when you answer the phone,' I said. 'No one's going to buy Denise's biltong. It sounds like shoe leather. You need something exotic. How about Denika's biltong?' And from that day Denise became Denika. I eventually managed to scrape together enough dough to help her open a beauty salon, Club Denika. The clients came flocking, including Gretel Pinniger, Australia's most notorious dominatrix, who lived in a huge mansion nearby. Gretel was a shocking sight, dressed head-to-toe in latex with horrible, pointy rubber boobs and garish mascara. Denika was speechless when Gretel marched in and slapped a very large wad of cash on the counter and ordered Denika to make her beautiful within three months, in time for her election campaign as a candidate for her own independent party, the Extra Dimension Party. She'd have been better off paying a plasterer.

We were both working flat out, but there was no light at the end of the tunnel for either of us – no end game. I didn't want to spend the rest of my life jumping from one to project to another, constantly worrying about where I was going to make my next buck. One evening, my frustrations came pouring out over a glass of wine at her place, where I was now living permanently because both her sons, Tim and Troy, had moved out.

'Where's this all leading?' I asked her. 'I've slogged my guts out to get nowhere over the last twenty years. I don't have the energy to be doing this twenty years from now. I could be heading for a nervous breakdown at this rate. We know only too well that it's been affecting my health. And you don't want to be doing facials and massages for the rest of your life, do you? Surely there's more to life than this.'

'But that's what people do, Dave,' Denika replied. 'This is real life. It can be a struggle sometimes. What's the alternative?'

'I don't know. Something radical. Why don't we pack it all in and go and live on a deserted island?'

'Yeah, alright, Dave. Another of your schemes. I've heard it all before.'

'I'm serious. Other people have done it. It would be just you and me, nobody telling us what to do or when to do it. There'd be none of this constant arguing, because we'd be in it together. We could grow our own food, catch fish, keep chickens. We could even sell our own produce. I'd lose weight, you could read books. What's stopping us? Can't you see how amazing this could be?' I insisted.

'Okay, I'm not promising anything, but we can't just pack up our bags and pitch a tent somewhere. Where would we find an island? Don't forget, we've no money,' Denika said.

'I know just the man,' I said. 'Trust me, this is going to be one of those life-changing conversations. I'm excited ... very excited. Living on an island, eh? Very, very excited!'

***

Bluey was no stranger to out-there ventures in the middle of nowhere. He had recently returned to Sydney after setting up a dive school in Papua New Guinea, where he also built a yacht and promptly shipwrecked it before the diving business also went belly-up. Before that, while running the Cairns LJ Hooker real estate agency, he came across a remote five-acre beachfront property at Bloomfield River, about sixty kilometres south of Cooktown on Cape Tribulation in Far North Queensland. Here, he developed a fishing retreat called Bloomfield Lodge. Cooktown was widely regarded as an unfenced reservation for lunatics, the Wild West of the north-east, so this venture was not without risks.

The finance came via merchant bank Ward Knight and Dunn, and that's where it all became very murky. Ward Knight and Dunn were later proven to have links to the notorious Federated Ship Painters and Dockers Union, a criminal organisation masquerading as a trade union. Apparently this mob used Bloomfield Lodge as the hub of their marijuana trade and it was dubbed the 'Painters and Dockers Holiday Lodge' by the media. Bluey swore that he was a totally innocent bystander whose business was targeted by these crooks because it was so remote.

Nevertheless, Bluey had an eye for discovering unique locations, and he owed me a favour or two. He was also at a loose end and in search of a new adventure of his own. As soon as I mentioned the plan for Denika and I to find an island, I could see that his brain was scrambling for ways to deal himself in. 'Look, we want somewhere as far away from the rat race as you can find,' I told him. 'And it's got to be beautiful. Great beaches. Like a desert island, but with trees. And not too many flies. Denika hates flies. Fresh water would be good. Maybe just a cabin already there. It'd be good if there was a natural harbour, too. And a garden. A telephone, too, perhaps. Oh, one more thing, we've no money.'

'Woah, woah, woah!' he protested, laughing. 'Hold your horses, Glash. Let me make sure I've got this right. You want me to find paradise. And it can't cost a cent! Do you think this place even exists? And, if it does, don't you think someone might already be there?'

'Yep, that's basically it. We want to live in Woop Woop. But on the water! Come on, Bluey, I know you won't let me down.'

The first place Bluey identified was Hicks Island, about 150 kilometres south of the very top of Cape York, the northernmost tip of Australia. There was no denying that it was a beautiful spot, although a few things put us off. There was an airstrip, which meant that outsiders could come and go too easily. The anchorage was really poor, too, plus we were told that the bugs and mozzies were a menace. But the main issue was that it was owned by a consortium of around five people, including Roy Turner and his wife, Ana, who also owned Haggerstone Island just to the south, which has since been developed into a luxury resort. Several years before, Roy was cooking lunch on his boat while some of his employees and their families swam in nearby Margaret Bay. A three-metre croc grabbed the arm of one of the girls and, without a second thought, Roy leapt from the boat onto the croc's back and gouged at its eyes until it let go of the girl. Ever since then, Roy has been known as 'Gouger'. Buying the twenty-year lease to Hicks seemed too complicated for us, even if we could have somehow raised the $600,000. Although Bluey had been on the right track, we soon lost interest. Today, Hicks Island is home to five or six luxury private properties.

Next, Bluey heard about another island one hundred kilometres south of Hicks: Restoration Island. I liked the sound of it immediately. We were all in need of some restoration. I called it Resto, in the true Aussie tradition of cutting a word in half and adding an 'o' – like servo (service station), fisho (fisherman) or Davo (David Glasheen). At more than one hundred acres, this island (latitude -12.6177, longitude 143.4667) was much bigger than Hicks and only accessible by a ten-to fifteen-minute boat ride from a tiny bay on the mainland called Cape Weymouth, which in turn was about forty kilometres of rough track from the Aboriginal community of Lockhart River, the northernmost town on the east coast of Australia with a 700-strong population. Resto was much less accessible and exactly what we had in mind. Its only inhabitant was a caretaker who looked after part of the island for a company called Restoration Island Pty Ltd. *Denika and I can do that,* I thought.

When Bluey investigated further, he discovered that this company was owned by a consortium of three men: Colin Lindsay, Dewar Goode and Bruce Hattam. Colin was a businessman from Ballarat and owned five of the eight shares; Dewar Goode, who owned two shares, was the son of Arthur Charles Goode, the founder of 1970s financial powerhouse AC Goode and Bruce Hattam was a real estate agent and owned the final share. In 1979, they had purchased the thirty-year lease for the whole island for $156,000 from another businessman, Peter Huybers. Their plan had always been to turn it into some form of tourist resort, but Colin Lindsay quickly realised that the eastern two-thirds of the island had no potential for development. There was no chance of landing a boat on that section of rocky coastline, which was totally exposed to the elements unless the water was dead calm. So, in return for an extension of the lease from thirty to fifty years, Colin cleverly offered this portion of Restoration Island back to the Australian government's National Parks in 1989. Doing so effectively returned this wild two-thirds of the island to its traditional owners, the Kuuku Ya'u people, who knew Resto as Ma'alpiku Island National Park. One of the key conditions of the extension was that the consortium had to spend a minimum $200,000 on 'deemed island improvements' within five years. A longer lease meant a more valuable lease, and the upfront asking price for the head lease on Colin and his consortium's habitable third of the island was now $1.2 million.

There was no way Denika and I could scrape together that kind of money, so we needed to find financial partners if we were going to take it any further. Obviously, Bluey wanted a slice of any action. None of this was part of our original plan; we'd just wanted to live in isolated tropical bliss, not embroil ourselves in another convoluted, high-stakes business venture. It had seemed all too simple when Denika and I were dreaming, or maybe pipe-dreaming, but something was drawing me to this place. Surely, it couldn't be too hard to become long-term custodians of the island without getting too tangled up in all the commercial stuff? Without capital, it was all academic, so Bluey and I put out some feelers and we managed to attract a wealthy investor who liked the sound of owning part of a tropical island. He agreed to come on board if anything came of these early talks. With this loose commitment in place, it was time to talk turkey with Colin Lindsay. So, in November 1993, I set off for Cape York with Bluey and his brother, Pete, the architect who designed the Painters and Dockers Holiday Lodge and a good friend of mine from school and yacht racing. None of us had a clue what to expect.

***

Lockhart River was only a short flight on a twin-propeller plane from Cairns – about one hour and forty minutes – but the views out of the window sent shivers down my spine and the time flashed by. I had seen images of the Great Barrier Reef taken from outer space, but those amazing shots didn't do justice to the brilliant colours on display from this vantage point. The intensely blue waters of the Coral Sea were mesmerising. And the reef, with its hundreds of tropical islands stretching on and on forever, captivated me. It was hard to imagine that I might soon make my home in one of the seven natural wonders of the world. My forehead was glued to the window for the whole flight, until we banked sharply towards the mainland and the plane descended into a thick cloud. Then, just as quickly, we emerged from the cloud, scarily close to Mount Tozer, just north-west of Lockhart River airport.

While we waited to be picked up from the 'terminal' – a glorified hut, really – I read about the history of the airstrip. It was built in 1942 during World War II. The Battle of the Coral Sea earlier that year had made Cape York an important defensive position in the fight to keep Japanese forces out of Australia, and also a strategic point for launching attacks on enemy positions in Papua New Guinea. The airport was almost built at a tiny nearby coastal settlement called Portland Roads, but the surrounding land could not be cleared to accommodate up to 12,000 American and Australian troops. So the current site was chosen about thirty kilometres south. It was hard to imagine so many people ever being crammed into this lush, remote corner of the world, where it seemed only trees could thrive.

After a short wait, a rickety old four-wheel drive pulled up to the airport and John Pritchard, the botanist caretaker of Restoration Island, introduced himself. He seemed shy, perhaps a little nervous, but I guessed he wasn't used to meeting new people. Cape Weymouth, where we would pick up the boat to the island, was a good hour's drive along some very ordinary track. November was just before the wet season, so the road was only really muddy when it passed under the canopy of trees, where sun couldn't penetrate. Even so, some of the ruts were knee-deep and permanent, and we were tossed around in the back like rag dolls. John kept to himself in the front as I drank it all in: the landscape, which alternated between panoramic views across the greenery and the suffocating density of the rainforest; the air, pungent with sweet eucalyptus and heavy with humidity after a short, sharp shower; and the wildlife, with exotic parrots bursting out of their camouflage in fright, termite mounds as big as houses, and the various roadkill – a couple of wallabies, countless squished cane toads and one unfortunate long-dead feral pig.

I was transfixed, but snapped out of the daze when John swung a violent left down a steep track that was barely worthy of the name. *How the hell would we ever drive back up this?* I thought. After a few minutes, we pulled into a clearing that led down to the small beach, where John's tinny was bobbing in the shallow water. 'That's where the Chippendales live,' John said, pointing to a small property set back from the clearing, his first words since we left the airport. 'They're good people.' We unloaded our bags from the car and took them down to the boat, pulled off our shoes and hopped in while John weighed anchor.

'That must be the island,' I said, pointing to the only island in view.

'Nah, completely the wrong direction,' John replied, with a slight smile. 'That's Rocky Island. Much smaller.' He was probably thinking 'more city dummies'. And his opinion wouldn't have changed much when Bluey shrieked, 'What's that in the water? It's a croc!'

'It's a log,' John answered, pithily.

'It's moving, though!' argued Bluey.

'No. It's not. The water is moving, the log is stationary,' said John. Nevertheless, Bluey's eyes stayed trained on the shore until we left the mangrove swamp that skirted the shallow bay and emerged into the choppy sea. My gaze was fixed in the direction of Resto. Once we passed a rocky outcrop, there she suddenly was: strong, majestic and slightly mysterious. I felt weirdly overcome with emotion. I had been so excited to finally see the place, and it had exceeded my expectations. It was like going on a blind date and finding that the woman at the bar was drop-dead gorgeous. 'Pretty special, isn't she?' I declared to the rest of the boat. John grunted in agreement, while Bluey and Pete ignored me. These guys were here for a business venture, not an extreme lifestyle makeover.

I had already seen an aerial picture of Restoration Island. Its shape wasn't dissimilar to Ireland, but with a little green beak of flat land, framed on two sides by white beaches, poking out the western shore where County Mayo would sit, and without County Kerry jutting out at the south-western tip. As we approached, the brilliant white sands of the north-facing beach came into view, while the island's grey-green spine loomed imposingly, over one hundred metres high. Nearer still, and we could pick out a figure on the beach. When John cut the motor and we glided gently onto the sand, Colin strode down to meet us with the confidence of an emperor greeting his loyal subjects. 'Colin Lindsay,' he announced. 'Welcome to my island.'

Colin led us through the row of enormous palm trees that lined the shore, interspersed with a few sheoaks. We emerged to about five acres of flat land, and I could see the living area, about one hundred metres across this clearing. Then it struck me: *This place is a shithole.* There was rubbish strewn everywhere and I could make out at least five dumps that had been burned and not cleared away. Then I spotted a derelict caravan with the door falling off its hinges and the windows smashed. What the hell was the caretaker doing here? *I could definitely take much better care of this place,* I thought.

When we reached the 'house', we found a run-down converted fibro cement boat shed, about twenty metres long and three metres wide with an open front that led into a living area with very basic amenities. There were only two shabby deckchairs at the front, which Colin and John took, with nowhere for the rest of us to sit. It wasn't exactly a warm welcome. 'Right, why don't you fellas tell me all about this investor and what you have planned?' Colin said.

What!? We'd barely set foot on the island and he wanted to talk business? How about a cuppa? Or a biscuit? How about actually seeing a bit of the place first? I'd waited weeks for this chance, and I wasn't about to wait until morning. 'Hope you don't mind if I sit this one out,' I said. 'I'm going to have a look around.'

'Where are you heading?' asked John.

'Well, the best spot to get a feel for a place is usually the highest point,' I said. 'Can I get up to the top, there?' Again, Colin and John exchanged a knowing look.

'You can ... theoretically ... but it might be best to wait until morning,' John said.

'No, thanks,' I said cheerily. 'No time like the present. Have you got a machete I can borrow?' For sixty metres or so, there was pretty dense-looking vegetation, beyond which the bald summit poked through. I couldn't imagine that this pair had been keeping the tracks very clear. John recommended that I take some pink surveyor's marking tape to tie around the trees so that I could find my way back down, and he also handed me some clippers. He showed me over to the best spot to start the climb, where the water had gouged a vertical scar through the shrubbery during the wet season.

'It's been years since anyone's gone up there, so you're going to have to bush bash your way through. Traverse across to that first big rock there, turn right and you should be able to find your way to the Incredible Rocks,' he said.

'Why are they called that?' I asked, realising immediately that it was a stupid question.

'They're incredible,' John smiled. 'From there, you can go three ways. Straight on is Green Ant Gully. I recommend you don't go there. Before you ask, it's full of ants. To the right is the Road to Nowhere. It doesn't go anywhere. But to the left, there's a little track that leads to the summit.'

'Does it have a name?'

'Summit Track.' Silly me.

Within a minute of scrambling up the rainwater gully, I spotted a hole at the centre of a spider web that looked like a small gramophone speaker. It was the tell-tale home of the funnel-web spider, one of the deadliest spiders on the planet. *Thanks a lot for the warning,* I thought. At the top of the gully, I tore off a strip of marking tape and wound it around a branch, then started to climb across to the left to the first rock. The light would start to fade soon, so I didn't want to dawdle at every vantage point. I pressed ahead, following a vague semblance of a track, thrashing first with the machete, and then clipping any stubborn branches or vines away. Every time I took a slight deviation one way or another, I left some more marking tape to be on the safe side. It was tough going, especially for someone not used to strenuous exercise, and sweat poured down me and into my eyes. But I was glad I had kept my long-sleeved shirt on, because thorns and spikes were attacking me from every angle.

When I reached the rocks the view was, indeed, just incredible. North was partially obscured by the vertical rock that created this natural viewing platform, but facing south, the Coral Sea sparkled and dazzled for as far as I could see. To the east, out towards the Pacific, the intense blue was punctuated with golden sandbanks and the subtle shades of submerged reef. And west, inland, every contour was underscored with striking shadows, which contrasted against the sun-splashed greenery. Could any spot on the planet be more inspiring – more uplifting? Was there a more complete picture of pure, natural beauty? It was literally breathtaking – and I had very little breath left to give after the exertion of the climb. I raised my arms out wide at shoulder height, and filled my lungs with the deepest inhalation, then slowly let the air escape my body. It felt like all my worries and stress had dissolved onto the breeze with that breath. My shirt was drenched, so I peeled it off, stood up straight and let the fresh sea air cool my body. I must have looked like Christ the Redeemer overlooking Rio de Janeiro, as I slowly revolved a full 360 degrees with my arms outstretched.

The Incredible Rocks were only two-thirds of the way to the top, and I was still determined to reach the summit. I took John's advice and steered clear of Green Ant Gully, but I was curious about the Road to Nowhere. I'd never been afraid to go off on a tangent. So I hacked my way through to a cosy, flat clearing that must have been totally obscured from an aerial view by the dense foliage. The view over to the hinterland was also dazzling, and I earmarked this as a spot for future seclusion and meditation. Then I retraced my steps and tackled Summit

Track with my last ounces of energy. The track actually stopped about five or ten metres from the very summit, so it wasn't as easy as I'd hoped to appreciate the scenery. I felt on top of the world, nevertheless. Just a few hours on this island had restored my faith that the rest of my time on this incredible planet would be full of new adventures, new challenges and new dreams. And I wanted the world to know that I was back. So I turned to face towards Sydney and, to anyone who'd listen, I yelled out the loudest, proudest, 'Coooooeeeeee!'

Chapter 3

Go home

For three frustrating years after that first visit, it felt like I was treading water. I jumped from project to project just to earn enough to live on, and Denika and I continued our capricious relationship. But that first visit to Resto had affirmed my commitment to find a different way of life: one beyond the vicious cycle of pressure to earn enough money for a lifestyle by which other people measure your value and success. With Resto, it had been love at first sight. There was no point looking at other islands; this one was matchless. However, over those three years, I realised that our original vision of disappearing together to our dream island might not be achievable in the short term; I would have to compromise to ensure that Resto became my home in the long run. Nevertheless, it was exasperating that Resto remained always just out of reach, especially when the development plans became very complicated.

***

The signs were there from that very first trip in 1993 that I viewed Resto in an entirely different light to the others. While Bluey, Pete and Colin Lindsay spent their days planning their eco-resort, I immersed myself in the island. When they got out the theodolite to measure up potential construction sites, I got out a fishing rod. I was in my element and John Pritchard, the caretaker, was always happy to take me out in his boat. When he fancied a break for a beer or a smoke I used a handline to fish from the beach, collected delicious oysters from the rocks when the tide was out or explored the rest of the island on foot. There was so much more to this place than met the eye.

If the first night's effort was anything to go by, dinner on Resto was no big event for these guys. Supermarket bread with processed cheese and jam and a couple of beers was not my idea of an island feast.

Dinner had always been the highlight of the day for me in Sydney – a chance to unwind and connect with people. Slowly. City people shovelled their food down their throats. It was like their eating had to match the breakneck pace of the rest of their lives. Whatever happened to chewing your food, savouring it and digesting it? Here on Resto, there was no excuse. I couldn't understand why, with the sea and beach a short stroll away, we didn't eat at the water's edge instead of at the house. On the second night, I suggested that we cook the fish that John and I had caught – several nannygai, two beautiful parrot fish and a coral trout – on a camp fire on the beach. There were a few mutterings about it being a lot of effort, but I was more than happy to build the fire and prepare the fish while they continued to discuss their grand plans.

    As I was looking for firewood along the north-facing beach of Resto's natural harbour, I discovered a patch of land marked by some old string, loosely tied around sticks to create a rectangle. John later explained that it was an

Aboriginal burial site, believed to be for two women and a child. It was the first time that it struck me that white fellas were only very recent custodians of this land. When I came to the granite rocks that marked the end of the beach, I turned in through the trees, back towards the house. Again, it was overgrown, and I hadn't brought a machete, but I clambered through the undergrowth and stumbled across a sign for Huybers Highway, pointing further into the trees.

I'd already heard about Peter Huybers, who owned the island before Colin and had an impeccable reputation in town. Peter was a successful businessman who owned Queensland Pastoral Supply, a provedore company. When he branched out into construction and agreed to a fixed-price contract to build the modern mining town Weipa, further north than Lockhart River on the west coast of Cape York, he lost money and was forced to sell Restoration Island.

Apparently the place was in pristine condition in those days, and all the rogue vegetation was stripped back to a minimum. Now the native hibiscus, which local people used to cut and trim to make spears for fishing long ago, had grown back thickly with vines criss-crossing the track in a tight mesh. I managed to battle through and came to a sign for Web Walk, off to the right. Either Mr Web was another previous island owner, or this was a warning about the track's inhabitants. I stopped there to catch my breath for a moment, when I heard the deep-throated *wup-wup* of a bird in the undergrowth. When I ventured further in, there was a rustle of branches, followed by silence, then another *wup-wup* just a few metres away. I followed the call again and the same thing happened. *This bugger's playing hide and seek,* I thought. The light was fading fast, so I turned around to go back. When I did, the huge bird was inches from my face, staring straight at me with piercing, goading eyes. I nearly jumped out of my skin and instinctively shrieked. That freaked him out and he started flapping like a demented fruit bat. I panicked even more and thrashed my way out of there and into a clearing.

'Ah, you've met Old Swampy,' said John with a laugh, when I told the others about my stalker. 'He's a pheasant coucal, a member of the cuckoo family.' John knew everything about the wildlife here. 'That's how he hunts, by creeping up on his prey – frogs, lizards and big bugs. He's totally harmless, but he does like to play games. You'll come across much scarier than him here, though, if you hang around.'

After another two days, the 'developers' seemed to have reached an agreement on how to move forward. Pete had made some initial sketches, which looked to me like the plans for an aerodrome, not an eco-resort. If they were going to build accommodation for up to sixty people here, surely it had to blend in with the landscape? I had imagined airy, graceful structures made from the region's natural timbers, protected from the sun by huge shade sails and sheltered from the elements by natural contours, not this monstrosity. Where would all the staff stay? Where, for that matter, was any kind of forward planning? But I was trying to stay out of it. I couldn't bear the thought of this place being a rich man's playground. This short time on the island had convinced me that Resto was somewhere I could live in utter contentment. Spending the day fishing and the night yarning was my idea of bliss. It would be a perfect new start for Denika and me – I just wasn't sure how I was going to make that happen. For now, the development was another crazy Bluey idea that wouldn't happen in another hundred years. I had to bide my time.

On our last morning on the island, there was just time to take one last dip and catch some bait fish in a net as a thank you for our hosts' – very basic – hospitality. John had warned me about crocs, of course. Morning is the best time to be in the water, because you can spot the buggers from a lot further away. It was a cloudless day and the sea was calm and crystal clear, a brilliant turquoise laced with golden streamers of light. I waded in up to my knees and dared to let myself float on my back for a few seconds, then stood up quickly again to check if any beady eyes had broken the surface of the water. I was right at the point of the spit, where the north beach forms a sharp angle with the strip of sand that faces west across to the mainland. I felt totally isolated and enclosed by sea – it was that classic deserted island image of white sand and a single palm tree in the background. I spotted a small shoal of sardines in the shallows and ran back up the beach to grab a bait net, and then crept back into the water, hoping the shoal had not moved too far.

My gaze was fixed on the sardines beneath the surface, but I remembered to look up as I waded out up to my waist. That's when I spotted the fin. Not the reassuring curve of a dolphin fin bouncing through the water. This was the angular fin of a shark stalking his prey at what looked like one hundred kilometres per hour. It took a microsecond to process this information, and the same amount of time to decide not to hang around to find out whether the shark was after the sardines or me.

My first few thrusts through the water were not graceful. Luckily, the seabed slopes quite sharply at that point and after a few thrashing strides, I could just about lift my legs above the surface and practically hurdle my way to safety. Bent double, gulping in air, I watched in terror as the shark continued to power towards the shore. He only stopped in the very shallow water, where I could clearly make out that it was a hammerhead. With a couple of petulant thrashes, he turned tail and sulked his way back out onto the reef. *Jeez,* I thought. *With predatory cuckoos one minute and sharks the next, you needed to watch your step in this place.*

'Sh-sh-shark! H-h-hammerhead! Out there!' I spluttered to the guys, breathlessly pointing to the spit, running back to the house. 'Four metres. Huge. Chased me right onto the beach. Is anyone listening?' There was barely a twitch of acknowledgement, even from John, who would have known that these great hammerheads were quite rare here, compared to the more common smaller hammerheads.

'Behave, Glash,' said Bluey. 'With talk like that, you'll be scaring the visitors away before we even have a chance to build a resort. Pack your bags, we need to catch the tide.'

***

It turned out that sharks were the least of our worries. There were choppy waters to negotiate over the next few years and we were barely seaworthy. The broad plan was for John to stay on at Resto as caretaker, answering to Bluey, while we returned to Sydney to try and raise money for the planned joint venture development with Colin's company. The first step was to form a new company, Longboat Investments, which would be the legal entity involved in any contracts with Colin's company. Bluey, Pete and I were all directors and equal shareholders, along with our other investor, who agreed to stump up around $300,000, which wasn't a lot of money to him, to help fund the development approval. Then we discovered that in order to be granted development approval, we would have to carry out a full environmental impact study, or EIS. No one had factored this into the equation and, if we were going to have to cough up for this, we wanted something concrete in return. So Colin agreed to give Longboat one of his five shares in the company that owned Restoration Island. It was becoming far more complicated than I had ever intended, but at least I now had some legal standing on the island.

Bluey was our project manager on the ground and was paid to keep an eye on all the botanists, biologists, anthropologists and any other opportunist who cashed in on the environmental survey by counting lizards and birds for months on end. Soon we lost John as caretaker, along with his useful ties in the local community, after Bluey – not a people person at the best of times – donged him during a drunken argument. Then, when we heard that there were problems over bank interest payments, we felt we had to negotiate a formal sublease from the owners to provide more security for our investment. This all wasted a lot of time and energy. Finally, nearly three years after our first visit, the development application for a sixty-bed eco-resort on the habitable part of the island was submitted to the Cook Shire Council and approved.

Pete's initial design was never improved on, and I hated it – so much so that I personally paid for my first-ever girlfriend, Brit, and her husband, Peter, both trained architects, to submit an alternative design based on the traditional long houses of Papua New Guinea. I met Brit at Clover Moore's house – the same Clover Moore who's now the longest-serving Lord Mayor of Sydney. Clover was friendly with one of my mates and went to school with Brit. Brit was upside down when I first met her, but she was a beautiful, slim blonde-haired goddess from Norway, whichever way you looked at her. When we arrived, the girls were in the middle of a yoga session and my eyes nearly popped out of my head. Upright girls were fascinating enough, but girls doing headstands were mind-boggling. And then Brit opened her mouth and this deliciously exotic-sounding Scandinavian accent tumbled out: 'Do you please mind to stop staring at me?' I was in love. We spent two wonderful years together until she received some bombshell news. Her dad, who was top dog in a Swedish engineering company, had been offered a job in India. Brit had no option but to move with her parents, and then she was accepted to study architecture at Cambridge University in England. It was too good an opportunity to refuse, so we were forced into the longest of long-distance relationships. We wrote to each other every month and I still have all her letters here on the island. When she returned to Australia with Peter years later, we kept in touch and even holidayed as a group on Fraser Island, although Sylvi preferred to stay in the resort rather than camp. Brit and Peter became regular visitors to Resto, even though their two-storey long house design was rejected by the rest of my group.

I wasn't the only one who hated our initial design. Just a few weeks after the council decision to approve the plans, the people of Lockhart River launched an objection. How the hell had we completely overlooked the thoughts, feelings and dignity of the people who truly owned Restoration Island? My other shareholders were about as connected to this island as I was to the moon. We had been just as arrogant and ignorant as so many before us, ever since Europeans first arrived in Australia and began to systematically abuse the rights of Indigenous people. All the time that we'd been plotting and planning, the Kuuku Ya'u people kept their counsel, waiting to be consulted. That invite never came.

So, with no other option but to use white fella bureaucratic methods, Lockhart River Aboriginal Shire Council lodged an appeal on behalf of the traditional landowners. The appeal was sponsored by a powerful Indigenous organisation, Balkanu, run by Gerhardt Pearson. Gerhardt is the brother of Noel Pearson, a prominent lawyer, academic, Aboriginal land rights activist and the chairman of Cape York Land Council. Noel was a man who had strong admirers and detractors in equal measure.

The initial basis for the appeal was that we didn't own the land, but that was thrown out immediately. A legal lease document will always carry more weight with a judge than tens of thousands of years of history. Separately, the Aboriginal community also objected to not being consulted – and this challenge clearly had good grounds. But I wanted to avoid another legal battle – I'd already had enough of them to last a lifetime. Plus, I didn't want to be the bastard arguing against the land rights of Indigenous people. We needed another solution.

There was no point sending Bluey back up there to try and mediate. He'd already managed to piss everyone off, including the local hippy community based at Chilli Beach, opposite Restoration Island on the mainland, who he called 'ferals' in a court document. We had literally no allies in the area and the animosity towards us was spiralling out of control. So, in May 1997, armed with just a suitcase containing a mountain of documents, three shirts, two pairs of shorts and swimmers, a decent torch, a couple of books, a jar of chilli powder, some toothpaste and my toothbrush, I returned to Restoration Island, expecting to stay for a couple of weeks. I never truly left.

***

'You have to talk face to face. No phone calls. And try and find a mediator who they trust,' said my elder brother Mick, when I sounded him out for advice before I set off. We called him Guru Mick because, even as a boy, he was wise beyond his years and had life, with all its mysteries, figured out. He looks like a hippy Gandalf, the wizard from *The Lord of the Rings,* and is part of the landscape around Sydney's Northern Beaches, where he lives. We look similar, we're both talking machines, and neither of us has ever been scared of challenging normality. Mick studied architecture and was personally mentored by the American icon Buckminster Fuller, who was famous for inventing the geodesic dome. But Mick's real passion and skill was understanding Indigenous Australians. He made a film called *Uluru* for which he shot footage of an elder of the local Pitjantjatjara people walking around the rock telling traditional stories. Mick needed a wheelbarrow full of battery packs to make it all the way around. Then, he formed the Bush Video group of filmmakers, artists and technology experts who produced highly experimental video art on Indigenous themes. Some of their work won awards at international showcase events like the Cannes Film Festival. There was nobody better than Mick to advise me on how to approach a crisis meeting with the local Aboriginal people of Lockhart River.

'Listen and learn and work out where they are coming from,' he told me. 'Forget the businessman in you. Start by drawing in the sand with your finger or a stick. This is their place to talk. Let them figure things out for themselves. That's when good things will happen, not before. Don't complicate things. And make sure you know about these people. Learn their history. If you don't understand that, you will never gain their respect. But you should also be aware that, after the way this has already been handled, it will take you a decade to earn even a scrap of trust in their eyes.' Struth! My chances of making progress sounded bleak.

There was an obvious choice as mediator: the white CEO of the Lockhart River Aboriginal Shire Council, Dave Clark. He was trusted by the local people but, as a civil servant, had to stay neutral. What's more, he understood the Kuuku Ya'u. When I telephoned from Sydney to ask for his help before I made the trip back to Resto, he suggested we should meet in the council offices.

'How do you get to Lockhart River from the airport?' I asked.

'What? You didn't come into town when you were here last time?' he asked, incredulous.

'Errm, no, I don't think we did,' I mumbled. 'We were on a pretty tight schedule.' This sounded terrible, even to my own ears. We had been so wrapped up in our own agenda that we didn't even spare the time to set foot there. I wasn't going to make the same mistake twice, so I drove the four-wheel drive that Colin had left for me at the airport straight into town. What an eyeopener. The people there looked so dispirited. They had a haunted appearance and wouldn't make eye contact with me. To them, I was yet another white fella tourist, gawping at them like they were some kind of exhibit. I was so shocked that people were living in modern Australia in such poor conditions. I soon discovered prices of basic commodities like milk and bread in the town's one food store were way higher than what I would have paid in Sydney. I couldn't imagine there was much in the way of work out here, so I wondered how the locals could afford to pay those prices. I realised that my understanding of Indigenous issues was shamefully poor. I was all ears when Dave – a genial bloke with the leathery, weathered look of someone who's spent a long time in these parts – sat me in his office and told me all about the local history.

The region had originally been home to five different clan groups, each with their own *ngaachi,* or land. For example, the *ngaachi* of the predominant clan, the Kuuku Ya'u, stretched from Lloyd Bay to the Pascoe River, including

Restoration Island and Restoration Rock. Then the Europeans arrived and shattered the status quo. First on the scene in 1848 was Englishman Edmund Kennedy. Six of the eight men Kennedy left behind at Pascoe River starved to death after refusing fish and other food from the Kuuku Ya'u people, while Kennedy himself died further north, after copping a spear in the belly. 'What d'ya reckon, Dave, unprovoked attack or self-defence?' Dave asked with a wry smile.

In 1880, Dave explained, a Queensland government geologist, Robert Logan Jack, discovered Lockhart River on an expedition and named it after his close Scottish friend, Hugh Lockhart. By this time, fishermen in luggers were looking for sea cucumber, sold as a delicacy in China, and mother-of-pearl sea snail shells, or trochus, which were sold for jewellery. 'This was known as "lugger time",' Dave told me. 'Some captains paid Aboriginal family groups as little as $1.50 a month to dive for this stuff, even though it was worth a fortune. These people were exploited from day one.'

A sandalwood trader, Hugh Giblet, came to the rescue; he protected the locals from unscrupulous lugger captains and rewarded them with food, clothing and a bit of booze for a Christmas party. The Sandalwood King, as he called himself, objected to plans to build an Anglican Church mission near the river until he died in 1923. 'He was hit by a *woomera,* a wooden spear-throwing device, during an altercation,' Dave explained. 'It broke his jaw and the wound became infected. It must have been pretty wild up here in those days.'

A mission for about eighty Aboriginal people was eventually established in 1924 at the waterhole at Orchid Point, next to Giblet's old camp, and is now called Old Site. The local Aboriginal people were suddenly denied access to their country and forced to live alongside strangers and, in some cases, clan group enemies. But the mission briefly flourished and sustained its residents by catching fish, dugong and turtle and growing garden produce. Then more people from as far away as the Flinders Islands of Princess Charlotte Bay, about one hundred kilometres south, were brought to the mission. Only a few Indigenous people in the north-eastern area remained in their traditional lands, while the mission's population soared to almost 400.

When World War II broke out, the white folk fled back to the safety of the south and cynically advised the Aboriginal people to 'go bush' to escape air raids. The Indigenous people were happy to spread out and reconnect to their land. Two years after the war ended and peace was declared, the mission was re-established but it was described by Australian novelist Kylie Tennant as an 'insanitary and poverty-stricken little pesthole' and 'the worst mission of them all'. People were dying faster than babies were being born – until the arrival of a new superintendent, John Warby.

'You'll hear his name a lot around here,' said Dave. 'They call that period "Warby Time". He taught people to run their own cooperative trochus businesses and improve their own living conditions. For the first time, mission residents had a voice. It's what we try and encourage now. This fight over Restoration Island is one of those rare times when the community comes together as one.'

Then the market crashed. Not the stock market, the trochus market. Warby left and the Anglican Church handed over the mission to the Queensland Government, which tried to relocate the people to Bamaga, a small town forty kilometres from the tip of the peninsula. I was getting the picture. Why on Earth would the Indigenous people want to be uprooted again, so far away from their traditional lands? Quite rightly, they refused to go. Some reports suggest that the Old Site church was burned down by the authorities, under the guise of containing a tuberculosis outbreak. It forced them out. Apparently, the residents weren't given notice to even clear away the place settings that had been set for dinner. Most people believed that the fire was started deliberately, so that the residents of the mission would accept a compromise move from the coastal Old Site to the current location of Lockhart River, further north and two kilometres inland. Was it any wonder that this clumsy, callous move created friction that lingered to that day?

'You've got your work cut out, that's for sure,' Dave said. 'I wouldn't want to be in your shoes, the way the locals are feeling right now.'

It was a lot for me to digest, but I was in a much better position to engage with the locals in a meaningful way. The meeting was scheduled for two weeks later, on the island. This gave me a chance to get to know Resto again. And I finally had her all to myself.

Bluey had left a small tinny for me at Cape Weymouth and seeing the island again sent a tingle down my spine. Then, having moored the boat, my heart immediately sank. Another three years of rubbish had accumulated. The lawn area was overgrown. Dead palm fronds littered the beach, which had not been tidied since I was last there. No wonder the local people wanted us out of the picture.

Light was fading fast and there was no point making a start straight away, so I just swept the kitchen, tidied up the house, grabbed a reasonably clean sheet to place on the not-so-clean mattress, and plotted my course of action for the next two weeks. On the previous trip, I had slept in the space shuttle, a grey, fibreglass domed pre-fab near the generator shed at the foot of the hill. The design was not dissimilar to those my brother Mick had studied. It was totally out of place here – an ugly stain on this canvas of potential beauty. It was too claustrophobic for my liking. Ever since I was a child, growing up during World War II and sleeping in a room with windows blacked out to prevent another Japanese attack on Sydney Harbour, I have hated rooms with little natural light. I felt much more at home in the house than the space shuttle. The warm breeze was a soothing relief in the sticky night, and a zillion stars were visible through the windows. But the best part of being in the house that night? I couldn't hear the constant background babble of business bullshit, just the gentle flop of the waves on the beach – nature's sleeping pill.

My priority for the next two weeks was cosmetic repair. I was determined to present the island in the best possible light for the big meeting. Almost at first light, after a breakfast of muesli, fruit juice and coffee with powdered milk, I found a wheelbarrow and rusty spade in the shed and started the arduous task of shovelling the remnants of rubbish fires into one large natural gulley that, if not filled with rubbish, would empty out onto the southernmost tip of the beach during the rainy season. This was May, only a month after the rains, so the concrete tank midway up the hill was full and I didn't have to worry about water supplies.

After two hours of gruelling toil I was whacked – and I'd barely made an impression on the first of perhaps ten mounds scattered across the island. I was in the worst physical health of my life, overweight by a good twenty-five kilograms and smothered in middle-aged spread. My sweat was torrential and my clothes were saturated. Then it hit me: what the hell was I wearing clothes for anyway? I felt a delicious freedom when I let it all hang out. Most of my skin was used to the sun from so much time spent around yachts in Sydney, but I was careful not to overexpose the newly exposed areas.

Clearing the rubbish took a full week. Whenever I needed a break, I went for a fish, either in the boat or from the beach. Buying from the visiting trawlers, I also built up my stores of prawns and crayfish in the freezer, which was run off a cranky old generator in the shed, and collected plenty of oysters ready for the welcome feast. Then I turned my attention to mowing and weeding the five acres of flat land, which mostly stretched out in front of the house but also surrounded the sides and rear. There was no chance of achieving such a feat in a few days, but I could at least make it look more presentable with the hand mower. Those blades would have struggled to slice through butter, and it was another killer task. I kept my thongs on most of the time. It was almost impossible to walk barefoot because of the rusted star pickets, pointed metal posts used for holding fencing or tying a tree, that were buried under the soil surface and impossible to spot. Step on one of these and it would easily pierce deep into the soft flesh of the foot, and always resulted in a trip to the clinic for either a tetanus injection or antibiotics. They were little booby traps of agony, on par with the caltrop bindi-eye weed. Its spiny thorns grow out of a woody burr and can penetrate a rubber thong, as I soon discovered. I leapt a mile high and it was a good job that no one was around to hear my colourful assessment of the situation. The weeds were all over, too, probably covering two-thirds of the ground, but were pretty easy to spot because the runners can grow for metres. Clearing them would have to wait for another time.

Every day, I forced myself to walk further and further without anything on my feet because I knew I needed to toughen up, physically and mentally, to meet the island's challenges. Finally, I removed the sticks that marked the Indigenous burial site and laid white stones neatly around the edges. It was a symbolic gesture of my new-found respect for the history of this place.

There was just time for one more trip into town to stock up on fresh items for the salads ahead of the meeting. It was then I realised I hadn't spoken a single word to anyone else in two weeks. I'd been perfectly happy in my own company and had not felt lonely once. I left town with my shopping without speaking to anyone, too. Either my isolation was making me paranoid, or word was out that I was the big-city bully who wanted to steal the locals' land.

The Lockhart River delegation consisted of about twenty members of the Kuuku Ya'u clan, some of whom I had agreed with Dave Clark to pick up in the tinny at Portland Roads, a tiny picturesque settlement a few kilometres up the coast from Cape Weymouth. Portland Roads had safe anchorage, protected from the south-easterlies for commercial fishing vessels and passing yachts, and was more accessible by dirt track than Cape Weymouth, too. Several senior male members of the delegation came back with me, while the others brought their own boats to the island. I was nervous. Should I shake their hands? Would it be too familiar? I'd read that it wasn't really a part of Aboriginal culture. But would they be offended if I didn't? I opted to offer my hand – a couple accepted, some didn't. It was a sticky start and my boat group only spoke a few words to each other on the trip across to the island. They were clearly tense, too, and I could not have felt more like an outsider in their company.

The leader of their group was Sweeney Hobson, one of the elders of probably the most influential family in the clan. But another of the fellas in my boat had much more of a presence. Jerry 'Wolfie' Pascoe didn't say a word, but he made my hairs stand on end. He had an aura that exuded dignity and commanded respect. When we landed, Jerry headed straight for the house, where I had prepared the fresh food and built a makeshift barbecue from a few bricks and some wire grating that I found in the shed, ready to cook the fish on. Wolfie grabbed one of the two chairs and told me, matter-of-factly: 'When I come here again, this is my chair.'

'Yes, sir, whatever you say,' I said, smiling.

When I asked Dave, who came in another boat, what time I should start cooking, he told me to leave my visitors to do everything. Those who didn't cook sat talking to each other, while some wandered around the island. I hoped they would notice my work on the burial site. Dave introduced me to everyone individually and I told them all that I was there to listen. I brought out a few beers, but not too many. I didn't want alcohol to obstruct the real business at hand. Then, with our stomachs full, it was time to move to the shade under the palms by the beach, sit down in the sand, and talk. Dave explained their position in detail and I started to tell them about our plans, drawing in the sand as Mick had instructed. When I looked up to scan their faces for approval, my glance met with a uniform scowl.

Then Sweeney suddenly took over.

'This land, this ocean, is my birthright,' he said. 'We don't want your mob here. Go back to the city. Go back to your money. That is your life. There is nothing for you here.'

'Yes, I understand,' I replied. 'We have made mistakes. We have been thoughtless. But we're not trying to take what's rightfully yours. Let's find a way of working together. It has to be a better way than going to court.'

'Bugger working together,' Sweeney barked. This went down well with the group.

'Look, believe it or not, I'm on your side,' I said. 'I actually want you to *win* if we go to court. But you won't win. These are white fella rules in white fella court. Colin Lindsay's company has the lease and that's all that matters to lawyers.'

'No white fellas talk to us about development,' said Sweeney.

'I know, and I'm sorry about that. Honestly, I am. That can't be changed now. But we can start talking.'

'Bugger talking,' grunted Sweeney. More appreciative murmurs.

I was devastated that I hadn't been able to make any progress. I had been banking on my negotiating skills to persuade them to reconsider their objection. The atmosphere in the boat back to the island was frosty and, on the small beach at Portland Roads, I just thanked the men for their time and for listening to me.

Then Wolfie spoke up. 'When we win in court, we ask this old fella here to look after the island. Davo is like Warby. A good man,' he said. Old fella? That was a bit harsh! But I'd made an impression on one person, at least, and I later learned that the term 'old fella' was a sign of respect.

'It would be an honour to do that,' I replied. 'A real honour.'

Chapter 4

Nature's bounty

After the meeting with the Kuuku Ya'u, I decided to hang around and make myself useful on the island. There was nothing urgent to attend to in Sydney, and my first two weeks on the island made me realise just how much work was needed to restore Resto to its former glory. It would also be good for the locals to see that I was here to stay, and that I hadn't just flown in to deliver a few empty promises. If they could see I had the island's welfare at heart, perhaps I could win them over. I wrote a letter to thank them again for the meeting, to spell out the differing positions and also to offer the local community an equity position in Longboat, hoping it might make them feel sufficiently invested to call off the court case. Despite all of this, their objection went ahead and, of course, we won. It was a pyrrhic victory. We had won the battle but started a war, as I discovered on my next trip into town for some essentials. Determined to retain my dignity, I smiled at everyone I passed on the street. Most people just turned their backs. Inside the store, when I went down one aisle it instantly cleared. There was even silence at the cash register when I paid for my goods. Then, while carrying my bags to the car, I passed a group of men and women. 'White cunt,' one muttered, loud enough to make sure I heard. Jeez, this was going to be a bumpy ride.

 I drove round to the council offices to talk to Dave Clark, but I felt that even he wanted to keep me at arm's length. It wouldn't be good for him to be seen to be fraternising with the enemy. However, he did tell me that Rolf Harris was bringing a TV crew to Restoration Island in a few days to film a documentary about Captain Bligh. *What?* Rolf Harris was coming to Resto? It was unbelievable. *Tie Me Kangaroo Down, Sport* was more famous than our national anthem. This bloke was a cultural superstar. He was a bigger Aussie name around the world than Dame Edna Everage, even Crocodile

Dundee. And he was coming here? The timing could not have been better. I needed something to look forward to.

'That's exciting,' I said. 'But why are they filming something about Captain Bligh on the island?' I asked, quite innocently.

'You still have a lot to learn about this place, don't you?' Dave laughed. 'It was Bligh who named it Restoration Island. Apparently there are some carvings in the rocks at the top of the island that were made by his men, too. Here, read this.' He handed me a copy of the book *Mutiny on the Bounty.* Back on the island, I finished the book in one sitting. I already knew the bones of the story, but nothing about what happened to Bligh and his eighteen loyal men after Fletcher Christian had booted them off the *Bounty.* It was one of history's most incredible feats of endurance, seamanship and leadership.

Bligh and his men had barely enough food for a week, four cutlasses, and a quadrant and a compass, but no charts. They were crammed into the launch like sardines, with water almost coming over the sides. His intended destination, Timor, the nearest European colonial outpost of the Dutch East Indies, was almost 7000 kilometres away. Despite the odds stacked against them, more than three weeks later – and with the men on death's door from starvation and dehydration – Bligh spotted the Great Barrier Reef. On Thursday 28 May 1789, he navigated the boat through an opening towards an island with a 'bay and a fine sandy point'. If he did manage to do this without charts, it was an unbelievable feat because Bligh's Entrance, as it's now called, is such a narrow gap.

After mooring the boat and staggering onto the beach, Bligh immediately felt nervous when he spotted the remains of camp fires. He'd had trouble with unfriendly South Pacific natives in the past. There was just enough light for some of the men to gather a few oysters but they couldn't build a fire, so half of them slept back on the boat and the others slept on the beach so that if one group encountered danger, at least the other would survive.

The following day Bligh found wiregrass and realised that the soil must be moist. In true castaway style, he stuck a three-foot stick into the earth, found water and dug a well. According to his journal, he then found two 'ill constructed' huts and a catapult, along with kangaroo tracks. After lighting a fire using a magnifying glass, the men cooked a stew with some bread and tiny pieces of pork from their rations. They cut down the tops of some small palm trees and ate the soft, fleshy hearts, and also tried – unsuccessfully – to roast fern roots. Bligh warned his men not to eat the berries – but you try saying that to men on the brink of starvation. He described one fruit as like a sweet gooseberry, another like elderberries growing in clusters, and a third like a blackberry.

Despite their ordeal, Bligh's journal was upbeat and jaunty and, just before noon on that second day, 29 May, he wrote: 'This being the Day of the Restoration of King Charles the 2nd, and the name being not inapplicable to my present situation (for it has restored us to fresh life and strength), I named it Restoration Island, for I think it probable Cap.n Cook may not have taken notice of it.'

Bligh and his men gathered meagre supplies for the trip ahead to Coupang (now Kupang in Indonesia), which would last another sixteen days, and prepared to set out to sea again late on the Saturday afternoon, just as native people began to gather threateningly on the mainland shore.

This information mesmerised me. The book had transported me back in time. I could clearly picture Bligh standing proudly at the sandy point of the beach and writing in his journal, although the high water mark would have been much further inland in those days, because the beach grows every year due to wind and wave action. The palms that Bligh referred to would have been about seventy metres from today's high water mark, but have long since fallen.

It's possible they found a spring, too, because in late May there would not have been much water left in the soil from the rainy season. The only natural water here today is a soak on the rocky side of the island, marked by a palm-like pandanus tree, and it would surely have been impossible for these men, in their physical state, to have climbed around to that point. They definitely wouldn't have been able to climb to the top of the island to make any carvings in the rocks. So, if these carvings *did* exist, it would cast a lot of doubt over Bligh's official account of those days here. Two days was no time to recover their strength and health for the next leg of their voyage.

Much of his retelling was easy for me to relate to, though. There is a gooseberry-like fruit which still grows here. It's deliciously tangy. And our native grapes do look like clusters of elderberries. He discovered ants' nests that were 'webbed like a spider's, but so close and compact as not to admit rain'. This might actually have been a funnel web. Perhaps the Indigenous people bred kangaroos here so that they were easier to hunt, which would explain the camp fires, the catapult and the huts. And the fact that he named this place Restoration Island was uncanny. It restored Bligh and his men to fresh life and strength. After just three weeks on my own here, I was already feeling like a new man, despite all the unpleasantness surrounding the development approval. The future was very uncertain, but I was intent on making the most of my time on Resto.

I became obsessed with the possibility that there were carvings at the summit. They could have real historical significance. I had bashed my way back up there before the meeting with the locals, and it was obvious nobody had been there since my first visit three years earlier. Strips of the pink marking tape still clung to the trees. From then, I made a point of climbing to the top every few days. It was good for my soul. And I scoured every inch of granite, every nook and cranny, in search of something to indicate that Bligh's men had made it up here. Nothing. But I didn't have any clues to follow. If Rolf Harris was bringing a big TV crew with a team of researchers, perhaps he might be able to shed some light on it. I would be sure to ask him.

The weather on the scheduled day for filming was dreadful: overcast with storm clouds building up over the sea. In the morning I received a rare call on the radio phone, which picked up a signal from the tower in Lockhart River via the antenna on the roof of the house, from one of the producers. He asked if I could go to Portland Roads to help take some of their equipment over to the island. I was happy to help, but the wind had whipped up, the rain was coming down in sheets and it really wasn't safe for me to take the boat over there. A promise is a promise, though, so I battled the elements to reach Portland Roads, very relieved to be back on solid ground. The storm was raging and there was no way I could risk trying to get the crew across to the island with their expensive equipment until it had blown over. *In any case, where is everyone?* I wondered. I could see all their vehicles, but there were no other boats and no people. 'They set off half an hour ago,' shouted Geoff Pope, who ran the small Australia Post office there. 'Wanted to miss the worst of the weather.'

'Charming! Nobody told me,' I said. 'Suppose I'll sit it out here, but then the tide will be out. I'm stuck here like a shag on a rock for the afternoon.' Our group had been just as unpopular among the white folks as it was with the Aboriginal people, so there was nobody for me to turn to for a cuppa or a beer, or even for shelter from the rain, so I slumped under the biggest palm I could find. Soon the storm blew over and the skies cleared, but all I could do was twiddle my thumbs for four or five hours until the tide came in far enough to allow me to return to the island.

I moored the boat at Resto just as the crew was packing their gear into their boats. Rolf was heading down to the water to leave. 'Excuse me, Mr Harris,' I panted. 'I'm sorry that I missed you this afternoon. Not my fault, I should add. Bloody weather. Loved *Jake the Peg,* by the way. And I've got a sheet of tin over at the house that might make a good wobble board. Anyways, do you have a few minutes? I wanted to pick your brains on something of historical interest about

Bligh.' The prick just stared at me like I was something he'd stepped in, and carried on towards the boat without a word. No thanks for allowing them to use the island, no apology for wasting my whole day. I was speechless. It shattered my illusions of him but, of course, it wasn't too long before the real Rolf Harris was revealed to the world as a mongrel paedophile. Perhaps his time in the big house has taught him some humility, too.

***

A few days later, I was preparing for another day of hard yakka, with a breakfast of cereal and some extra chopped banana for energy, when the phone rang. *Two calls in a few days – I'm becoming more popular,* I thought. 'Is that Mr David Glasheen?' asked a very serious-sounding man. 'We have your daughter Erika at the police station in Kings Cross. Could you come down here, please, straight away?'

'Err, not really. I'm in the middle of nowhere. I could perhaps make it for late this afternoon, but even that would be pushing it. Is she okay? What's happened?'

'Not really. Look, as one dad to another, she needs you here as soon as possible.'

'Okay, tell her I'm on my way.'

Shit! The next flight to Cairns was in two hours and the tide was on its way out. This was going to be tight. I rang the airline, Aero-Tropics in those days, and grabbed the last seat on the afternoon flight out of Lockhart River. I could sort out the Sydney flight once I was in Cairns. I needed to be in the boat within minutes or there was no chance of making it to the airport in time. I threw a shirt and a pair of shorts into my bag and ran down to the beach to find the boat grounded. *Shit, shit!* I knew pushing it out through the mud would take too long, if I could manage it at all. Luckily, I had combed the beach the previous day and left anything that might be useful in a big pile. There were two sections of sturdy plastic piping, so I shoved them under the boat's front, a metre apart. It was much easier pushing the boat onto the first roller, and then onto the second, than heaving it through the mud. The hardest part was dragging the first roller back out from underneath to place back at the front once I had got it rolling, because I had to tip the boat forward with my bodyweight while holding the pipe. I really was becoming something of an athlete. After I had repeated this move a couple of times, I calculated there was just enough water to take the motor. Thankfully it started first time, which wasn't always the case, and I was away.

Nearly seven breathless hours later and I was banging at the front desk of the station at Kings Cross. Ricky had been in an argument with her girlfriend, a Canadian as cold as the North Pole. It was a toxic relationship and, apparently, it had turned very ugly. At one stage they took restraining orders out on each other. On this occasion the police were called to reports of a domestic incident, and found Ricky out on the street while her partner hurled her possessions out of the window from four floors up. Ricky had been charged with assault and needed me to bail her out.

It had been apparent to me for some time that her drinking was a problem but, while her personal life was spiralling out of control, her career hadn't suffered and she had been making a name for herself as a chef. Soon after moving back to Sydney from Brisbane, where Ricky briefly lived with a boyfriend, she started to run a fancy restaurant, Barrenjoey House, while the owners disappeared for winter. By all accounts, she was a tough cookie who sacked suppliers when necessary and was never afraid to cut costs. When I was in Sydney, we would meet up occasionally for a drink, but I never saw her actually drunk. She was careful about how much she drank in public – and then secretly carried on in private.

In a stroke of luck, my Uncle Norm, Mum's sister's husband, said that he would build Sylvi a new house in Berridale, a small place near Jindabyne, the last town before the Snowy Mountains snowfields. Samantha and Ricky moved with their mum to make a new start together, approximately two years after I first visited Resto. The deal was that Sylvi would look after Uncle

Norm in his old age. He was a sprightly old fella and was still driving at the age of ninety-four – on the wrong side of the road, mind you, but still driving. Ricky found work in nearby Cooma and the ski resorts, before she went on to become the number-two chef at the number-two restaurant in Canberra. Then, a few years later, celebrity chef Bill Granger took her on at his Woollahra restaurant, one of his three Sydney eateries. Ricky was the first chef to be employed by Granger who hadn't been through his training program.

At first, everyone tried to keep her sexuality from me. I have no idea why. What went on behind closed doors was none of my business and didn't change my love for her. I guess all parents dream of their children finding a nice husband or wife and having lots of beautiful little grandchildren, but I really didn't care whether she was straight or gay, as long as she was happy. It was clear to me, though, that she wasn't happy in this new relationship with the Ice Woman. Ricky ran in some interesting circles and drugs were clearly an issue, but I figured most people experiment with them at some point.

There were other signs of her inner turmoil, too. She self-mutilated and had lots of tattoos, including a Japanese one that meant 'be warned'. Ricky was tiny but very strong and could clearly handle herself in a fight. As I led her down the steps of the police station, I decided it was time for a heart-to-heart chat. I wanted to go somewhere well away from prying eyes and her old influences, so I took her down to La Peruse to watch the sunset, hoping to replicate the tranquillity of Resto. 'Ricky, there's only one way out of this,' I said. 'You need to get out of this city, it's bad for you. Please, come and stay with me on the island. Just give it six months and see how you feel.'

'I'm fine, Dad,' she said. 'I know I need to change. This has been a wake-up call, honestly. But please don't worry about me. I promise I'll come to the island soon.'

I couldn't force her to go back with me, she was far too headstrong for that. The only practical thing I could do to help was to scrape some money together and hire one of my barrister mates to fight the assault charge. But our heart-to-heart had been illuminating for me in another way. I was talking to Ricky about Resto as home, and for the long term. I couldn't wait to be back there away from the trauma of city life. Denika still appeared keen to join me, as long as I could convince her that she wasn't going to be closing the salon and moving away from her two sons on a whim. It took me one day to place my belongings in storage and this time I headed back with two suitcases, filled with all my cherished personal items like photos and books. For me this was a one-way ticket – there was no going back to civilisation. Whatever the eventual outcome of all the development plans, I was intent on becoming the island's permanent custodian.

***

If this island was going to be my permanent home, I had to stamp my mark on the place. My first project was a no-brainer: I had to revolutionise the eating arrangements. It beggared belief that nobody had thought about creating a dining area down at the beach. Why hang around the house when nature had created the perfect picnic spot just a stroll away? Within a few weeks I was receiving the occasional visitor, usually one of the trawler captains who often moored in the sheltered bay. They were always keen to swap a box of prawns for a few beers, as their rations of grog disappeared quickly. I wanted to really get to know these guys, and where better for them to open up than around a camp fire down on the beach? The fire is the critical element. It's an ageold tradition in many cultures, especially in Aboriginal ones, to sit around the fire and tell stories – but this custom is fading in modern society. When you look into a fire, you clear your mind of debris. People – fathers and sons especially – lose their inhibitions, reconnect and open up. When visitors shared this island, I wanted to make it easier for them to share a piece of themselves, too. We needed a place that could nurture those connections. Cooking on a camp fire is never too easy though, so we needed to build a proper cooking area with shelter and a few seats. We needed a beach shack.

I wouldn't have known where to start. Fortunately, though, another of the early visitors was Hippy Richard and his family, who had used Resto as a base for fishing weekends for some time. Richard de Ruiter, nicknamed Hippy Richard for his flowing locks and long beard, not unlike my own, was a Dutch maths teacher who lived at Mission Beach, just south of Cairns. The man had amazing bush skills. His sideline work was construction, and he excelled at making incredible living spaces out of concrete. And, unlike our mob's efforts, his constructions blended in with the environment. No project, in any location, was too great a challenge for Richard. His wife, Sandra, was a strong, resilient woman and his grown-up son, Emile, was studying architecture. They either camped on the island or, on calm nights, slept on the trampoline nets of their trimaran.

'We were hoping to stay for a couple of weeks, if that's okay, Dave,' Richard said. I was thankful to see a friendly face up here, so I welcomed them with open arms. 'What can we do in return?' he added. 'I can see you've started tidying the place. There must be something we can build.'

'Funny you should say that,' I replied, and told them about my plans for a beach shack.

'Leave this to me,' said Emile, confidently. 'I know just the spot, right on the sand spit there.'

'No, I don't want it there,' I said. 'It's too on display. Every man and his dog will be dropping in. I don't want anyone to know I'm here.'

'Err, David. You are talking to a trained architect here. I think I know the best place for it,' Emile said.

'And I think I know where I want it. Just set back in amongst the trees. We'll still have a clear view out onto the water, but we'll be much harder to spot.'

It was too much for Emile's pride to handle and he spat the dummy. He built his own little camp site at the southern end of the beach and we didn't see him for two days. Meanwhile,

Richard, Sandra and I set about building the shack.

First we needed three strong logs, each about the same thickness, for the three pillars of a triangle. By now, I knew every washed up log on the island and they were all high above the water on the windward side of the island. Richard and I took the boat in as close as possible to the shore, and took turns swimming in with a crowbar. We tied rope around one end of the logs, then levered them into the sea, tied the rope to the boat and floated the logs round to the beach. Next, we had to dig three holes, each a couple of metres deep, using just a spade. It was tough going. The sides of the holes remained stable but moist, so we had to lay planks around the top of the holes so that we didn't accidentally step near the openings and collapse the walls. Thankfully Emile was back on board, because it was all hands on deck to drop in the logs, which we had sawn down to the correct length with a rusty old blade. There was no way I could have done it all on my own. For a shade sail, I found an old boom cover on a boat that had been abandoned in the bushes near Cape Weymouth, and we tied it to the pillars through holes we had hand-drilled in the top of them. A few years later, with the help of two Dutch wwoofers called Chris and Daniel, we added another post to make a rhomboid shape, so that more people could sit in the shade. Finally, we needed to make the place homey with some maritime shabby chic. We draped fishing nets over the posts, hung lanterns and lifebelts from the nets, laid thick rope along the shade, and created a few seats from crates. For some reason, crates for bottles of home-brew from Japan were a regular treasure find, probably offloaded into the sea by fishermen. This alfresco dining project took a week, and I sometimes had to physically stop Richard and Sandra from working. I couldn't have been prouder of our creation.

Running in parallel was our barbecue-building program. We made the pit out of a forty-four-gallon oil drum, sawn in half lengthways with a hacksaw. I had forearms like Popeye after that! Inside, we placed the metal rim of a truck wheel to give the fire area some structure, and also to help retain the heat. We then filled the area around the truck wheel with sand for insulation. Finally came the stainless-steel grill, which had once been used as a sieve in a mine but had been thrown out because of a small hole. It had somehow made its way over here before my time on the island, and I soon realised that visitors often brought random gifts like this; I always find a use for them. To light the fire, I use a few heat beads and then add wood or dried coconut husks. There's an endless supply of them, which I leave to dry in four wooden pens under fishing nets so they don't blow away. One wheelie bin full of dry husks is enough for a good meal. On his next visit, Richard brought some welding equipment to add a rotisserie frame and handle. Initially we had to hand-turn the spit, but I later bought battery-operated motors, and kept our original spikes.

The fruits of our hard labour were sensational. The first fish on the barbie was a huge mangrove jack with salt, chilli flakes and olive oil rubbed into the skin, and served with a lovely fresh salad and a cold glass of chardonnay that the de Ruiters family had brought. Straight away, I picked up the subtle coconut flavour from the husks in the meat of the fish. I felt like jumping into the boat and catching another then and there, even though it was pitch black. For the rotisserie, Sandra had brought a lamb shank, basted in olive oil and garlic, and stuck some sprigs of rosemary into the meat. I parboiled the veggies – sweet potatoes and carrots – pricked them with a fork and coated them in salt, wrapped them in foil and stuck them in the fire. Although I like to eat slowly, this meal didn't touch the sides. Everything was melt-in-your-mouth tender and oozed flavour.

Over the course of a few weeks and months, the island started to look a lot more homey. There was a huge amount still to do, but I could now invite Denika and be confident that she would see the potential. I made a big effort to add some female touches, too, like sticking little pieces of coral in between the bricks of the house. I even carved 'Welcome Denika' into a piece of driftwood, which I painted and hung over the entrance to the house. I'd never done anything handy like this around the family home when I was married to Sylvi, and married to the job. I can't remember ever using a hammer or paint brush on our house. Sylvi was lucky if I mowed the lawn once a month. Here, I was determined to keep on top of all the regular chores. The only difference was that it now took me the best part of a week to mow the five acres of flat ground. It was risky work too in those early days, because all sorts of metal fragments – bits of wire or shards of glass, blown all around from the rubbish dumps – would fly up from the mower. I soon learned to wear shades and a lap-lap for protection. A lap-lap is a style of loincloth from Papua New Guinea that looks a bit like a nappy when folded neatly around my groin to cover anything that might cause offence to visitors. All that time in the sun had bleached my hair blond and my matching white beard was starting to take shape. I had a great all-over tan, and the physical labour was paying dividends for my physique, too. I had already lost about twenty kilograms and, for the first time in my life, I had a six pack – a home-brew six pack, but it looked much better than the beer belly I arrived with.

The amazing effects that island life can have on a man's health were not new to me. Fraser Island, with its incredible 123-kilometre stretch of pristine beach, had been a regular getaway spot for me and my advertising mate, Roger Richmond-Smith, when I worked for a company called Queensland United Foods (QUF) in Brisbane. We camped up at Sandy Point or Middle Head, out of the way of tourists, and once we finished our respective annual marketing and advertising plans there, we flew them express back to Brisbane to meet our deadlines. The following year, Roger was experiencing some health problems and his doctor told him to cut back on the booze and fags. 'The best place for you is Fraser Island,' I told him. 'And I could do with a break from the booze, too. We'll take two bottles of wine, that's one glass each per night. And no ciggies. I'm in charge!'

Apart from fishing tackle, all we needed then were two kilos of rice, some salt and pepper, a couple of limes and a cooking pot. Nature would provide the rest. Fresh water came from the clear creeks and we could collect pipis and beachworms for bait. When we arrived at Middle Head and picked our spot, I noticed Roger rummaging around in the back of the car. 'What are you after, Smithy?' I called.

'Nothing mate, just lost a thong.'

'What do you need thongs for?' I asked. Nobody wore thongs here.

'Err, no reason, really,' he said sheepishly. There was something fishy about this, so I went to investigate. The bugger had brought his own supply of grog in an esky and was swigging a cheeky beer or two before we headed off for a fish. Then, hidden under another blanket, were ten packets of smokes. 'Right, you know the rules,' I said, snatching the bottle out of his hand and pouring the contents into the sand. 'One glass of wine a night, we said. If you won't take responsibility for your health, I will. Touch one of those fags and I swear the rest will go on the camp fire.'

'You prick!' he yelled. 'We're not bloody married, you know.' Smithy stormed off and our tiff lasted for two whole days. We fished at different spots, ate at different times and didn't speak a word to each other. By the third day he was running up and down the sand dunes like a teenager.

'I've never felt better in my life,' Smithy said, when he finally opened up to me around the camp fire as we cooked the day's catch, usually jewfish or tailor. 'I need someone to be strict with me. Reckon I owe you an apology, Glash.' He even refused his one glass of wine, which meant one more for me. Fraser Island was a magical place and, as I fell asleep that night under the stars to the soothing sound of Smithy snoring like a camel in labour, I remember thinking that I could get used to this island life. A few days there set Smithy on the road to recovery, but I caught a disease that's impossible to cure: islomania, an obsession with islands. It's a blissful yet intense form of intoxication and I hope I never find a remedy.

***

I couldn't wait to show Denika what a few months on Resto had done for my health. But, out of the blue, I received a weird call from her. 'I've got a friend who has just got divorced and is at a loose end,' said Denika. 'We wondered whether she could come up to Resto for a few days. She's called Jenny.' (Names have been changed to protect *my* innocence.) The penny didn't drop until Jenny arrived and within five minutes asked if I minded if she went topless.

'Knock yourself out,' I said. And she very nearly did knock herself out when she bounded down to the beach.

'Do you want to give me a massage?' she purred, back at the house.

'I suppose I don't mind giving you a massage,' I said, and spent about thirty minutes nervously prodding her calf muscles and ankles.

'Don't you like me, Dave?' she asked, tentatively.

'I don't dislike you. But you've only been here two hours. I don't really know you.'

I was buggered if I knew how to react. Jenny didn't appreciate my caginess one little bit and the atmosphere was as frosty as it can be in thirty-five-degree heat for the rest of her stay. Shortly after this visit, Denika called again. 'I hear you and Jenny didn't hit it off. Would you mind if Barbara spends a few days up there? She's going through a bad patch.' Had I become some remote drop-in centre for fallen women? Or was Denika trying to set me up so that she didn't have to make a commitment? If it was the latter, she wasn't doing a very good job.

'Carry me to the boat,' pleaded Barbara as she wobbled from the car to the beach at Cape Weymouth in her high heels. Even with my new-found strength, I couldn't have managed that task.

'What was that?' she shrieked, slapping at her arm. 'I felt something bite me!'

'Probably just a mozzie,' I told her impatiently.

'That's just great. Now I've got malaria. Take me to the nearest doctor!' she howled. It was going to be a long few days. In the boat, she scared off every gull from here to the top of Australia with her screams each time spray splashed over the side. Barbara couldn't help with the cooking – she only ate in restaurants. She wouldn't drink powdered milk – it upset her constitution. She couldn't wash up – it would ruin her nails. She didn't want to swim in the water – it would spoil her hair. She didn't want to sleep alone, but she didn't want to be in the same room as me, either. 'There's going to be no hanky-panky,' she said. 'You're not wrong there,' I muttered under my breath.

By the time Denika finally did arrive for a visit, a few weeks later, I was as toey as a Roman sandal. She travelled up on the supply barge from Cairns, which was captained by a tyrant called Captain Bob and his blonde commandant girlfriend. I often tell city people to sail up here. They need those thirty-six hours to unwind and set their body clocks to Resto time. When they come straight from the city by plane, the static electricity from their stress sets my beard on end. The boat trip absorbs all that negative energy.

It was not exactly a relaxing experience for Denika, though. She wasn't used to being told what to do, and she struggled to conform to some aspects of Captain Bob's strict regime, like waiting until the captain sat at the head of the table before she could start her dinner. She also noticed that the crew received bigger servings than the paying passengers, and had access to all the best snacks. Rebellious as ever, Denika sneaked into the galley at night-time and was literally caught with her hand in the cookie jar. She copped a spray for that but it was nothing compared to when she went in to bat for a young Aboriginal girl, another paying passenger, who was being treated like shit by the crew. Denika was practically confined to her quarters after that confrontation.

She was still spitting feathers about the Neanderthal crew as I unloaded her bags onto the beach at Resto, having picked her up from the barge at Lockhart River. 'And you'll never guess what happened next...' she started to say, but couldn't finish her sentence before this caveman dragged her straight into the bushes. Remember that not too long before, I'd been struggling in that department. So when I pounced on her again before we'd even made it back to the house, Denika was understandably astounded. 'Jeez, what's got into you, Dave?' she squealed. 'You haven't been sticking needles in your dick again, have you?'

'No need for needles up here,' I said. 'This place is all the stimulant I need.' It was true: I felt invigorated on Resto. I had room to breathe, space to think, freedom to feel human again. Blood was surging through my veins once more. And over the next week, we left no stone unturned. We had sex on the rocks, sex in the sea and even had a go in a hammock, with disastrous results. It wasn't one-way traffic, either. Denika was as keen as mustard – up to a point. 'I'm not complaining,' she panted, 'but this is exhausting. I actually need a couple of days off.' It was a perfect week, one which reminded us how good we could be together – in the right circumstances. If Denika had any doubt about coming to live here permanently, I reckoned I'd given it my best shot to persuade her.

Chapter 5

Father time

It was a terrible day to be off-loading a large quantity of roofing iron. There was a strong southerly, with gusts probably up to forty kilometres per hour. The sea was rough and I shouldn't have even been out in the tinny, but the mothership needed to deposit the iron sheets here before taking other supplies, which were weighed down underneath the iron panels, further north. The delivery ship captain, Paul, was adamant that the job couldn't be put off for another day, when he moored the mothership 200 metres off the beach in the lee of the island, partly sheltered from these winds, and left his crew and me to do all the hard work while he jumped in his dinghy to come ashore and take a quick dip with his wife and daughters.

'Are you sure?' I checked. 'It's going to be hard enough to even pull my tinny up alongside your boat, let alone off-load the panels. And your crew want me to take two loads at a time. There's no way I can do that. Have you seen the size of my tinny? I don't care if it takes us until next week.'

'Dave, we've done this a thousand times,' he assured me. 'Just listen to Buddha over here,' he gestured to his first mate, 'and we'll be out of your hair in no time.'

I needed the roofing for a number of new projects that I had on the go with Hippy Richard. Some of the panels on the house badly needed replacing because I was running out of buckets to catch the leaks during heavy showers. We'd also planned an extension on the side of the house for a new kitchen area that would require roofing. Plus, I was outgrowing the shed with all the bits and pieces I was collecting or had been given, so I needed to build a new one. And finally, there was an ambitious project in the pipeline to build a tiki beach bar on the mainland-facing shore. So I ordered four packs of six panels in total, each about eight metres long and a metre wide, bound together in plastic. And they were heavy.

My fears were confirmed when I positioned my tinny under the winch of the mothership. My boat thudded against the side and I struggled to stay in, let alone stand up. The spherical first mate, Buddha, and a young lad cautiously lowered two packs into my tinny as I sat nervously at the stern. When the packs were in position, lengthways, I clambered on top of the panels to tie them to the bow. One decent wave and I would have gone overboard, because the plastic covering was slippery with sea spray. I tentatively coaxed the boat to shore and heaved the packs of panels up onto the sand using rollers. There was no way that I could repeat this, so I went back to the skipper. 'Look, Paul, I'm really struggling here. I need a hand. This is bloody dangerous,' I pleaded.

'Okay, okay,' he said, irritated. 'Tell Buddha to let the young fella go in your boat instead. He won't have any trouble.'

When I pulled alongside again, I climbed onto the mothership and the young bloke clambered down into the tinny. It looked even more precarious from the safety of the ship. We tied the next pack onto the winch and lowered it down in the same way. But the young bloke was standing midway between the stern and bow at the starboard side, next to the ship. 'You want to move from there, mate!' I yelled. 'Get to the stern! If the iron slips, you'll be in big trouble.' He just gave me a thumbs up and, as the packs of panels settled on the boat's seats, another wave slapped the tinny against the ship and dislodged them, pinning the young man's thigh to the side of the boat. The boy was screaming in agony as the tinny tilted over, taking in too much water. 'Untie it at the bow and loosen the stern rope,' I yelled to Buddha. 'This bloke's going to lose his legs. Sink the bloody boat now.'

Buddha frantically let go of the rope and the boat and panels sank like stone. We had expected the iron to dislodge and in the water so the young fella could wriggle free. But there was no sign of him. Now it was panic stations – he was obviously still trapped. Buddha and I peered over the side of the ship, freaking out, but we couldn't see anything in the choppy water. Ten seconds turned into twenty, twenty seconds into thirty. Still no sign, so we both jumped in. The water was opaque from all the sand churned up from the sea bed, and I couldn't see a bloody thing. Just as I came up for air, up popped the young fella, spewing water from his lungs.

'Fackin' roofin' iron,' he spluttered. 'Leave the fackin' stuff down there, eh?' He had scraped a layer of skin off both thighs as he prised himself free when the boat settled on the seabed. He was taken to the boat's sick bay to check that nothing was broken and I could tell he was in severe shock.

I wasn't too bothered about rescuing my tinny because it had been leaking beforehand, but the motor was valuable so we tightened the stern rope and pulled the boat up on board. We then unscrewed the motor and Wally, the mothership's chief engineer, got to work. A motor can be under water for a month and will still work perfectly well as long as it is fixed and fired up as soon as it's pulled out. All you need to do is to rinse the motor in fresh water, pull out the spark plugs and dry them, pour petrol or metho into the engine and pull that through, then replace the spark plugs and crank it up again in water. A couple of ribs of the tinny had broken against the side of the mother ship during this chaos and it was like sailing a banana skin back to shore. The panels are still on the sea bed to this day. After this incident, the mothership changed their health and safety rules and refused to deliver roofing panels, or anything that had to be handled by more than one person.

***

At least we didn't need to keep an eye out for crocs during that mayhem. They will usually stay clear when there is a big boat around. All the commotion would have put them off, too. By then I had been on the island long enough to have spotted a few salties. But the golden rule is that the most dangerous croc is the one you can't see. So I grew accustomed to picking my time to have a swim, and I also kept the beach clear of large logs. Already, while beachcombing I had occasionally wandered towards a large grey piece of driftwood, excited about its possible use in some new project, only to almost crap myself when the 'log' scurried back into the water. There was little chance of crocs venturing above the high water mark so, as long as you kept your wits about you, it seemed to me that these amazing creatures posed no great threat – even with a baby son to consider.

Yes, that's right, Resto had worked her magic during Denika's first visit and instantly transformed my impotence into virility. In May 1998, I found myself racing down to Sydney to be present for the birth of Kye Glasheen. At fifty-four, around fourteen years older than Denika, having more kids had not been in the script for either of us but, for me, this was a chance to atone for my previous parenting mistakes. We were considering the name Kye even before I found out that it meant 'restoration' in Japanese. Bringing up a child in this environment could help us avoid all the pitfalls of modern-day parenting. He would eat healthily and learn to grow, catch and cook his own food. When he was old enough, he would develop practical bush skills and make his own entertainment, without relying on a computer or smartphone. We could school him ourselves and teach him about real life, not Latin declensions or Greek mythology.

That was my theory, but persuading Denika was a different matter. Crocs were just one of the hurdles. How would we protect him from all the dangerous creatures in Far North Queensland? What would happen if he fell ill and we couldn't reach the mainland? Where would he find friends? Valid questions, but my time on the island had already taught me to find solutions, not look for obstacles.

Our differences erupted in another almighty row and I returned to the island on my own. It was heartbreaking to leave my baby boy back in Sydney, but the relationship between Denika and me was volatile at the best of times. I hated arguments and it wasn't in my nature to scream or throw pots and pans. Some people can forgive and forget the hurtful things that are said in the heat of the moment, but I could never do that. I was easily wounded and my way of dealing with fights was to run. But running had never been more difficult; I would be missing out on those special early months of my son's life. I would be so far away and unable to help out the way a father should.

I knew they were both in good hands, though. Through the salon, Denika had become very friendly with a wonderful, elegant elderly lady called Mrs Goodwin, or Mrs G for short. Mrs G was the eldest of thirteen children and lived in a retirement home, but she was super fit and still very proud of her appearance. She was keen to help in every possible way, including financially, because she thought her own children did not deserve the legacy from her husband's newspaper business. Mrs G often looked after Kye during the day but, despite this help, Denika was exhausted from working full-time as a single mum. That's when she remembered our original dream of escaping the daily grind. Denika was showing signs of coming round to the idea when she had a brainwave: Mrs G could come, too.

I loved Mrs G and had no doubt that she would also thrive on the island. It was Denika I was worried about. She had been born with a silver spoon in her mouth in the old Rhodesia, with servants at her beck and call. It was one thing for her to come for a romantic getaway, but another thing completely to start a new life here. I knew I had the mental fortitude to cope with the isolation, the extreme weather and some of the hostile wildlife, not to mention the hostile locals. For me, the island's beauty and serenity more than made up for any downsides. The surrounding water was like an amniotic sac, protecting me from the harsh realities of the outside world. It was a girdle of constant support, wrapped snuggly around this symbiotic entity that the island and I had become. I felt the sea absorb any encroaching negativity.

Denika simply had to give it a try and, at first, our new family unit functioned just fine. I was doing what every dad dreams of: spending quality time with his son. I'd never had this opportunity in the corporate world. I was lucky if my daughters were awake before I left for work and they would be in bed and asleep by the time I came home. Here I could frolic in the water with Kye, kick a ball on the grass, fish from the beach and build castles in the sand. When it was time for his nap, I wrapped him in a makeshift papoose, strapped him onto my back and he dozed off while I mowed the grass. He was a happy, healthy little boy.

Seeing Kye in this natural setting reminded me so much of my childhood. I had always been a beachcomber and would often catch an early train to primary school, St Aloysius' in Kirribilli, to head down to Sydney Harbour at 7am, before my dad, Max, was even awake. Catching fish in a jar or discovering a kaleidoscopic shell was far more rewarding than reciting my seven times table. My boarding school, the prestigious and strict St Ignatius' College, Riverview, was like a prison for me and I spent most of my time at the back of the class, doodling and daydreaming about girls' bras, not algebra. I counted down the days to our family's annual six-week summer holiday in Huskisson, on Jervis Bay. It was a blissful time of self-discovery. We rented a shack called Lingalonga, and I would have happily lingered much longer each year. It was a slice of the idyllic life that foreigners associate with growing up in Australia. Sun, sea, the wind in your hair, the sugar-soft sand between your toes – the great outdoors. Dad allowed us boys free rein to do as we pleased, but we didn't ever abuse it. There was no need to look for mischief, there was too much fun stuff to do. Mick, my younger brother, Phil, and I joined four or five mates from other families and we disappeared from dawn until dusk. Dad bought us a dinghy that doubled as a sailboat and taught us how to row over to the sandspit on the other side of the river, where there was a dazzling white beach that stretched for miles. At low tides we collected worms, pipis and yabbies in oyster jars for bait for our simple lines – no rods, just a hook and a line with a cork float. I was a boy scout, so I was good with my hands, but Mick was a more natural fisherman. We caught flathead, whiting, bream, jewfish

– you name it. We didn't spend a cent. All the while Dad sat on the balcony of the RSL, reading and relaxing over a few beers with my mum, Valda, and the other parents and their younger kids, like my sister Kate. Yet Dad always kept an eye out to make sure that we were safe. When we returned, sun-kissed, salt-crusted and exhausted, to our parents, we'd build a fire and cook our catch, and often fall asleep under the stars.

This was the kind of freedom I imagined for Kye, but on his doorstep. Do parents encourage that self-sufficiency nowadays? Sure, the currents were strong and there were a few bull sharks and tiger sharks lurking in the murky waters. But we were never going to capsize that dinghy. Dad knew that, and there were plenty of adults around on the beaches or in other boats. Besides, if kids aren't allowed to make their own mistakes they end up mollycoddled and spoon-fed. I love to watch the young fellas of Lockhart River entertain themselves. At the age of just three or four they could teach other much older Aussie kids a thing or two about fishing. They don't go running to Mum and Dad for help, they figure stuff out. These kids don't need to buy the latest computer game or app to keep themselves happy. The treasures of this country – their country – are enough to delight them. I have no doubt those blissful days in Huskisson inspired my own life choices.

On Resto, Mrs G was also living the dream. It was as though we had tunnelled her out of the retirement home and she was determined to make every second count while she was on the loose. With both Kye's parents around, there wasn't a lot for her to do with him. So she was happy to read books during the day and sip champagne – or Lockhart River's nearest equivalent – down at the beach shack with Denika as the sun dropped behind the mainland mountains. Denika spent those early days adding a woman's touch to the house. She painted a couple of chairs, brought some order to the cooking area, and did the washing for us all. When word reached the hippy community – the non-Indigenous horticulturalists, as we called them –

on Chilli Beach that a beautician was living on the island, there was huge demand for her skills. Denika's biggest challenge was combing the dreadlocks out of their hair. These girls had no cash, though, and could only pay in dope. Denika liked a joint and it took the edge off. Mrs G gave it a go, too, and we didn't hear another word from her for two days. She just sat there, away with the fairies, with a grin from ear to ear.

I wasn't into marijuana. I'm not saying I never had a drag, but it didn't float my boat. I'm talkative, but I don't think I am any more or less talkative after a few beers. The words just come out more jumbled and maybe a bit faster! After a joint, I withdraw into myself and I don't contribute to the conversation so much. That defeats the objective of being in a social setting for me. It's a big part of the culture up here, though. Life can be tough in these parts and a smoke maybe provides some temporary relief when the realities of the remote tropics kick in.

The novelty of island life soon wore off for Denika. All the little jobs became chores to whinge and moan about. She wanted to shower in warm water, not the scalding water at the shuttle, which was so hot because the ground-level plastic pipes warmed up in the sun. She soon tired of washing clothes and sheets by hand, but a washing machine wasn't exactly practical here. She was paranoid about Kye playing in the water, even though I assured her I was on constant croc alert. Then, cracks started to appear in our long-term vision for bringing up Kye. I wanted him to eat the fish I was catching and the fresh food that we were starting to grow in the garden area that I'd cleared. Denika thought he should be having Coco Pops for breakfast from the store in Lockhart River, which meant regular calls to the one taxi service and a $150 round trip fare. It was cheaper than running a car, but still more than a bit unnecessary. She was fearful about Kye's health, but didn't want to go to the doctor in Lockhart River in case he caught something in the waiting room.

It was increasingly clear that we were on different pages. I probably had more in common with Mrs G than I did with Denika. After six months, she decided that enough was enough. 'This life just isn't for me, Dave,' she said. 'You're in your element here. I'm not. This is no place to bring up a kid. He's not getting any social interaction with other kids his age. It's not healthy for him. He's going to grow up feral. You can't say I haven't given it a go – I told myself I would give it six months, and I have. But things aren't going to improve and we're arguing all the time again. That's not good for Kye, either. Look, he's your son and I always want you to be part of his life. I know that can't happen in Sydney, so I'm willing to try and start afresh in Cairns. I'll open another salon there – Mrs G will help. That way you can visit and I can bring Kye up here occasionally.'

For once I couldn't argue. She had given it a good go. But you can't fit a square peg in a round hole. Denika was high maintenance and this was a life of near self-sufficiency. I was almost relieved that her decision drew a clear line in the sand. Our relationship had been too fragile for too long and a clean break would at least give me the chance to find another soulmate – somebody who truly shared my dreams and my ideals. But I was devastated to lose the chance to really bond with my son. Lots of people say that those formative years are the one chance you have to truly connect with your children. If you try to pick up the pieces later on in their lives, you're always facing an uphill task. Kye was too young to understand what was happening when we said our goodbyes at the airport. He wouldn't have noticed that, as I squeezed him too tightly so I could hide my tears, I filled my lungs with the deepest breath, hoping that his sweet, intoxicating smell would stay with me forever.

***

Glash, you need a dog, I told myself on the way back to the island. All my life I'd owned a dog and one of the hardest things about moving up to Resto was leaving Claude, our Dalmatian, behind. But he was too old and domesticated to adapt to island life, so Mick took him in. I needed a dog that was island savvy and had survival instincts in its genes – an animal that would be protective and faithful, but would also keep me on my toes. What I needed was the canine equivalent of the Cato character in *The Pink Panther* movies. This loyal manservant attacked Inspector Clouseau when he least expected, as a way of honing his master's self-defence skills. But Cato always came off second best, often demolishing the apartment in the process. I didn't want to be attacked and I didn't want the island to be wrecked, but a Resto dog would definitely need his wits about him. I paid a local a bottle of beer for Cato, a brown puppy that looked like a cross between every male dog that had ever lived in Lockhart River, with DNA mostly from kelpies, ridgebacks and pit bulls. He was a friendly little bloke and followed me everywhere, excited about every new project.

There was plenty to keep us both occupied, too. As part of our lease conditions, we had to carry out improvements to the island and the first priority was to completely remove all the rubbish that had accumulated over so many years. It was a huge task – too much for one man – and the only locals talking to me were the younger fellas, who were not interested in the legal battles. Fortunately, I heard about one sixteen year old called Shiva, who was at a bit of a loose end and happy to work in return for somewhere to stay now and again, along with a good feed and a couple of beers after a hard day's work. Together, over about twelve months, we removed 200 cubic metres – the equivalent of about twenty removal vans – of heavily compacted rubbish with weekly trips to Portland Roads in the tinny, which I had stiffened up with pieces of timber screwed to the side after the roofing iron chaos. Often I would find one rusting VB can and dig down a little further to find hundreds more. One dump site alone, which connected the southern end of the beach with the old shed, was sixty metres long, eight metres wide and more than a metre high. The way the island had been treated – a 'burn, bash and bury' mentality – was environmental terrorism.

Sometimes, we had to break down the bigger items, like parts of the derelict caravan, fridges or large batteries, with sledgehammers or hacksaws. It was brutal work. Anything that could be salvaged for a rainy day was split into four piles: timber, stainless steel, nets and buoys. At Portland Roads, we piled the rubbish neatly out of view and another bush kid, Albie, who was already driving his dad's truck at the age of thirteen, took it to the tip for $60 a visit. Transporting this amount of rubbish down to Cairns by hiring a barge for a four-day trip, as we were supposed to, would have cost a fortune. It was amazing what we found in or around our dumps. One day I stumbled across a precious wentletrap – the highly valuable ornamental shell of a predatory snail. King Louis XIV of France once paid £300 for one of these pure white spiralling cones, and I have no idea what one might be worth now. It would have washed up out of the deep water during a cyclone and could have been here for thousands of years, beautifully preserved.

As the big clean continued I also started work on a garden. To be successful, I knew I needed chickens. Not only would they help clear up any unwanted weeds, but they would also fertilise the soil. But I had a huge area to clear and fertilise, which meant a fixed pen was not going to work so I constructed a square frame on wheels that could be moved from spot to spot, once the birds had done their job. It was covered in a double layer of wire mesh, as much to keep snakes out as to keep the chickens in. It failed. Within a couple of days my chicken population was down from six to five. I'd started with three brown females, one beautiful white girl and two roosters called Bruce and Sheila (Bruce was the dominant male but Sheila seemed very wimpy and effeminate for a rooster). A Children's python, a pretty species with red or brown blotches on its skin which I had often seen hanging from trees near the beach shack, managed to slither underneath and wrap itself around one of the brown chooks, basically squeezing and stretching it to death. In case you're wondering, the snake's name comes from the person who discovered it, not from a diet of young Australians. I heard the commotion in the pen and tried to bang the snake on the head with a bit of wood, but he wasn't going to give up easily and the chicken was already dead, so I allowed him the reward. This incident freaked out the other chooks and they refused to return to the pen, perhaps thinking they stood more of a chance free-ranging. Now I faced the problem of trying to find the eggs. When I heard the *cluck-cluck* clue that one had been laid, by the time I found the spot, the chicken would be long gone and the egg could be anywhere in a ten-metre radius. They were laying eggs on the chairs in the house, in the dunny, under my bed and in any number of other hiding spots on the island. Nobody told me that I should replace any fresh eggs that I found with a ceramic egg, so that the chook would come back to the same spot. Nevertheless, I had more eggs than I could eat.

Then another of the hens died of natural causes. For someone who bred budgies as a boy, you might have expected me to be more of an expert at rearing birds, although I had one notable failure back then, too. My 'super-budgie' project was inspired by a friendly retired scientist who lived a few houses up the road and grew spinach that you needed an axe to chop down and tomatoes as big as pumpkins. At the time, I was fascinated by nature, wanted to become a vet and already kept a couple of budgies in a homemade cage that I had cobbled together from some wood and wire mesh. Two budgies became four, four became sixteen and so on, until I had to expand my aviary to accommodate about 400 budgies, parrots and cockatiels, all properly tagged and documented. Watching the professor got me thinking: if he can create super-veggies, why can't I create a super-budgie? So I picked the two biggest budgies in my flock, and let nature take its course. Sure enough, out popped an egg the size of a golf ball. The bird that hatched was big, but looked awful – like a cross between Henny Penny and Godzilla. It could barely fly and it struggled to move around. I felt terrible, set all the survivors free immediately and cancelled Australia's first, highly unethical, genetic engineering program.

Although the chickens on Resto were a struggle, the garden was taking shape nicely. I grew sweetcorn, sweet potatoes, yams, kiwifruit, wong bok, bok choy and herbs like coriander, basil and Chinese allspice in ceramic pots. For a while, a banana tree flourished. A lime tree produced rich, green fruit until I poisoned it with pee. Lime trees love the nitrogen from the urea in urine so I asked any willing visitors to pee in a bottle, but evidently overdid it. I grew a pawpaw tree behind the dunny and left the fruit to dry before grinding it down to shake over a salad, but the tree grew too tall and blew over in one of the cyclones. I nurtured the native bush cherry trees, or *ilnti* as the locals call it, and always intended to make my own jam from this sweet, rich fruit. A mango tree grew in the gulley, but took up too much space for me to consider more there, and the soil in the paddock, where there was space, was too sandy and lacked nutrients. The eggplants were attacked by nematodes, which disappeared with one spray of white oil insecticide. Grasshoppers as big as small mice were a constant problem and would nip me when I tried to shoo them away. When water was available, the garden, which was split into five separate allotments, flourished. During the dry season, it was almost impossible to keep everything alive. It was labour-intensive and, at times, soul-destroying. Self-sufficiency came at a high price.

Today I have a new solution. She's called *Jepidanimo,* the tinny that sank with the roofing iron. I told you – I find a use for everything eventually. No longer seaworthy, the boat has made a beaut boat garden. It was a project for four German girls – *Jepidanimo* is an anagram of the first two letters of our first names – who were visiting the island and wanted to help. The general rule is that one German girl is as productive as two Australians. When I suggested we build a boat garden, which I had seen in someone's greenhouse in Portland Roads, they were all over it. First we dragged it over to the side of the house using plastic rollers and pulled it onto some old tyres, laid flat, so that the boat garden was lifted off the ground and out of the reach of unwelcome visitors. Then we scrubbed it with wire brushes and sugar soap; that stuff will clean anything. Next we drilled around a hundred holes for aeration in the bottom, like a colander, using a battery drill. Then, I raided my supply of paints, which I'd picked up on a shopping trip to Cairns for next to nothing because there was a printing error on the tin, and the girls chose a deep royal blue. Once painted, we lined the bottom of the boat with volcanic pumice for more aeration. The next layer was an old shade cloth, to help retain moisture, followed by around eight inches of lawn clippings and another ready-made organic fertiliser: twenty years' worth of dried poo, which a previous visitor had shovelled out of the blocked concrete sealed septic tank at the back of the dunny. It was never too whiffy down there because the sun dried it off almost immediately. I'd just hope no one would say my cooking tasted like shit, because I wouldn't have been able to keep a straight face. Then came a layer of soil for the herbs to grow in, followed by a layer of seaweed, which I constantly replenish when there's been a big dump on the beach. It stops the soil in the boat garden from drying out and the results are amazing. Basil, perfect for an evening mojito, was soon flourishing and I expected some cherry tomatoes to do the same.

My tree-planting program – which included numerous frangipani, poinciana, casuarina and dwarf palms – was more manageable than my early veggie and fruit gardens. Not only did the trees add to the aesthetic appeal of the island, but their roots also helped to bind the sandy soil and prevent unwanted erosion. The exotic and entrancing frangipani are my favourites and I have nine of the seventeen species here. There's one called a fruit salad with four different colours, a pink one, a pure white one, a blood red one and the only evergreen, the Singapore frangipani, with white flowers and a yellow centre. A delicious creamy, peachy smell sits in the air when they flower and, up-lit against the night sky, a frangipani looks like branched coral, frozen in time by a photographer's underwater flash. Only the flamboyant deep red poinciana can rival the prettiness of a frangipani. The palms develop their own personalities. Those exposed to the southerly winds turn their backs and rock in stubborn rhythm with the gusts, or bend double when defiance is pointless. On calmer days the breeze whispers through the casuarina, a blissfully hypnotic sound second only to the slosh of the waves.

Cato understood the brilliance of his playground. Each evening I would tell him what a lucky boy he was and he would listen attentively, his head cocked to one side and tail wagging gently in agreement. He was such good company that I made the mistake of allowing him to sleep on my bed, something I have never done since with my dogs as I didn't want them to think he or she was the leader of our pack. Then, one morning when Cato was still just a few months old, I woke up and he was dead on the bed. There was no evidence of a snake bite on his little body, so it was probably a spider. It could have happened during the night, in which case I had been lucky, or the previous day. But I heard no yelp and he appeared perfectly healthy at bedtime. Someone suggested it might have been parvovirus, but Cato hadn't been in contact with other dogs for a while and parvo, which attacks the gut and heart, usually kills within a week. The poor little fella had such a lust for life, but it can be tough in the wilderness. It was my first major setback, but resilience was essential for my survival. So I buried the pup, wished him well and, hearing that furtive *cluckcluck,* set off to hunt for another egg.

Chapter 6

Boxhead

The beach shack has always been my favourite spot for a cold beer after a hard day's work. Over the course of an hour or two, the sea dances in a symphony of blues and greens – turquoise, emerald, sapphire, aquamarine, mint and cobalt – as the setting sun melts behind the ridges of the hinterland. It's when I truly connect to this place, when isolation is a blessing. I was in this trance-like state when, without any warning, a young Aboriginal fella appeared on the sand spit. He had no idea I was there, so I wandered over.

'Cooee,' I called, and the poor bloke nearly jumped out of his skin.

'Shit, man, you scared me,' he laughed. 'I didn't know anyone else was here. Any ideas what to do with this croc out here? Just came over from Weipa for some crayfish with a mate and this croc trapped us. We can't get back to the boat. Bugger won't budge.

We know crocs. But this croc don't behave like other crocs. This bugger not even scared of rocks, man.'

'Sounds like you've met Boxhead,' I said, as we wandered down to the southern tip of the beach, where their boat was moored off the rocks, about one hundred metres from the shore. The young fella's mate was hurling rocks in the direction of the boat.

I'd heard all about Boxhead: the meanest, hungriest, ugliest, and most cunning and respected croc in the whole of Cape York. For a start, he appeared different. His head looked as though he had run straight into a wall and his snout had been concertinaed back into his skull. It was much squarer than normal, even for a saltwater croc – a bit like Boofhead, a character in an old *Sydney Daily Mirror* cartoon strip, who had a pronounced forehead. His colour was different, too. Most salties are a dull grey, but Boxhead was much darker.

His behaviour was definitely different. He hated humans, ever since he was shot in the paw by a bloke who spent a lot of time out at the Aboriginal outstation at Wongai Point, named after the luscious wongai plums that grow there. This was disputed territory for Boxhead; he thought he ruled over the area, and this bloke lost three or four dogs before eventually wounding the croc. The injured leg also created a distinctive lopsided swimming style. Everyone in these parts had a story about Boxhead. And they often involved him cracking the shits, because he was not one to back down from a challenge.

This pair of young fellas had arrived just after midday and, after their first dive, they surfaced to discover a croc between them and their boat. They climbed onto the rocks and then, from the beach, tried throwing rocks to scare him away but he just sat there, biding his time, knowing they had to swim back to their boat. The stand-off had lasted for four hours. As soon as I spotted the croc from the beach, I knew it was Boxhead – he matched his identikit perfectly. Jeez, he was a freak. 'That's Boxhead alright,' I said, and went to fetch my tinny from the bay. The two blokes jumped in and I took them out to their boat but, even with the noise of the motor, this bugger still didn't budge. He'd waited this long, he wasn't going home without his supper. *You bastard,* I thought, *we need to sort this here and now.*

So I gunned the motor and we headed straight for him. He didn't bat an eyelid and I had to swerve at the last second to avoid a collision. Then I made some figures of eight all around him. Nothing. I didn't like this one bit. If I'd had a gun I would have tried to pop one in his tail, because it was obvious he wasn't the slightest bit scared of us. The two blokes were extremely careful when climbing back in because Boxhead had kept his beady eyes on them. Only when they were out of sight did he admit defeat and disappear from view beneath the surface with a petulant splash.

Normally, I don't mind so much when you can see crocs in the water. That's much better than not knowing where they are, because they can stay underwater for a couple of hours at a time. They're just as effective on land, too, and can outrun a human. The only thing they are not so good at is changing direction. So, here's a top tip: if you are ever being chased by one, run in zigzags! And here's an even better tip: don't put yourself in that situation. Having just one croc in the vicinity is bad enough, but very occasionally I've seen two or three together on the beach, sunning themselves. You definitely wouldn't want to be around if a territorial dispute was brewing, but I've never seen that happen on Resto because no croc had a claim on this island – although Boxhead clearly thought that he had. *I've not seen the last of you,* I thought.

***

Without Cato for company, and still with so many plans for improvements to the island, the idea of a ready-made supply of willing labour through the wwoofer program was really appealing. It was Hippy Richard's suggestion and he was still a regular visitor, always willing to throw his construction talents into my next project. Clearly, Resto was no organic farm, but as long as I was seen to be growing some of my own food, I met the WWOOF movement's criteria and objectives: 'To help build a sustainable global community by linking volunteers with organic farmers and growers to promote cultural and educational experiences based on trust and non-monetary exchanges'. When I first included my details in the wwoofer handbook, I wondered whether anyone would want to come and stay on a remote island, but I was surprised by the number of applications. The first to arrive was a great bloke from Canada called Chris. He stayed for the first Christmas after Kye and Denika had left, along with Richard and Emile. It was great to have company over what could otherwise have been an emotional period.

Chris created a little pot plot of his own next to my garden and, within a few weeks, the plants were flourishing so he offered to make a cake on Christmas Eve containing a 'secret' ingredient. One scrape of the bowl with my little finger, just before washing it up, was enough to make me a bit woozy. On Christmas Day, we divided up the tasks for the main meal. Richard was to prepare the salad, Emile and

Chris would go out in the boat to catch some fish, and my job was to find crayfish. I don't often eat crayfish – I prefer to watch them in the water – but I do have a crayfish pole with a noose on the end, which loosens by a button on the bottom. When you spot some feelers sticking out of an underwater crevice, you slip the noose further in and over the body, and tighten it to pull the crayfish out.

On this occasion, Chris suggested that we try some of the cake before tackling our respective tasks. By the time I reached the beach, I was feeling tingly. I did a quick check for crocs, but the water was like glass and there were none around, so I slipped on the snorkel mask and waded out with my pole. Beneath the surface, the pandemonium of colours seemed more mesmerising than normal. My head was spinning as I tried to make my body swim. Then I spotted two feelers and I loosened the noose on the pole. But then, the crayfish started to talk to me. 'Please, Uncle Davo, don't eat me today,' it said. 'How would you like to be dragged out of your home by the neck and stuck in boiling water? Not very Christmassy, is it?' *Shit, it's got a point,* I thought. *And it's so cute, like a watery, baby bunny.* I stood up, and Resto was on the move. Either there was an enormous earthquake underway or Chris hadn't stuck to the recipe. By the time I reached the house, I could hardly string two words together, but I remembered I had arranged to ring Kye to wish him a happy Christmas. 'Kye, it's Dad. Hoppy fish face, son,' I garbled, followed by helpless giggling for the next hour.

***

The next big project was to add an eating area onto the side of the house, which would be useful for when I couldn't build a fire down at the beach shack. Before any help arrived, I dug holes for three posts, around three metres from the side wall. I found three more logs, cut them to the same size, dipped the bottom ends in sump oil to prevent termites, cut a notch in the top for the cross beam, and lowered them into the holes. There was no need for cement – sand is more stable. It took me three days to level and straighten them up using a spirit level and a piece of string. Whenever two were perfectly aligned, the third would slip. It truly tested my patience, and I'm normally pretty calm. When the Hippy Richard cavalry arrived, we hoisted up the crossbeam and lashed it to the three poles with twine, and then lifted on some new roofing iron – delivered by road this time and brought to the island on a bigger, borrowed boat – and screwed down the panels.

    Formica benchtops, rescued from the Portland Roads tip, were fitted along with a twin-ringed cast-iron gas stove, picked up second-hand from an op shop for next to nothing, and shelves for non-perishable foods, complete with hooks for all my pots and pans. I repositioned the sink and food preparation area, which had been outside, in the main living area. This is where I wash up, which I do meticulously after each meal. You can't just leave scraps of food lying around, because the place would be inundated with ants. I'm also very careful to wipe the dining table very clean after each meal.

I use a wok for a lot of my cooking, and I reckon I throw a decent meal together. A spicy Thai prawn stir-fry is up there with my favourites: sweet chilli, red hot fresh chilli, fresh coconut milk, lemongrass, ginger, garlic, freshly squeezed limes ... and then a bit more fresh chilli. Or I like to fry up some lamb chops, to serve with a fresh salad, when the trawler boys deliver my meat from Cairns. An omelette is always a reliable late-night fall-back option, too. For lunch, I will often take an old jam jar down to the beach when the tide's fully out and collect several dozen oysters using a hammer and screwdriver. There's nothing better than freshly-shucked oysters with a slice of bread and some homemade seafood sauce: Worcester sauce, fresh lime juice, black pepper, either egg mayonnaise or fresh cream and tomato sauce. Mm-hmm.

The next big build was the bath and shower area. The lack of a decent shower had been a bone of contention with Denika, and I wanted everything to be perfect when I finally found my island soulmate. This was when Richard's freestyle construction skills were really useful. First, we had to pull down the old rusted metal water tank that backed onto the new dining area, clear the ground with spades, dampen it, and then level it with rakes. To build the bath, we broke up polystyrene foam into chunks, which we covered with mesh moulded into an oval shape. We then packed the inside of the wire frame with concrete, let that set, and then added more polystyrene before cementing the outside and smoothing it with our hands. We added a powdered ochre to the cement to provide an authentic terracotta colour. Built into the walls of the bath was a small wooden seat, and two holes just the right size for champagne flutes. I've used the bath once! The sea is my big blue, ever-welcoming bath.

Fortunately, just weeks before, a Telstra engineer was on the island to install a monster of a satellite dish for an internet connection. In his boat was a mini Dingo digger and, with a spare hour to kill, he asked if there was anything he could help with. So I set him to work digging a small trench from the water tank at the bottom of the gully to the house. This trench would hold the underground plastic pipes that would keep the water cool, but I realised some people would want a hot shower, too, so we created a separate water line by rolling up a stainless-steel sheet and pushing a copper tube inside. Next, we cut a hole in the stainless-steel sheet and placed that over a chip heater, to be filled with chips of bamboo cut from the shoots that wash up on the beach. Bamboo burns hotter than coconuts to heat the copper wire and, when the shower is turned on, it quickly warms the water to a good temperature. With a chunk of creativity – and lots of trial and error – most challenges can be overcome with limited resources.

***

Chris the wwoofer was a willing worker and learner. He watched me fish, asked lots of questions, then went off and put what he had learned into practice. One day, he disappeared in the boat for what seemed longer than usual. Eventually, I spotted him staggering back to the house. He was slumped forward, one hand holding the other arm across his chest. *Shit, he's broken his arm,* I thought. I ran over to him and could see from his contorted face that he was in agony.

'Shit, Dave, this hurts real bad,' he said, wincing and lifting up his hand to reveal a tangled mess of fish hooks, wire and ripped flesh. That's when I fainted.

I came round to find Chris bending over me, wafting the air with his T-shirt, which he must have somehow eased over his injured hand. 'Dave, wake up!' he shouted. 'I need some help here. You need to pull yourself together.'

'Urgghh,' I groaned. 'Okay, just keep that thing away from me. How the hell did that happen?' Once I managed to sit up and compose myself, keeping my eyes off Chris's hand, he told me that he had been using a lure with three treble hooks. These hooks, each with three deadly-sharp barbs, are used for catching the bigger fish, and Chris had wanted to make sure that the big one did not get away. He had snagged a good-sized coral trout but, while trying to unhook one of the trebles, the fish had made one last desperate thrash for freedom and the other hooks on the line had locked into his hand. There were at least seven separate points of entry through his fingers and palm. And once one of these barbs goes in, it doesn't easily come out. An experienced fisherman would always use pliers and heavy-duty gloves to free a treble from a fish. I accidentally caught a seagull on a couple of occasions and always had to cut the hook to free the bird.

There was a rusty pair of side cutters in my medical kit, but I'm not good with blood and gore at the best of times, and there was no way Chris could tackle this himself. He would have needed both hands. I knew the medical clinic in Lockhart River had a quality pair of side cutters, so I poured him a beer and rolled him a joint to help ease the pain, and wrapped his injured hand in a clean towel and then taped a plastic bag around to keep it dry, before shakily driving into town. Lynn, a paramedic nurse and boss at the clinic, was on duty and rushed out. 'Dave, what the hell's happened? You look awful,' she said, helping me out of the car.

'No, no, not me,' I whispered, ready to either throw up or faint again. 'It's Chris, there.' When Lynn unravelled my handiwork even she was taken aback, and the clinic must see someone with a hook fixed in them at least once a month. Chris was sedated with a strong painkiller and all the barbs were cut. If any of the barbs had not penetrated right through a finger or palm, another cut was made in the flesh to pull it out the other side. I didn't watch.

***

One of the first regular visitors to the island was Toby, a lovely bloke and a hardy farmer who had a great family, and tried his hand at managing livestock and many different types of agriculture at the Wattle Hill cattle station, inland and north of Lockhart River. A two-hour boat trip down the Pascoe River to Resto was the easiest way for Toby and others from Wattle Hill to travel to

Portland Roads, where they met the barge for their supplies. The tides often meant they came down the previous night, so they needed somewhere to sleep in their swags. The mozzies would have eaten them alive at Portland Roads, so Resto was the perfect spot to moor their boats overnight. We only have problems here with flies at the start of the rainy season, when they can drive you crazy. The nastiest bites come from horse flies – the black ones are slow and dumb and easy to bash, but the green-eyed horse fly is a smart little bastard with eyes in the back of his head.

    Toby told me that he would be bringing five piglets on his next trip. Four were already spoken for, but I could have the fifth for $50. 'It'll be like a free worker for you,' he said. 'These things eat anything and everything. It'll soon clear any stubborn weeds.' Bindi-eye was still a problem, constantly floating overland from the Gulf of Carpentaria. Other weeds occasionally sprang up at the water line, one with pink flowers and a black one that smelled like aloe vera. A pig would be perfect for keeping the lawns clear, and would provide more fertiliser than the chickens could ever produce.

The plan was for all five piglets to stay overnight on Resto, and the spoken-for four would be picked up at Portland Roads the next day. The old chicken pen would make a perfect piggy hotel. 'Don't worry,' Toby told me. 'They'll be exhausted after a two-hour boat trip. You'll not know they're there.' One of them wasn't there. The first four poked their heads sleepily out of their brown hessian bags as we transported them, two at a time, by wheelbarrow from the sand spit over to the pen in the garden. The fifth, with a piercing, defiant squeal, made a bid for freedom. We chased him this way and that for about ten minutes, trying to throw the bag over him when he paused for breath, but we eventually lost him in the undergrowth. 'He'll be back,' said Toby. 'He'll want to spend the night with the others.' We never saw him again. He may have even swum back to the mainland. But I couldn't be sure that he wasn't living in the bushes and, for the next week, I had nightmares about a porker the size of an elephant, wearing a red bandana, breathing fire from his snout and dripping blood from his tusks, returning to eat me up.

My pig must have witnessed this act of rebellion with envy, because she became a frustrated escapologist. I called her Houdina – a female Houdini. She wasn't subtle and soon learned that she could smash her way through the pen. When she wasn't trying to escape, she was eating: scraps, weeds, lizards and witchetty grubs dug from the most nutritious soil. Kye was just a toddler when Houdina acquired her taste for adventure, and she often bowled him over if he was in the way of her food. Denika was paranoid that she might try and eat him, too. It wasn't difficult to lure Houdina back, though. A few scraps of food, laid Hansel-and-Gretel style back to the pen, always did the trick.

Still, continual repairs to the pen were pointless; I had to try another method to keep her under control. So, I dug a big trench inside the pen, laid a plastic bag along the bottom and filled it with earth and water to create a wallow. She was as happy as a pig in

... mud. Apparently, rolling in the mud kills bugs on their skin and keeps them healthy, just like elephants and hippos. And the more she ate, the more she looked like a white baby hippo. Houdina was enormous – as big as a three-seater couch when fully grown – and way bigger than the rest of her litter. But she was the wrong type of huge, Toby told me on one of his visits. 'She's too fat, Dave,' he said. 'What have you been feeding her?'

'Everything,' I said. 'I go to the supermarket every Friday and pick up anything they are throwing out: bread, fruit, veggies. Some of it's good enough for humans but I can never bring back enough for Houdina. I can't keep up with her appetite.'

'Try feeding her more fruit for a few months before we slaughter her,' he advised. It was just coming into mango season and we had plenty. There were also a lot of mango trees in Portland Roads. I was still persona non grata with most of the community there, so I couldn't ask them to share their fruit. But ninety per cent of the mangoes that had fallen had been pecked at by bush turkeys, and were just left to rot on the ground. Again, perfect for Houdina, and she soon lost her puppy fat on this high-mango diet.

At the end of the mango season, the day of reckoning arrived. This was another act I couldn't bear to watch, and so I went to stay on a friend's trawler in the bay for the night while the Wattle Hill boys got to work. She was butchered humanely and hung from the branch of a tree overnight, so that her meat didn't settle like jelly. Then the plan was to scald the whole carcass in hot water in the other half of the forty-four-gallon drum, which had been used to make the fire pit, so that the hair could be easily scraped off. Houdina was too big for the tub, though, and had to be chopped into sections on a large tarpaulin. She kept us in meat – deliciously tender, mangoey meat – for many months and this was incentive enough for one more attempt at rearing this type of animal.

Piggy Muldoon was named after a prime minster of New Zealand, Robert Muldoon, whose droopy cheeks and portly figure combined to create a distinctly porcine look. Piggy Muldoon was part of a litter from a feral pig killed in the wild. Lynn from the clinic loved animals, and had taken Piggy Muldoon in as part of the family. She fed him from a bottle, tucked him in at night and read bedtime stories – hopefully none about the Big Bad Wolf. But Piggy Muldoon was another animal with a monstrous appetite. Because he repeatedly stole food from Lynn's pet dog and cat, she reluctantly found him a new home. 'I know he will be in good hands with you, Dave,' she said, somewhat naively. Lynn visited him regularly and, when she landed on the beach and called 'Here, piggy piggy,' Muldoon squealed, ran to her and rolled over on his back to have his tummy tickled, which invariably caused Lynn to break down in tears.

Piggy Muldoon also thrived on Resto but, when Houdina finally disappeared from the freezer, it was time for him to take her place. This time, Wye, the Vietnamese trawler captain, assured me that one of his deckies knew how to slaughter animals and would do the deed in return for a few choice cuts for the boat. I wasn't totally convinced, especially when this bloke pulled out a .45 Colt revolver that looked like it had last been fired during the Gunfight at the O.K. Corral, so this time, I forced myself to stick around to make sure that Piggy Muldoon met with a dignified end. The deckie told me to distract Piggy with a tasty last supper and then leave the pen. I'm glad I did, because it looked like he had his eyes closed when the deckie took aim, and the bullet went straight through Piggy Muldoon's neck and out the other side. Blood sprayed up into the heavens, but it could have been a mozzie bite for all Piggy Muldoon cared. He just carried on eating. 'You bloody idiot!' I screamed. 'He's supposed to be dead. Don't just leave him like that. Do something. Shoot him again.' But the deckie had frozen in horror. I couldn't bear to watch the animal bleed out, so I grabbed the gun, pushed the deckie out of the way, and shot Piggy Muldoon clean between the eyes. There was a startled *eek,* and then he toppled over onto his side. *Please don't faint,* I told myself over and over, as Wye and his crew took Piggy Muldoon to their boat to complete the butchery out of sight. This time, the carcass was skinned and I turned up to collect my share a little too early, because Wye's wife was still digging the brain out of the skull – another test for my delicate constitution.

***

Gradually, I was starting to build a network – mainly professional fishermen and people who used the island as a base for casual fishing, like Hippy Richard, or the younger fellas, like Shiva and Albie – without making much headway in the Lockhart River community. The Aboriginal people's resistance to our presence – and me, as the representative of our group – was entrenched. Some of the white community, and especially those who either lived close to Resto or who had no long-standing axes to grind, were coming round, though. They could see I was really trying hard to make a go of it here.

One of these people was Keith, a healthy, swarthy bloke, probably in his mid-thirties, who was looking after a camp in Cape Weymouth. He was also very practical – the ultimate odd-job man – and I began to rely on him for advice if I was ever out of my depth. Sometimes, when I was distracted by other projects, Keith helped me mow the lawn and then we chatted around the fire long into the night. He was something of a loner, who had recently been in and out of a couple of relationships, but he was very affable and never too intrusive. One night, he gazed wistfully into the flames and said, 'I'm thinking of leaving, Davo. There's nothing for me here. I've been offered a job in South Australia working on the powerlines and I think I'm going to take it. It's not as though anyone round here is going to miss me.'

'No, that's where you're wrong, mate. I'd miss you heaps,' I said. 'Who's going to fix my outboard motor or my generator if you go?! Shit, Keith, who's going to sit round the fire and talk like this? You're a real mate. But you've got to do what you've got to do. Know this, though. If you ever need anywhere to live, I'd be happy to have you here. You could build your own camp out in the bushes perhaps.' He smiled, and slipped back within himself, clearly battling with his emotions.

A few days later, Denika's youngest son, Troy, came for a visit and to look for a job. He had the typically headstrong, adventurous attitude to life that people in their mid-twenties possess. I had organised a few days' paid work for him with Keith, landscaping the grounds of a home that belonged to a couple called Louis and Fiona. When I picked up Troy in the boat on the Friday afternoon, he told me that Keith hadn't turned up for work that day. 'Perhaps he'd double booked himself,' I said. 'He doesn't have a phone, so he wouldn't have been able to let Fiona know.'

That Sunday, I tried to set up a new power inverter and didn't know whether it had to be earthed, so we jumped in the boat to go and ask Keith. On the way there, we passed Arthur Chippendale – 'Chips' – along with Neil McMahon, down on Chips's beach. Neilo was my nearest neighbour, and had helped me out while I was without a boat and stranded on the island for a few months. We developed a flag system so I could let him know when I really needed a lift to the mainland. Whenever I stuck a pole in the sand with a cut-up sheet for a flag, it signalled to him that I had to go into Lockhart. The flaw in the system was that sometimes he didn't see the flag for a week. Chips and Neilo were waving at us, so I waved back, but we were too far away from the shore to hear their shouts.

It was strange that when we moored the boat and wandered up the beach, Keith's blue heeler didn't bark or welcome us. His red ute was parked up, so he was definitely home. 'Cooee!' I called. Nothing. I knocked on the door, which was slightly open, slowly entered the house, and cooeed again. Still nothing. *Weird,* I thought, *the house looks even tidier than normal –* perhaps his mum was coming to visit. Outside again, I could hear the faint whimpering of a dog and, glancing up towards the shed about sixty metres away, I saw Keith hanging from a noose tied around the cross beam of the lean-to. 'Troy, quick!' I yelled. 'Come and cut him down. He might still be breathing.'

'He's dead, Dave. He's been dead for some time,' said Troy, quite calmly.

When I composed myself it was clear there was nothing we could do except notify the police. We headed back towards Cape Weymouth, but there was no longer any sign of Chips and Neilo, so we went on to Portland Roads and I asked Westy, a local mackerel fisherman, if I could use his phone to tell the cops. Chips had already discovered Keith before we had turned up, and was waving to stop us going any further. The cops had been quite dismissive when Chips called them. It was an open and shut case as far as they were concerned. But, typically, I couldn't accept it at face value. I wanted answers and, after the police removed the body, I headed back to the house to see if I could discover a suicide note. There was nothing. It just didn't add up to me. Only a few days ago, we'd been having a heart-to-heart and Keith was anything but suicidal. Maybe, on this occasion, the cathartic nature of camp fire had not been able to liberate his deepest demons.

Troy seemed to take it all in his stride – seeing dead bodies was not uncommon during his upbringing in Zimbabwe. But I had nightmares for weeks. This was the first time I had ever seen a corpse. I couldn't get that picture of Keith's lifeless, pallid face out of my head. I obsessed about his motives. But who knows what secrets Keith took to his grave? I thought he looked on me as a mate but, looking back, he had no real support network. For a loner, this can be a tough place to survive. I made a promise to myself, there and then, never to allow seclusion to turn into isolation.

Chapter 7

Quassi

Human friends were initially hard to find, but fortunately a new 'man's best friend' was easier to come by. After Cato's death I was keen to find another dog as soon as possible. I could go days and weeks with very little interaction with humans and I missed that unconditional companionship of a dog. The coconuts might briefly cackle at my words of wisdom after I tossed them into the fire each evening, but they didn't appreciate my ramblings like a dog would. So, I put the word out to my few allies on shore and word soon came back that Corrine, a schoolteacher in Lockhart River, had a pure-bred pit bull that had just produced a litter of ten pups. Once again, any dog in town could have claimed paternity rights.

Corrine was going to keep three and sell the rest back home in Darwin, because she feared they would not be well looked-after locally. I went to see the pups and when she opened the pen one came running straight to me, keen to be picked up and fussed over. 'This little fella would be great,' I told her. He was only a few weeks old and needed to stay with her for three more weeks before I could buy him for $100, which is a fair bit of money for a dog up here. When I returned a few weeks later, he looked so unhealthy and scabby that I wondered if it was the same dog. He looked like Quasimodo, the Hunchback of Notre Dame.

On the way back to the island, I caught a couple of fish for a celebration barbecue and he was fascinated. I had to shorten his rope or the fish would not have made it back to the mainland intact. It's a shame I didn't tie him up when I made the fire that night because, with my back turned for just a couple of minutes, he devoured them both – heads, scales, guts and all. I toyed with the idea of calling him Sushi but I liked Quasimodo – it suited this ugly duckling. And after a few weeks of running free around the island and wolfing down everything that I put in front of him, he no longer looked like a freak so I dropped the 'modo' and added an 's'.

Quassi was growing into a noble, powerful hunk of a dog. He had the muscular physique of his pit bull mum but a long, slender, body. Everyone loved him and he was incredibly affectionate. But I had to be careful, especially when kids were around. He was extremely playful but didn't know his own strength sometimes, and accidentally knocked many a young fella for six. He was also extremely protective, especially where I was concerned. If anyone had ever threatened me, he would have torn them to pieces, no question. So I was constantly aware that Quassi was a potential killing machine. Kids had to be warned to stay away from his mouth because one snap from those jaws could have taken a hand clean off. Sometimes the trawler boys or tourists would anchor off the beach and ask if it was okay for their dogs to stretch their legs or have a crap on the island. 'Not if you want it to be alive when you leave,' I told them. Quassi would not have taken lightly to another male dog on his turf, but he turned on the charm for one female staffy, Rosie, brought over by the region's psychiatrist, Ernest Hunter, a keen fisherman and social kayaker, who regularly visited the island with two kayaking mates, another psychiatrist called Geoff and a mental health worker, Chris. This bunch of crazy buggers called themselves Los Trios Bastardos and were always entertaining company. On this occasion Ernest was alone with Rosie and it was love at first sight for Quassi.

'Has she been spayed?' I asked Ernest.

'Don't worry, he'll never catch her,' he replied. And he was right. Quassi chased Rosie for hours and eventually collapsed on the beach, frustrated and exhausted. Knowing he was no longer a threat, Rosie came up to make friends and they played and licked each other until it was time for Ernest to go. Quassi whimpered on the beach when the boat left, while the staffy stood on the prow, howling back at him. I had never seen two dogs form such an instantaneous, almost human, emotional bond. It was really touching and made me realise that there was a tonne of testosterone surging through Quassi's body. He was getting more and more excitable. Even if I left the island for just an hour he was beside himself when I came back and either squirted pee all over me or tried to hump my leg.

So it was a surprise when, after a quick trip into Lockhart for some shopping essentials, he wasn't there to greet me on the beach. I called his name a few times. Nothing. *Shit, something's wrong here,* I thought, and started to jog back to the house, scared witless about what I might find. Then I heard a pitiful whimpering and spotted him, flat out in the shade of a palm tree. Two abject wags of his tail was all he could manage. Then I noticed that his front paw was bleeding badly from a wound with tell-tale jagged edges. I tore off my singlet and wrapped it firmly around the upper part of his leg to stop the bleeding. He wasn't happy, but he trusted me. As I carried him back down to the tinny, to go straight back to Lockhart, I noticed a bloke waving madly from a fancy yacht moored about one hundred metres off the beach.

Placing Quassi gently in between the thwarts, I gunned the tinny over to the yacht. 'Can't stop, mate,' I shouted as I cut the motor. 'My dog's been badly injured.'

'Yeah, I know, I saw it all happen through my binoculars,' the bloke said. 'I'd been watching this croc for a while. It was only small, about a metre long, so probably quite young. Anyway, it wandered up the beach there towards that little retreat in the trees.'

'Jeez, they don't normally venture up to the beach shack. That's where Quassi normally hangs out,' I said.

'Yeah, so this fella comes tearing out towards the croc, barking his head off and the croc shits itself and runs back towards the water. That's when he should have called it quits. But your boy was up for a fight and followed the croc into the shallow water and had a bite at the tail. The croc just snapped back and must have grabbed his paw. It was hard to tell what was happening at that point, but I saw the dog limp back up to the trees. I did try to see if he was okay but the second I stepped out of the boat he was on his three feet, growling like I was going to rob the place. He's a feisty one, alright.'

I thanked the yachtie and drove like a madman to make it into Lockhart just before the clinic closed. Looking after wounded animals wasn't in the nurses' job description but thankfully Lynn was on duty, and she wasn't about to turn him away and risk the wound becoming infected. She gave him an injection to numb the pain, cleaned up the wound and made about ten stitches. Quassi took it all in his stride – and probably enjoyed the attention. He was good as new in a very short time, back patrolling his beach with renewed vigour.

***

While Quassi was able to vet anyone daring to approach the island by sea, there was nothing he could do to prevent impromptu aerial incursions. More often than not, these helicopters were flown by Brazakka, one of Far North Queensland's many larger-than-life characters, who has that sea-dog,

Ernest Hemingway look: weathered face, glassy eyes and an untamed white beard. At twenty-one, Dennis Wallace cashed in on one of the first prawn trawlers in the Gulf of Carpentaria and soon made a name for himself in game fishing circles. Then he gave himself the nickname Brazakka, which he claims means 'wild man' in some Indigenous language, but that's probably a tall story. He was soon rubbing shoulders with the rich and famous; he counts Hollywood tough guy Lee Marvin as a close friend and once fished with former US president Jimmy Carter. He's now in game fishing's Hall of Fame – and don't we know it. He was actually one of the first people to introduce tagging to Australia, but it's not much better than killing the fish. Once released, these incredible creatures are often badly wounded by the tags and become easy prey for every shark within a hundred miles. When the appetite for catching big fish plummeted as people became aware of the ecological damage it caused, Brazakka moved into the helicopter business.

Most of Brazakka's visits to Resto were contract work – dropping off Telstra technicians or picking up materials for the lighthouse on Restoration Rock on behalf of the Australian Maritime Safety Authority. So I was curious when, one morning, he landed on Resto with a new passenger – an elderly bloke who spoke with an American accent and puffed on a cigar the size of a small island off Cuba. *Not another developer,* I thought.

'G'day Braz. What brings you here? Does your guest fancy a cuppa?' I asked.

'Got anything stronger?' the American asked. 'A whisky would be good.' Whisky at ten in the morning? Jeez, I knew that Brazakka knocked around with some hardcore characters, but it was a bit early for me. After Brazakka had taken him on a short stroll around the place, they soon left. It had all been a bit weird and secretive, but Brazakka rang later that afternoon.

'Davo, do you know who that was?' he asked, excitedly.

'Err, no. You didn't introduce us.'

'I didn't want you to put your foot in it,' he said. 'It was Fred Turner, the boss of McDonald's. Known him for ages through game fishing. He was doing a recon to look at bringing two groups of twenty here. The first group will be his top executives from around the world for some team building, and the next will be his best mates and some family. What d'ya think, Davo?'

'So twenty people here at the same time?' I asked. 'That's way more than have been here before. Where will they sleep? Where will we eat? What will we eat?'

'Look, there's a few bucks to be made here for both of us, mate. Let's not stress about the details, let's just make it happen,' said Brazakka. It was definitely appealing. My funds were at an all-time low and I badly needed some cash. If I charged them $1000 a head, that would be a total of $40,000. But to pull this off, I would have to buy thousands of dollars' worth of tents, mattresses, sheets, crockery, new generators, a new fridge, food and, of course, grog. If I was going to take this on, I wanted to do it properly. And my biggest worry was that there would be nowhere to sit twenty people for dinner. The beach shack would be too open to the elements. There was no alternative but to fast-forward one of my building projects: a brand-new tiki beach bar.

To catch the last of the evening sun, we positioned the tiki bar on the shore facing the mainland, just a few metres back from the high water mark. It was a bad spot, totally exposed to southeasterlies and northerlies and too close to the water to be safe from erosion. Colin Lindsay insisted on using his connections in the construction industry to source the steel struts. This was way off beam because steel rusts quickly in sea air. The floor was to be a slab of concrete, which was a baseless idea because decking works best for beach structures. The tiki bar didn't really stand much chance, though the creative concept was executed perfectly. There would be two bars: a 'posh' bar for cocktails and sundowners, and a 'public' bar for beers.

With the help of a few wwoofers, holes were dug by hand and the four steel struts were concreted into the ground. The beams came as part of the kit for a nine-by-seven-metre shed, and there was just enough roofing iron remaining. We tied together split palm fronds to line the roof's inside and create an authentic tiki effect, and we wound rope and netting round the steel posts. The counter of the posh bar was custom-made in Cairns out of a hard rosewood from Papua New Guinea, and it sat on a stainless-steel preparation area that I picked up from a bar that closed when the old Cairns Pier was pulled down. We built the public bar from heavy washed-up timber and topped it with chamfer weatherboards, sourced from Lockhart. The floor was laid by a professional concreter, who mixed terracotta browns and ochre colours into the ivory cement to match the colours of the landscape. Circular steps up to the entrance were designed to create a feeling of being washed inside from the beach by waves.

The tiki bar was perfect for entertaining the McDonald's mob, and the last palm was just being thatched as Fred and his guests, all with way too much luggage, arrived by helicopter for their retreat. It was a huge logistical exercise. An extra generator was flown in and we needed twenty drums of fuel for the helicopters alone.

Brazakka had been in charge of beer supplies, but only bought a couple of cartons, which I put on ice on top of the cocktail bar for when the guests started to mingle at 5pm sharp. I had made a plate of fresh sandwiches, too, to help their chef, who was busy unloading his equipment. 'Davo, you bloody idiot,' said Brazakka, dragging me to one side. 'Forget about the beer. These blokes are top executives – they drink cocktails, fine wine, spirits, not bloody VB. And there's no bloody lettuce on their sangers. Have you ever had a McDonald's without lettuce?'

'I've never had McDonald's,' I replied truthfully. Brazakka was frazzled. If this had been an event that I was managing in Sydney, I'd probably have been the same. But, my new-found inner calm was helping me to put life's challenges into perspective. A lettuce-less sandwich was not going to kill anyone. And wasn't going without some of life's 'essentials' part of this whole teambuilding exercise, anyway?

On that first night I set enough places for twenty-three people. Braz promptly removed three of the settings. *Someone's out of favour,* I thought. Then I realised that the skipper of one of their chartered boats, a popular bloke called Biggles, his deckie, Beau, and I weren't invited into the inner sanctum. *Think of the money,* I told myself, as we hung around outside like spare parts, waiting on them hand and foot. We were the dish pigs. It felt like I was a stranger in my own home, a horrible feeling.

The following morning the guests were served packet cereals at the tiki bar. I refused to eat that crap so I lit a fire at the beach shack and cooked myself some prawns and mud crabs. A few of them wandered over and asked if they could try what I was eating instead. It was a great chance to get to know some of them better. Then, when they returned from spending the day clay pigeon shooting or fishing off their chartered boats, swimming in waterholes, or heli-fishing, most preferred to assemble at the beach shack again for pre-dinner drinks. Not fancy wine or cocktails, but my home-brewed beer. Brazakka's supply of beer had disappeared in the first hour! When it was time for dinner, I set the twenty places again but Fred pulled me aside. 'Set another place at the top of the table next to me,' he said. 'You are the guest of honour tonight. Let's get to know each other better.'

He obviously felt uncomfortable that I hadn't been included. This was one incredibly astute bloke. Fred had actually just retired as chairman but still held the post of Honorary Chairman. You never truly retire from McDonald's and he was effectively still top dog. During his time in charge he'd been the man responsible for building the McDonald's reputation as a company that treats its employees well. He was also the architect of McDonald's folklore decisions, like making each burger precisely 0.28 inches thick. Fred didn't miss a trick and I could see why these executives were so keen to travel halfway round the world to spend time with him.

Before we'd finished our entrees, I was telling Fred all about my corporate career in food marketing and how a long-standing friend and colleague, Peter Lancaster, was now supplying all the dry mixes for McDonald's ice creams and thick shakes throughout South-East Asia, where fresh dairy supplies were hard to come by. Fred vaguely knew Peter but called over his South-East Asia man, Daniel Ng, who worked very closely with him. 'Let's call him up,' I suggested, and soon after dinner we had Peter on speakerphone, laughing about the fact that his key clients were staying on my desert island.

Fred and I were the last ones standing that night and, as the others dispersed to their tents, we took a bottle of whisky down to the beach shack and lit a fire. Brazakka wandered over at one point, but Fred politely suggested that he would appreciate some time alone with me and Brazakka shuffled off with his tail between his legs.

'I hope you don't mind, Dave,' said Fred, when the fire and whisky hit their target. 'When you were busy earlier I had a look around the house and saw the framed cartoon on the wall. How did the limerick go?'

'Ha, that old thing!' I said, chuckling. The drawing had been presented to me when I left QUF, and showed me holding a huge jewfish under a sign to Fraser Island. I was wearing my lucky green shamrock tie which, unknown to everyone else, I only wore to meetings when I expected resistance to my ideas. It was my Irish equivalent of the New Zealand haka battle cry. At the bottom of the picture was a rhyme that I easily reeled off for Fred:

> *There was a bright spark called Glasheen*
> *With a mind like a threshing machine,*
> *His thoughts flew so fast*
> *We were stunned by the blast –*
> *And the trail's still ablaze where he's been!*

'There's more to you than meets the eye,' Fred said with a laugh. 'Tomorrow night I want you to deliver a speech to these guys. I've already seen you with them at breakfast and at drinks. They love you! But I reckon they already know a lot about your life on the island and all about Bligh. Instead, I want them to really understand that you're not just some crazy old guy who looks like Robinson Crusoe, that you shouldn't judge a guy by his board shorts. Tell them something from your time working with Peter at QUF. But tonight, let me pick your brains, because I value your opinion. What do you think about putting more healthy options on our menu?'

'You don't want to know – you won't like what I think,' I told him, but he pressed for my opinion.

'You serve dog food, Fred,' I said. 'Macca's is where you go when you have a hangover and you want to fill up on fat and stodge. My son is only allowed crap food once a week. And I take him to McDonald's for that. Otherwise it's sushi or fresh salad. Health food and fast food is too much of a contradiction. It would take years and years to change that perception.' Fred was really receptive and didn't take offence, and I'm told McDonald's does take more of a responsible approach to nutrition nowadays. Imagine if my conversation that night played even a tiny part in that policy. Perhaps they should launch a McResto – fillet of barramundi, lightly grilled, with fresh lemongrass and a wongai plum jam, served on a thick slice of damper and wrapped in a palm leaf. Mmmm...

Keen to repay Fred's faith in me with an entertaining talk, I considered a few stories from my time in the food industry: how I introduced The Wombles to Australia to promote ice-cream; or the day I tried to sign one of Australia's golden boy cricketers, David Hookes, to promote milk, but ended up on the grog with Paul Hogan, of *Crocodile Dundee* fame. But I opted for an example that captured my approach to business and life: never being afraid to tear up the rulebook and tread a different path. I started my speech by explaining how QUF had poached me from British Tobacco to nationally launch their Pauls brand of ice-cream in a ridiculous nine-month time frame. This was familiar ground for some of the McDonald's mob and clearly piqued their interest. 'Brisbane was a business backwater in those days, and I had joined a company of dyed-in-the-wool fuddy-duddies,' I told them. 'Plus, we had a tenth of the budget of our competitors. To make any sort of impact we had to drop our duds in Pitt Street.' (A few puzzled frowns.) 'Err, what I mean is that we had to create a stir – in your country it would be like pulling down your slacks in the middle of Madison Avenue.' (Chuckles.) 'The local creative talent was weak, though. Their concepts for a TV ad were too parochial and I was losing patience, so I gave them a deadline: one more day or the agency was sacked.' (Appreciative nods.) 'Then a shy young bloke called Greg Daniel, who went on to run two major agencies, put up his hand and presented a couple of ideas that blew the rest out of the water. So I immediately placed the eighteen-year-old guy in charge, which pissed his boss off a treat.' (A few raised eyebrows.) 'This young fella knew that we needed to push new boundaries and target adults, not young kids. Firstly, we called the ice-cream Pauls Private Bin. Our print artwork abandoned the traditional colourful photography in favour of stylish, hand-drawn imagery. And we needed packaging that would stand out from the crowd, so we tried a black lid for all the flavours.' (Murmurs of agreement.) 'We tested this packaging with hidden cameras in stores and it worked, but we still had to raise awareness of the brand in the adult market. We needed a knock-out TV advertising campaign. And this was where we hit the sweet spot. What do all adults love? Sex.' (Sniggers.) 'But sex had never been used to sell ice-cream before. Even better, I thought. So, picture the scene: a couple has just finished a romantic dinner at home. The lady is dressed provocatively. She sweeps her long, flowing locks off her shoulders to reveal a cracking pair of hooters.' (More sniggers.) 'She serves the man a portion of Pauls Private Bin French Vanilla. "French Vanilla? How do you eat that?" her man asks. She responds with some suggestive flicks of her tongue that could, quite possibly, have been perceived as an act of oral pleasuring.' (Riotous laughter – I had this audience eating out of the palm of my hand.)

'This was ballsy stuff and I knew my neck would be on the line when I presented it to a board of directors who had probably never heard of oral sex, let alone experienced it.' (Suppressed titters.) 'I needed some figures to back me up, so we booked a movie theatre and wired up our volunteers to electrodes to measure their pulse rate. When we showed the ad for the first time the power surge almost blew the theatre's electrical circuit.' (Uncontrolled hilarity.)

'I didn't need any electrodes to gauge the reaction of the board. I could see their heads about to explode. But it wasn't only the sexy TV ad that had the directors frothing at the mouth. It was the black lids. They were a step too far. The TV station switchboards lit up with complaints when the ads first went to air. It was mainly the wives of our board of directors, I think.'

(Chortles.) 'I expected that reaction in Queensland and pulled it off air almost immediately. But the ad wasn't targeted at Queensland, it was aimed at the more open-minded markets of Sydney and Melbourne. And it was a huge success there. Sales were sensational and everyone was talking about Pauls Private Bin. That campaign set the trend for modern-day ice-cream marketing, which is often provocative. And look at the colour of the packing of modern premium brands like Connoisseur. They're black!' (Unanimous buzz of approval.)

I paused for breath and Fred seized the moment. 'Boy, that's a good tale, Dave, and thanks for sharing. It's what I've been telling these guys for a long time. McDonald's has to learn to take chances. There's no right way or wrong way of doing things. Sometimes you have to go with your gut. Look at Dave now. He's still taking chances. And with his calculated risk comes the reward of living in a place like this,' he said and the whole table burst into a spontaneous round of applause. It was touching and made me quite emotional.

It had been a while since I'd felt genuinely appreciated. I thought that perhaps this type of corporate opportunity, blending my business acumen with the lessons learned from this alternative lifestyle, might be a sustainable way of securing my place here.

Fred and I spoke every night around the fire and we often ventured into more personal territory. One night he broke down in tears over some hurtful comments that one of his family members, who was on that trip, had made about him wasting family money on this type of gesture for his friends and employees. Even billionaires can be vulnerable and sensitive. Fred liked me, and I liked him. The McDonald's team came back to Resto three or four times before Fred died in 2013, a day after his eightieth birthday. The guests slept in chartered boats after that initial trial run, but that luxury option couldn't have matched actually staying on the island. Resto had made an amazing impression on some members of that first party, who brought their children back to show them where they spotted their first croc, where they learned all about icecream and where they discovered that a life outside the corporate merry-go-round can still have clarity and purpose.

***

That first McDonald's mob loved my homegrown grog, a dark brown ale that I make from a standard Coopers home-brew kit. Straight from the freezer, it's like nectar after a sweaty hot day on land or at sea. The trawler boys go nuts for it. With all the ongoing building and clean-up work, I hardly had any time for fishing and I quickly worked out that it was much more efficient to gift them some beer in return for their fish and prawns. I stress it was a gift, not a trade – I don't want to start paying any historical duties or taxes. The size of the gift depended on the fishos' appearance. If they were crawling up the beach, tongues dragging in the sand and hauling a huge box of fish behind them, I knew I was in a strong bargaining position. It was basic supply and demand theory – they never knew how much I could supply, but I could see the demand in their crazed eyes. My brother Mick once swapped twenty kilograms of fish, worth about $400 at market, for twelve bottles of beer that might have cost $10 to make. That's a seriously good trade. I do try to be fair because many of these boys have become good friends. But I don't want to make the trade too attractive because all the boats would be here all the time and that defeats the objective of living in isolation.

One of the first trawler captains to visit regularly was Phil Fry, who grew up in Monkey Mia in Shark Bay, Western Australia. Monkey Mia is famous for its dolphins, which were basically his childhood pets. Now living in Cairns, Phil is a gentle giant with a fair Celtic complexion totally unsuited to his profession. He has become a good mate and a lifeline for me. When I go to Cairns once or twice a year for my big shopping trips for essentials, I load up my supplies, neatly boxed, wrapped and marked, on his boat, the *Diamond Lil,* ready for him to drop off here on his next trip north.

Before fishing season starts in March, he loves to kick back on the island and sometimes looks after the place for me. Like many fishos, he's a man of few words and probably prefers the place to himself, but with a fire crackling away, my dog for company and a couple of beers to loosen the vocal chords, he and I can yarn until the sun comes up.

Occasionally, for special guests like Phil, I might open my secret supply of spirits. Phil introduced me to a stainless-steel fabricator in Cairns who built a stills tower for $800. Since then, I have made a coffee liqueur like Kahlua, and I have some glass demijohns of rum and whisky that have been ageing for sixteen years. If we added local flavours like the wongai plum or the island's beautiful native bush cherry, I reckon we could launch a Resto brand that would help promote local produce and culture. Another great idea from the Glasheen 'threshing machine'.

Phil was an experienced operator, but even old hands can make basic mistakes. One such mistake roused me one morning when I was in that fuzzy period between sleep and wakefulness.

Out the window, through half-closed eyes, I saw the shapes of the island come into focus in the grey light of a new day. Palms stretched and yawned, the sea rinsed the night from the beach, and the sunlight restored the wildflowers' vivid colours.

Then there was an almighty blast that shook the house's foundations. *Shit, what was that? Am I still dreaming?* Another blare bounced off the walls. Quassi tore into my room and hurled himself under the sheet. The noise was coming from the beach and sounded like a gas horn. That usually meant trouble. As I jogged outside I could see a boat a way off shore but poking out of the water, although the tide wasn't out. It looked like Phil's trawler, the *Blue Riband. That's weird,* I thought. *Why doesn't he just come ashore in his dinghy?*

Phil was waving madly from the bow and, when I reached the beach, I could see that the boat was sitting on top of the reef. 'What the hell happened?' I asked when I reached him in my tinny.

'It was a full moon last night and that's shit for prawns. They don't come up from the bed because the moonlight makes it easy for predators. So I headed in early, about ten o'clock. But I lost my bearings,' Phil explained. 'I thought I was about a kilometre further out than I was and, next thing I know, I smashed into the reef. Sent me flying across the cabin and I whacked my head. Figured there was nothing you could do until morning. There's a massive hole underneath, though. The bloody thing's a write-off.'

I wasn't going to give up on his boat that easily, so I took my tinny further out to find help in the shape of another trawler boy, Sharkey, who ran the *Prowler*. We tied Phil's boat to Sharkey's and tried to drag her off the reef but it was a neap tide – when there's little difference between high and low – and the *Blue Riband* wouldn't budge. We were probably doing even more damage. Phil was resigned to the fact this schoolboy error had cost him his livelihood – at least in the short term. Thank goodness he was insured, but the insurer told him to just leave the *Blue Riband* there in the water. Since then we've stripped her for anything remotely useful. But, every day as the tide retreats, her mast stealthily breaks the surface, and then most of the wreck slowly emerges as a permanent reminder that it's not wise to drop your guard in these parts, not for one second.

***

Even for those few days the McDonald's crew was here, I'd missed the liberation of nudity. As I lay in the shallows, watching the sheening water slide over my body as Quassi chased shadows of seagulls, some of Fred's words resonated with me. If the chairman of McDonald's valued my opinion, perhaps it was time for my mob to listen to me and realise that, without the support of the local community, there wasn't a hope in hell of building their heavenly eco-resort on Restoration Island. And, if we didn't come up with the funds for that development soon, Colin Lindsay would be back at square one and want to sell. Where would I stand then? It was time to check back in with Bluey.

But all of a sudden, Bluey was difficult to track down. All my calls went to voicemail. Then I received a call from Dave Nissen. Not much happens in Cairns without his knowledge.

'Your company's called Longboat, right?' he asked.

'Yep,' I answered, warily.

'I've just seen that name and your company logo etched on the glass door of a fancy office in Cairns. You didn't mention you had an office here.'

'Err, we don't, to the best of my knowledge,' I said.

What's that bugger Bluey been up to now? Dave found the number for the office and, sure enough, Bluey had signed a tenyear lease in our name and was pursuing other project management opportunities from there. And we were being taken to court because we already owed the landlord $8000 in rent arrears. This was the last straw for me and him. 'How the hell did I know nothing about this?' I shouted down the phone when I finally tracked Bluey down. 'I'm a company director for Christ's sake!'

'We thought you had enough on your plate, what with Denika and Kye and everything,' Bluey said sheepishly. 'Besides, there wasn't much you could do from up there. Sorry, Glash, but everyone's kind of moved on.'

'Moved on? Moved on? This is my bloody home, you idiot! I haven't bloody moved on. And I don't want to bloody move on,' I said.

'If I can resolve this court case and settle the debt, you lot will owe me big time for this. All the Longboat directors will have to resign. If that happens, then you all have my word that I will try my best to involve you in whatever develops.'

The others agreed without hesitation. I hated being let down, especially by supposed friends. However, I was now the sole shareholder of Longboat and in control of my company's destiny. I could use my one share in the island to try to achieve my own goals. And they didn't include some monstrosity of an eco-resort. As the guardian of Restoration Island, I wanted to create something positive and sustainable for the people of Lockhart River. One significant hurdle remained: Colin Lindsay had bought out his partners and now owned the other three shares, meaning he now controlled seven in total, while Longboat – me – just had the one. But I would have to tackle that problem later.

Jeez, this was stressful. I thought I had escaped this constant wheeling and dealing. Thank goodness I was a resident in nature's rehab clinic; if I'd been anywhere but the island I would have been hitting the grog and losing sleep again.

Chapter 8

Miranda

On the first Tuesday of every November the Melbourne Cup horse race stops the nation. It's a public holiday in many parts of Australia and, all around the country, people dress up in fancy suits, dresses and hats to celebrate this sporting spectacle with friends and neighbours. Cape York is no different, although it's a bit easier to bring this region to a standstill, because the pace of life up here is fairly slow to begin with. For my first few years up at Resto, I had paid no attention to the Cup. Weekdays had rolled into weekends and public holidays came and went without me even realising. So I was really pleased to receive an invitation to a Melbourne Cup barbie from a Portland Roads couple, Geoff and Cheri. My wwoofer at the time, an Israeli girl called Roni, was also welcome. She was a pocket dynamo with a mischievous twinkle in her eye.

From the second I picked up Roni from the airport, she wanted to know all about her duties. 'Look, I don't have rules but it normally works like this,' I told her. 'If the weather's good, we play. If it's crap, we work. I want everyone to enjoy this place.' After her first night on the island there was a rap on my door at 6am. It was barely daylight. 'Dave, the weather is no good. We must work,' said this force of nature, whose endless energy reminded me of my daughter, Erika. 'Your coffee is ready in the kitchen. We will start work in ten minutes.'

'Yes, ma'am,' I groaned.

It was easy for Roni to choose her outfit for the cup because she only brought two dresses. To blend in, she made a fascinator out of palm fronds and yellow flowers from the garden. It looked really pretty. 'Dave, give me your shirt to iron, please,' she demanded. Iron? I hadn't ironed a shirt in years. Nevertheless, she managed to press it by using a frying pan and a towel to protect the shirt. We even managed to dig out the old snakeskin tie that I had rescued when my Uncle

Terry died and Dad burned all his possessions – an old Irish tradition. Then Roni found a matching flower to pin to my tricorne hat and we were all set. It was comforting to have a woman fussing over me and I appreciated the attention. The hosts were providing the meat and fish for the barbie, so we took an entree and some booze. Roni took over again and made a tray of traditional Israeli pancakes, which looked delicious, and I received a firm slap on the hand when I tried to sample one before we set off. 'You must leave these until we arrive,' she said.

We arrived an hour before the big race and joined in the sweepstake. The others had been on the turps since midday and were waiting for us to arrive with the entree before starting to eat, so everyone eagerly tucked into Roni's pancakes, which were delicious. Some people ate up to five, but I was saving myself for the meat and only tried one or two. Then it all started to go downhill. Another guest, who was normally very well-spoken, started talking in some strange tongue that sounded like Swahili. Cheri was in the garden hugging one of the palm trees. Other guests wandered aimlessly like zombies. Roni crashed out on the sofa, giggling at the TV as the horses entered their barriers. 'What's funny?' I asked.

'There are chickens in the pens. What is this Melbourne Cup chicken race?' Then the penny dropped. She had sneaked some dope into the pancakes that my previous wwoofer, Chris, had left behind. The house was a scene of total carnage and I was quickly losing my own grip on reality. So, when the winning horse started to talk like Mr Ed, I stumbled outside for some fresh air and loaded up a plate with prawns, fish kebabs and a steak. There was just one problem. Every time I tried to use my knife and fork the plate inched away. We had to get out of there quickly and I somehow shepherded Roni to the boat before the tide went out. At sea, white stallions were riding the waves alongside us and I was convinced that I was the steersman of a Viking warship. 'Row faster,' I bellowed at Roni. 'Faster, I tell ye!' It's a mystery how we made it back to Resto and it was late the next day before either of us surfaced. A day later, Cheri rang and tore a strip off me, but I took it on the chin and explained that I had no idea there was any ganga in the pancakes. 'How much did you put in?' I asked Roni later. 'I reckon you used the heads, that's the powerful trippy bit. Go easy the next time you make Roni's Rockets.'

'We only should have had one each. It's not my fault that Australians are greedy,' Roni said sheepishly.

Roni stayed a few weeks and left a strong legacy. She was a special education teacher and wise beyond her years, having just come out of the Israeli army. It was interesting to hear that most people's opinion of her country was clouded by the actions of a minority of religious zealots, just as the majority of peaceful Muslims are tainted by the few terrorists. Roni and I were kindred spirits and, as her departure loomed, she worried about leaving me here on my own. 'We need to find you a woman, Dave,' she said. Roni was right; I desperately wanted to find a romantic partner to share my life with.

Jeez, did I miss female company! I'd always hoped there might be someone out there with my ideals and my goals, someone who could see herself thriving in this environment. Did these women even exist? Most women I knew in Sydney just seemed obsessed with the latest beauty products and making themselves look pretty. There's no need for all that crap here. We exist in our own skins, without frills and adornments. I've had so much fun here when women have abandoned convention, let their hair down and maybe stitched together a couple of palm leaves to create a makeshift bikini. That's the type of woman I knew I needed: fun, adventurous, carefree. I wanted to experience the thrill of the chase once again, and preferably not to chase someone with a Zimmer frame. Perhaps the chances of finding this person become slimmer and slimmer as the clock ticks on, but I knew I'd always search for the love and respect of a woman. The second you give up that hope, there's not a lot left to keep you going.

'Just how are we going to find this woman?' I asked Roni.

'Internet dating,' she replied.

'What? That's for sad old misfits, isn't it?' I replied. Roni was silent.

'That was your chance to say I'm not a sad old misfit'.

'You're not sad and you're not a misfit,' she said with a laugh.

On the dating site RSVP, Roni set up a profile for me. It stated that I was looking for a 'feminine, intelligent, fit, adventurous woman with an open mind, aged between eighteen and 120.' I didn't want to mention the island on my profile. 'I'll just get a load of lonely old sheilas who want a decent holiday before they croak it!' I said.

'You have to mention the island,' she insisted. 'That's your unique selling point. The offers will come flooding in.'

Despite taking Roni's advice, the response was really disappointing. My profile had a few views, and the occasional 'like', but nobody expressed genuine interest. In some ways I was relieved. It's a time-consuming and costly trip up here. And I would have known within the first two minutes whether any connection was going to materialise. That's fine when you nip down the road to a pub in Bondi for a date, but I could be stuck with a woman for days here, as I knew from my experience with Denika's clumsy attempts to pair me off. We tried other sites, like Zoosk and PlentyOfFish, but the response was the same and Roni felt like a failure when she left to continue her travels.

Just days later, I received a call from a friend in Cairns, Cheyenne Morrison. What Cheyenne didn't know about islands could be written on the back of a postage stamp. If I'm an islomaniac, he's certifiably islo-insane. It was hard to budge Cheyenne from the beach shack on his first visit to Resto. And, boy, when those flames melt away his inhibitions, Cheyenne can ruminate with the best. 'Islands are metaphors for you and me, Dave,' he said. 'They are part of a larger whole, but separated from it, too. That larger whole sustains them, and they contribute their small piece to it. But they are also worlds unto themselves, with well-defined boundaries – a magic circle offering exclusion and protection. I dream of this existence. Most people dream of this existence. Very few realise those dreams. You're one of the luckiest men alive, David Glasheen.'

Cheyenne had called to tell me he had been approached by a young reporter from the *Sunday Telegraph* in Sydney called Katrina Creer. She had initially wanted to write a story on him as an example of someone who had undertaken an extreme sea change from the big city, because he was living in Port Douglas at the time. But Cheyenne pointed her in my direction instead. I wasn't too keen on the intrusion, but thought it would be a useful way to spell out my intentions for Resto to the world. The story mentioned my attempts at internet dating and was picked up by Margueritte Rossi, a presenter for *A Current Affair* on Channel 9, who flew up with a crew the very next day.

'We'll find you a woman, Dave,' she promised.

They spruiked the hell out of my segment on the show and it was a ratings winner. Within fifteen minutes, my dating profiles were being bombarded, although mainly by lonely old sheilas looking for a holiday before they croaked it. But Margueritte was true to her word and asked me to select candidates to film two blind dates in Sydney.

The first was a fashion designer. *A Current Affair* took me to a gents' outfitters to buy a nice new shirt, although I really couldn't see what was wrong with the one I brought down from Resto – apart from a few moth holes. It was strange being back in the big city – waiting for traffic before crossing the road and dodging people with manic intent in their eyes on the street. *I don't miss this one little bit,* I thought. I was also copping some strange glances from passers-by, curious as to why this untamed creature had been allowed out in public. In an effort to make me look more respectable, I was taken to a barbershop for a beard and hair trim. I actually quite fancied the Russian hairdresser, who unfortunately wasn't interested in a real date.

The venue for the first staged date with the fashion designer was the magnificent Strickland House in Vaucluse, where I waited patiently, cameras rolling, on the lawn with a fancy picnic. When my date arrived I nearly dived into the picnic basket to hide. She just wasn't my type and, although we spent a pleasant afternoon together, there was no chemistry. It was the same the following day except this time, unknown to Channel 9, my date at a fancy restaurant at the top of the Centrepoint tower was a set-up – she was the girlfriend of my Mongolian mate, Walter. It would have been embarrassing if I'd only been able to persuade one willing subject, so this woman agreed to make up the numbers. It was cheap TV but this stuff works. I once watched a series of *Married at First Sight* while in hospital. I reckon that show's perfect for me. Or *The Bachelor,* perhaps. *Love Island* even...?

'It doesn't matter that these dates didn't work out,' Margueritte insisted. 'When women see that other women are interested in you, they'll be queuing down the street,' she said.

'But there isn't a street to queue down. That's the trouble – I don't think it's me, it's my location,' I said.

There was a good response again after the dates broadcast, but nothing worth following up. Online dating wasn't working out. I would probably have had more success sticking a message in a bottle and hoping it would wash up on another island where a single woman lived, undiscovered, on her own.

But not everyone was disappointed by my romantic misfortune.

***

Miranda had been very understanding, waiting faithfully for me to return to Resto after my small-screen debut. She and I had been an item for several years and it was a mutually beneficial arrangement: she provided companionship, emotional support and occasionally joined me at the beach shack for a good yarn. In return, I provided her with a roof over her head and the clothes on her broken back. When we first met, it was a bit freaky how she just wouldn't take her eyes off me, as she stared into the cafe I was in from her wheelbarrow in the junkyard next door. I was buying Bluey a farewell coffee before his trip to Resto to oversee the environmental impact survey, back in the early days. 'Do you reckon you'll be lonely up there?' I asked him.

'Probably,' he said. 'I wouldn't mind having a sheila with me.'

'I might know just the person,' I said. 'Wait right there.' It was easy to persuade Miranda to accompany Bluey. For just $10 she packed up her things (just a torso at this point). It's true, she was nothing to look at – no arms or legs or hair, and a face like a smashed crab. But, with a wig and some lippy, I was sure she could scrub up quite nicely. 'Here, she's yours,' I said, sitting her on the chair next to Bluey. 'She doesn't say a lot, but she doesn't answer back, either. Treat her well and she will be good company for you.'

'You're a bloody idiot, Glash. The least you could do is to introduce us formally. What's her name, anyway?' Bluey asked, chuckling away.

'Miranda,' I replied. 'Prospero's daughter in Shakespeare's *The Tempest.* It's set on a remote island. And she looks quite stormy. Miranda, meet Bluey.'

'Fair enough, I like the name. But I'm not going to be seen dead with a woman with no arms or legs,' he said. 'And she's naked. People will think there's something wrong with me!'

'Okay then, we'll find some limbs before you leave,' I said, and trawled the cafe's yellow pages for costume shops. There was one nearby and it luckily contained a whole mound of random limbs, presumably in case a couple of blokes like us turned up wanting to put the final touches on their plastic better half. We selected an assortment of limbs that fitted her, approximately, and found a ginger wig, straw hat and a flouncy dress. Miranda was radiant, and I was ever so slightly jealous when Bluey plonked her in the front seat of his four-wheel drive and the pair waved goodbye. Was that a tear in Miranda's eye I noticed? It was an arduous trip for a lady of her breeding and, just north of Cooktown where the sealed roads ended, she had to be rescued by some bemused local fellas when Bluey tried, unsuccessfully, to cross a fast-flowing river. I'm not sure that John Pritchard's opinion of Bluey improved when he met the happy couple at Cape Weymouth for Miranda's first – and last – boat trip to the island.

Miranda featured prominently in the Channel 9 television reports, so she attracted every whacko from here to Timbuktu. One woman from Hawaii, a surfy type who called herself The Fairy and had grown-up children, tracked me down by email. She fantasised about island life and said she was going to send me a parcel as a thank you for corresponding with her. She clearly fantasised about other stuff, too. There were about twenty items in the box that arrived, all individually wrapped in hand-decorated paper, along with a five page letter about the importance of human connection and how I should share her gifts with my friends. The first present I unwrapped was a squeaky bone for Quassi. How thoughtful. Next was a new set of quality fishing hooks. This woman clearly understood island life. She also sent some tasteful marine-themed ornaments for the house. Then I unwrapped a bottle of massage oil – could come in handy, I supposed – followed by a bottle of paint. Edible body paint. Next came some lube, and I don't mean engine oil. An ostrich feather tickler amused me – figuratively, not literally, I might add. There was a tag on the next parcel that read: 'You will need me there for this one!' It contained a battery-operated contraption which looked like it could cause permanent mutilation. Freaked out, I resealed the box and stuck it under the bed, where it remains today. The Fairy died of cancer within a year, I learned on social media. Perhaps this care package had been an impish manifestation of her dying wishes. It certainly kept the trawler boys amused for years to come.

***

Quassi loved his new rubber bone, but the chickens were his favourite pastime. They mesmerised him. He could sit and watch them for hours, seemingly protecting them from any danger. Even when the roosters Bruce and Sheila had an almighty fight in which Sheila, usually the subservient one, won to rule the roost, Quassi impassively looked on. Goodness knows what was going through his head. The only clue came one afternoon when I was enjoying a well-earned cup of tea outside the house. The chickens were doing their thing, laying eggs in the most unlikely of places. Only that morning, one had hopped out from underneath Miranda's dress and, neatly between her legs, was a big, white egg. If I hadn't seen the chicken leave the scene, it would have freaked me right out.

Suddenly there was an almighty squawk.

I looked up to see Quassi trying to hump one of the hens. It was not a good biological match and the poor girl looked distinctly offended – and uncomfortable. 'Quassi, get off!' I shouted as I ran across the paddock. 'That's not appropriate.' It was all over in a flash, but his grip on the chook's back must have ripped out some feathers, because Quassi had tasted blood. Two quick shakes of the neck and the chicken was no longer a potential dinner date, she was dinner. After a few gulps all that was left were a few feathers floating to the ground. Quassi looked like he had been taking lipstick tips from Miranda. I could see him think: 'That was tasty, on to the next,' but I grabbed him by the neck.

It was D-day for my chicken experiment and the rest were soon condemned to the pot, which created a shortfall of natural fertiliser. Keeping on top of the garden was hard enough, even with the pigs and chickens creating a constant supply of nutrients for the soil. The main problem was water. In the dry season, we could go for months on end without seeing a drop. We relied on full tanks to see us through and the main concrete tank high up on the hill, which held about 120,000 litres, had seen better days. The water was fed through a washing machine drum, to filter out solids, before flowing down the newly laid underground pipes to the house. That tank was old and could have crumbled at any minute, and then

I would have been in serious trouble. So over a period of a couple of years, I invested in four new tanks – two 5000-litre and two 10,000-litre tanks – which I retrieved from the mothership and floated them over to the island behind my boat, taking great care not to tilt the opening into the water because they would have sunk like lead. From there, with the help of wwoofers or visitors, we used our tried and tested roller system to push them into position.

The annual rainfall here is about two metres, only a quarter of some parts of tropical Far North Queensland. That's why the tip of Cape York is known as the dry tropics and is far less humid than places like Cairns. The difficulty is that most of that rainfall arrives in huge deluges. Down the side of the hill these rains create dirty grey torrents, which wash all of the nutrients and compost out of the soil, while the storms' high tides suck sea water inland up the trench that was once the big rubbish dump. I needed a dam and a wide relief pipe with a reverse valve to retain the tens of thousands of litres of wasted fresh water and keep the salt water out. So I set about building Hadrian's Wall and scoured the island for decent-sized rocks that I could transport by wheelbarrow, often over impossible terrain, to pile up under wire mesh and cement in place. Dry-stone walling is an art form, and finding the right-sized stones is crucial so, feeling like the Hulk, I sometimes had to tip small boulders down from high rocky outcrops. I'd underestimated the task of building this wall, and it wasn't a favourite with the wwoofers. I never intended to create a labour camp, so I shouldered most of this burden myself. To this day, it's a work in progress with about a quarter of the sixty-metre wall still to build.

***

The stability of this initial section was first tested by Cyclone Ingrid in 2005. Hadrian's Wall survived, but plenty of the island's other features didn't. Quassi and I emerged from the old generator shed to an eerie scene. The whole island was a mess of palm fronds and coconuts. Water was raging down the hill – over, around and probably under that first part of the wall – creating a surging funnel in the trench. The garage was completely flooded, and I would have to assess the damage there later. Hesitantly, I made my way over to the house. Thankfully it was standing proud, but the pawpaw tree was down and, at the front of the house, two of my favourite frangipanis had vanished. *No real dramas yet,* I thought. My tarpaulin system in the house had worked a treat and the roofing was all intact. The internet was out, but that was to be expected and the satellite dish was still up. Next, it was time to check on the boats. My new fibreglass Stinger I'd bought in Cairns and had been towed up by one of my trawler mates was fine, although a huge palm tree had crashed down onto the beach just metres away. It was going to take a good few hours with a sand pump to empty her of all the new sand she had taken on board. I was ready to congratulate myself on a successful cyclone-proofing operation when I remembered my promise to Dave Nissen. *Shit, his boat's gone.* It wasn't a big surprise, but he was going to be pissed. Then the other casualty hit me like a punch in the guts: me. I was totally buggered after the exertions of the previous day and a terrified, sleepless night. It was mid-morning and I did something that I had never done on the island: I took myself back to bed to rest up for the big clean.

Post-Ingrid, Nanako and Asami were none the worse for their cyclonic baptism and were happy to help unpack my secured items and restore the island to her former glory. Their replacement, who arrived a few months after the girls departed, was not so keen to pitch in. He was a budding Austrian artist who'd asked to spend four weeks here with his family, but the request didn't come through the wwoofer organisation. I had just assumed he realised that he and his wife would have to earn their keep. Nah! He didn't lift a finger to help and spent all his days down at the water's edge painting landscapes that looked like Jackson Pollock had suffered an epileptic fit. Also, this fella wanted ten showers a day and needed a constant supply of water for his own private veggie garden. To make things worse, his visit had coincided with an algae bloom in one of the 10,000-litre tanks. Blue-green algae can be toxic and although the water was only slightly discoloured, I wasn't about to take any chances. Nor did I fancy pouring bleach or chlorine into our drinking water, so I decided to empty the tank. This meant we were about 8000 litres of water down and, despite Cyclone Ingrid, the rainy season had not been especially wet. There were months and months to negotiate before a potential top up. It was a worry. So I dragged the Austrian up to the old water tank to show him the water level, and where it would be in a couple of months if he carried on using water at that extravagant rate. 'How do you say in Australia, David? There is no worries,' he said with a chuckle.

'No, I'm serious,' I replied, raising my voice. 'If you want water for the garden, you have to wash in the sea. Don't even pee in the toilet – go round the side of the house. But pick a different spot each time so that it doesn't attract vermin.'

'Pah! I am not animal. I would rather leave than pee on your ground.'

'That's your choice,' I said, hoping that he would piss off that afternoon. But he didn't and he even had the nerve to complain about the Chateau Lockhart wine I provided for dinner that night. It was the straw that broke this camel's back. 'Look,' I eventually told him. 'This can't carry on. If you want to drink the best stuff, you have to contribute.'

'I already tell you, David. I will paint a beautiful picture of Resto and sell this to the finest gallery in New York for $20,000. Half for you, half for me. Just you see,' he replied.

'Great, I look forward to it. In the meantime, can you draw a few postcards and sell them to the tourists at the airport for $2 each please?' The postcards didn't materialise and nor did any help, so his days on the island were numbered and I was happy to ask him to leave.

'You are an old fool, David Glasheen,' he said, when I dumped them unceremoniously at the airport.

'Just you wait until I am famous.' I'm still waiting.

***

Dealing with the Austrian artist was an exasperating experience. Resto normally absorbed any of my negative emotions like a sponge, but on this occasion I needed to vent my frustrations and Miranda wasn't in one of her more receptive moods. So when three sea kayakers arrived sometime later, using the island as a pit stop on their trip to Thursday Island, I had a captive audience around the camp fire.

'...And, to cap it all, he called me an old fool,' I finished, finally coming up for air.

'Yeah, yeah, we hear ya,' said Dave Winkworth, a seasoned sea kayaker with shoulders chiselled from granite and forearms that put Popeye to shame. 'But listen, we've got an early start in the morning so, if it's all right with you, we might call it a night.'

'Okay, but I probably won't see you in the morning and I want to leave you with one word of advice. There's a huge male croc claiming every uninhabited island from here to the tip of Cape York. Just watch your step,' I said.

'I'm sure we'll be fine,' Dave replied.

A couple of days later and about sixty kilometres north of Resto, Dave stopped for lunch at one of the tiny Macarthur Islands along with his friend, Arunas Pilka, a civil servant from Canberra, and their other mate, Mike Snoad. It was midday with cloudless blue skies, but there was a strong wind and the water was very choppy. Dave had gone for a swim and was back on the beach, basking in that slice of paradise under a palm tree, when Arunas waded in for a dip. Then there was an unholy commotion. From all the froth and foam, Dave instinctively thought Arunas had been attacked by a shark. He quickly realised that a four-metre-long croc had Arunas's right leg in its mouth and was trying to spin him round and drag him under the water in a death roll. Arunas jabbed his fingers in its nostrils then tried to prise open the jaw, managing only to slice open his hand. Without a thought for his own safety, Dave ran into the water, jumped on the croc's back and grabbed hold of its belly, clinging on for dear life until it let go of Arunas and swam off. Arunas's leg was torn to shreds but, amazingly, no arteries had been severed and it wasn't bleeding too heavily. Dave hauled the poor bloke out of the water and onto the beach, where he placed a plastic bag under the wound to prevent sand from entering the thigh. They kept their eyes peeled for the croc's return, because this bastard would be fuming that he had missed out on lunch. Dave and Mike made Arunas, who was barely conscious, a cup of his favourite black tea, and then let off an Emergency Position Indicating Radio Beacon, or EPIRB. This signal is detected by satellites and monitored by an international group of rescue services, including the Australian Maritime Safety Authority (AMSA) based in Canberra. There's a huge penalty for setting off an EPIRB without a life-threatening cause, so AMSA knew it was serious and a plane was immediately dispatched to investigate.

Two hours later, the crew spotted 'CROC ATTACK – ONE EVAC' scrawled in the sand. There was nowhere for them to land so a helicopter was sent and, in the meantime, Dave and Mike cleared a makeshift helipad on the island and rolled out a big plastic 'H'. The chopper flew Arunas off to hospital on Thursday Island, where his wound was stitched up and he spent a week recuperating. He was so lucky to escape with just a huge, ugly scar as a reminder of his brush with death, but he was more than happy to show it off on a later trip to Resto. Dave was awarded the Governor General's award for bravery for rescuing his mate, and is now widely known as Crocodile Winky.

Chapter 9

Sink or swim

'The background noise is our wind generator protesting at being run at 160 kilometres an hour when it's meant to do fifteen or twenty,' said Colin, talking to the ABC from the phone at the tiki bar. It was April 2006 and Cyclone Monica was due to hit, and the radio news wanted an eye-witness account. 'I think it's called *Survivor Restoration Island* at the moment, but without the prize money. But I built the structures here so I'm confident we're in good shape.' I half-expected him to give out a 1300 number for anyone wanting a quote for construction work.

Colin was visiting the island for a few days with his daughter, Kate, and her boyfriend, Chris. Kye was here with me, too. Nobody planned to be here during a cyclone, especially one with wind speeds predicted to reach 280 kilometres per hour. But Monica was changing direction like a drunk bouncing off the walls of an alley, and Lockhart

River hadn't initially been in her path. Now she was heading north and due to cross the coast forty kilometres south of the town. Again, I checked in with Dave Nissen and he confirmed our worst fears. 'It's currently a Category 4 cyclone, but it might be upgraded by the time it reaches you,' he said. Just as with Ingrid, only one year earlier, this news came too late for evacuation but, having survived my first cyclone relatively unscathed, I still believed that the old generator shed was the safest place in the whole region for me and Kye. Colin had other ideas. He decided to board himself and his family behind the cocktail area of the tiki bar with marine plywood, but the walls of the tiki bar were made of polycarbonate sheeting. 'You're mad,' I told him. 'A coconut will zip through that stuff like a bullet through tissue paper. And if any of the roofing iron comes loose it will slice your heads off.'

'Jeez, Dave, that's a bit dramatic. We're happy to take our chances,' Colin replied.

'Okay, don't say I didn't warn you. See you in the morning, I hope,' I said.

Ingrid had been an effective dress rehearsal the year before and, as evening approached, I started to work on the boat first so as not to make the same mistakes twice. This time, rather than drag it up the beach, I half-filled it with water and removed the motor, then tied it to the nearest tree. Then I rebuilt the mound of loose possessions in the house and jammed the doors shut with weights. With plenty of time to spare, Kye, Quassi and I took our food, chairs, blankets and books over to the shed. Quassi was super-nervous; Kye was super-excited. As the noise gradually rose to a deafening crescendo, much louder than I remembered during Ingrid, Quassi was like a cat on a hot tin roof and would not settle. If the door had opened, he would have bolted, so I had to tie him down. Initially, Kye wanted to stick his head out the door to see what was going on but, after a few missiles thudded into the shed wall, he started to lose a bit of confidence – not surprising for an eight year old. I needed to take his mind off what was happening outside. 'Do you know the Cyclone Song?' I asked.

'No, Dad,' he replied.

'Well, it's the same tune as "Time Me Kangaroo Down, Sport" but with different words. It goes something like this...'

> *Tie the Quassi dog down, Kye*
> *Tie the Quassi dog down*
> *Hear the noise of the wind, son*
> *Hear the noise of the wind*
> *That's the roof of the house, gone*
> *There's no roof on the house*
> *Altogether now!*

We must have invented twenty verses and it kept us amused for hours until Kye, still humming the tune as I tucked another blanket around him, somehow drifted off to sleep. Monica didn't last as long as Ingrid and, in comparison, we breezed through it, even though gusts of around 400 kilometres per hour were recorded near Gove in the Gulf of Carpentaria. Morning on Resto revealed the expected carnage of palm fronds and coconuts, but only one of the newly planted palm trees had fallen. There were even signs of life over at the tiki bar, and I was relieved to count three heads still attached to their necks. Chris, so relieved to have survived his first cyclone, proposed to Colin's daughter on the spot. The roof of the house was intact, too, contrary to the Cyclone Song. And I had been vindicated in leaving the boat in the water, because the tide had encroached way beyond the high water mark that I would have dragged her to.

Then, at low tide, the one significant piece of damage was revealed. It had not entered my head that my new trawler, the *Moreton Mist,* would be in danger. It was a big boat, about fourteen metres long, which I had bought from a salvage guy called Jason for $1 just a few months earlier. The trawler sank after hitting the reef about seventy kilometres north of here and Jason's options were to try and float it down to Cairns and risk the trawler sinking another two or three times; to repair the damage himself and sell it on; or to sell me the boat and collect a decent fee for removing it from the Marine Park. It was a no-brainer for him – and a great opportunity for me.

There were signs that the Aboriginal community's hostility towards me was beginning to subside. Whenever I asked anyone in the white community who to approach for help, one name always came up: Paul Piva. He was originally from the Solomon Islands but came to Lockhart River at a young age when his dad became the local priest. His mother, Veronica, was involved with the local council and was very well respected, too. Like many young fellas around here, Paul left home at an early age but found his way back and, like me in some respects, was treated as an outsider for a while. He was a black fella talking white fella ways. Then he met his partner, Laney, a member of the Kuuku Ya'u clan, and built a successful business repairing motors and renting out cars to visitors. But Paul was not prominent socially. He stayed away from the canteen, the communal building in Lockhart River which used to serve alcohol at restricted times, because he could not bear to see the clan infighting. When Paul was eventually elected to the local council, his ambition was to provide a better future for the local kids. He and Laney adopted or fostered as many as six children to live alongside their own four. That's a *really* full house, but Paul knew that these kids would be at risk if they left Lockhart River.

That house was actually featured in a promotional brochure for the area. Paul and Laney stood proudly on their verandah, with a green backdrop of lush, dense vegetation. From that picture it was hard to imagine that, just a few kilometres away, an area of several acres looks like it has been napalmed. In the early 1960s, as military activities intensified in Vietnam, the Australian Army designed an experiment called Operation Blowdown to simulate nuclear explosions at various heights above the rainforest of the Iron Range here, which closely resembles the vegetation of South-East Asia. About fifty tonnes of TNT were detonated: a destructive force equivalent to wind speeds of 1600 kilometres per hour, so it's not surprising that several acres were completely flattened.

Anyway, Paul sounded like someone who spoke my language, and I invited him over to the island to fish one weekend. Both Quassi and I were working over at Hadrian's Wall, the furthest point on our flat part of the island from the north beach, when Paul moored his boat. So we didn't see him approach until we heard a 'cooee' which measured about 2.5 on the Richter scale. There was a partial solar eclipse as he waved hello. Paul Piva was a man mountain. 'Let's keep on his good side,' I whispered to Quassi. It was mid-afternoon before either of us realised there was no time left for fishing. We had been engrossed in chat and found that we were perfectly in tune about the issues that faced the Lockhart River community, namely the hopelessness of the young people. Until these young fellas found meaningful jobs, another generation would be lost to the despair of life on perpetual welfare. *Here's a deeply committed human being and someone who could lead this community to better things,* I thought. 'How can I help?' I asked. 'I own one-eighth of the island on my own now. I'm not interested in eco-resorts. I love this place and I want to stay here, but I want the island to give something back to the traditional owners. Let's create something together that can generate jobs for some of the local kids.'

'That's good to know,' said Paul. 'Let me speak to Wolfie and the others. Let me talk to the council. This bad blood with you has gone on long enough. It's time to work together.' Within days Paul rang to ask a favour. A group of locals needed to travel north for a meeting and it was much easier by sea than over land, but they had no boat. Could I spare mine for a couple of days? It was never good to be without a boat here, but this was the rainy season and I tried to limit my trips to the mainland at this time of year because the muddy roads were difficult to negotiate. It was also a chance to make a concrete gesture of reconciliation. Two days later I received another call from Paul.

'Do you want the good news or bad news?' he asked.

'Err, bad I suppose.'

'Your boat filled with rain while it was moored and sank. Instead of rinsing the motor through these blokes just stuck it on the barge to Cairns, thinking someone would fix it there, and hitched a lift back to Lockhart. It'll be rusty as shit by the time it reaches Cairns.'

'And the good news?'

'They now owe you one!'

In any other circumstances I probably would have cracked the shits. But it was an old tinny and I'd been meaning to buy a more versatile fibreglass boat anyway. And at least I was starting to make inroads with the Aboriginal community. If I could build on this momentum, there was a chance of making genuine progress towards collaboration. Buying the *Moreton Mist* provided a perfect opportunity to go one step further.

Paul and I came up with a plan to repair the trawler sufficiently to sail her down to Cairns, where the damage would be repaired properly. Then we would train some of the locals to run the boat as a commercial line-fishing or cray boat. Profits would be shared collectively – a win-win for everyone. And those responsible for sinking my tinny could help drag the trawler just beyond the high water mark under Paul's direction, so that I could start the repairs. When we started, the atmosphere was still slightly strained, but after some hard work and a good feed, they were able to see me in a different light – as a human being who was going to be around for a long time, not a ruthless developer.

It took six gruelling weeks to fix the hole on *Moreton Mist* with a temporary patch made of timber, Visqueen and silicone sealant. With the help of Gregor, a shipwright from Portland Roads, we tipped her over at low tide and worked like crazy for a few hours before the tide came back in. I had also salvaged everything I could from the *Blue Riband* – like the steering wheel, ship's bell, rigging, stainless-steel shackles and chain – to use on the *Mist* and also to create a *Blue Riband* area over in the tiki bar. One man's rubbish is always another's treasure around here.

The *Moreton Mist* was almost ready to be booked into the boatyard in Cairns when Cyclone Monica torpedoed our grand plan. Even with a two-metre admiralty anchor and half a tonne of chain, the boat was dragged from her moorings and tossed onto the reef like a piece of cork. When the tide receded the morning after the cyclone, I put on some rubber sneakers and scrambled over the reef to assess the damage. My repairs had been obliterated and there were new holes in the hull. Our plan for a joint venture was right back to square one. Fortunately, some wwoofers were due to arrive a few weeks later and would be able to help fix me her up again.

***

Laura and Lizzie were two chalk and cheese English girls. Laura was quite posh and Lizzie was a more down-to-earth character from the industrial north, but both were bubbly and full of fun. They arrived on a Friday and it must have been a full moon, because a few trawler boys were making the most of the downtime. I am always a bit wary when fishos and wwoofers are thrown together, especially after the blokes have had a few drinks. These guys have been starved of female company for weeks on end, so I watch them like a hawk. One bloke in particular had taken a shine to Laura and Lizzie, who were both very pretty. I knew this bloke only too well, and had a bad feeling about him. So when the girls told me that he had invited them to go to Forbes Island for the weekend on his boat, my protective instincts kicked in. 'Look, I'm not your dad,' I told them. 'So I can't tell you what to do. But I can advise you. And I'm not sure about this bloke at all. I know these fishos and I know what they are capable of. I'd feel much better if you stayed here.' The girls were happy to take my advice.

When he arrived to pick them up in his dinghy I was waiting for him at the beach, and the girls stayed back at the house. He was unrecognisable: clean-shaven, wearing a fancy shirt and carrying two roses. But the cheap aftershave couldn't mask the smell of grog on his breath. 'There's been a change of plan,' I told him. 'The girls aren't going with you.'

'C'mon, mate,' he said. 'Share and share alike, eh? Just wanna spend a bit of quality time with two pretty sheilas.'

'Look. Firstly, I'm not your mate. Secondly, I'm not "sharing" anything. These girls are my guests, not my possessions. And as long as they're staying on this island, I'm responsible for their safety. And I don't think they'll be safe with you.'

The fuse was lit. 'I don't know what the fuck you've told them but you're a fucking liar!' he yelled, as he edged menacingly towards me, then stepping back abruptly when Quassi bared his teeth.

'Is something bothering you?' I asked.

'Watch your step, mate. Cos I will fuck you over, be sure of that.'

This explosion confirmed everything I told the girls, who were scared that he might come back to the island, so we accepted Phil's invitation to spend the night out at Curd Reef, about ten kilometres out from Resto.

Curd Reef is one of my favourite spots on the whole Great Barrier Reef. It's postcard perfect. The gleaming white crescentshaped sand bank is an ideal point for snorkelling; here the Inner Reef explodes into a dazzling palette of blues, reds, pinks and yellows. Cheeky damselfish and clownfish dart between brain coral, staghorn and soft coral, like Gorgonian sea fans. Much further out is the Outer Reef, with great spits of roller-flat sand, like Long Sandy Reef. Stand waist-deep here on the ocean side, and you can peer over the edge into a black abyss that can reach 2000 metres deep. It makes me feel really dizzy to teeter on the edge of a huge, staggering, underwater precipice, imagining the vast array of marine life out there, known and unknown.

When we approached Resto the following morning, the breeze carried an acrid smell into our nostrils. As we rounded the rocky headland I could see small wisps of smoke. Then we saw what was left of the *Moreton Mist:* a charred skeleton of a boat, poking angrily out of the water. This was either the first boat ever to spontaneously self-combust, or that prick had torched her. His boat was nowhere to be seen but a couple of Phil's deckies were waiting for us on the shore. 'Call the cops, Davo, we filmed everything,' one said. 'He waited until the tide was out, climbed aboard and emptied a gallon drum of diesel everywhere and then lobbed a Molotov cocktail from his dinghy and she went up like a Roman candle, right down to the waterline. Looked off his nut, he did.'

'Nah, I'm not calling the cops,' I said. 'Dobbing him in will just start a running feud. We don't want that round here. That's the end of it. Just tell the prick never to show his face here again if you see him.'

***

Routine is the enemy of the castaway. No two days are the same here. There's a skill to letting the day take its course and staying blissfully unaware of the passing hours until the body clock sounds the alarm that it's time for a cold one. I repeat only one task each day and that's to wander down to the beach as soon as I wake up to check that the boat's still there. Then I might swim, I might go fossicking on the beach for a while, or I might make breakfast and a cup of coffee. Hell, on some days I might have two cups of coffee. The weather often dictates the pace of the day and the direction that it takes. Heat and humidity mean light chores. A steady breeze is conducive to harder work. I take trips to the mainland for essential supplies rarely when it's windy or rainy. But the only time I will look at a clock is when I need to know the times of the tides. The reason for checking the tides might be something very simple. If I fancy a few oysters, then there's no point going down to the rocks when the tide's coming in. The maximum yield occurs fifteen minutes either side of the low tide, so I check on the Bureau of Meteorology website for the times, which are usually pretty accurate. I also need to know the times of the tides when I need to be in Lockhart River at a certain time.

Growing up around water, I have always understood the importance of tides. It came in very handy soon after I moved to Brisbane to start work for QUF. Late one Sunday night I received a call from my manager. 'Glasheen, get everyone down here straight away,' he insisted. 'The rain's coming!' The rain in question was Cyclone Wanda and the river systems, already full, would be stretched to bursting point. Our office was right next to the river and, when we assembled at midnight, my boss was organising everyone on the ground floor to move their files onto the top shelves. 'Excuse me, sir. Do we know whether the tide is coming in or out?' I asked.

'What kind of a bloody question is that?' this dinosaur snorted. 'Don't bloody worry about building sandcastles now. I know you've only been in Brisbane a few weeks, but the sea's miles away. I assume you weren't here for the last floods in 1938? Well, I was. And we managed very nicely, thank you.'

Actually, I wasn't born in 1938, but I wasn't born yesterday either. If this was low tide, then we were going to be in serious trouble when the tide turned. As the others made their way home, I asked a couple of blokes to help me move my whole office to the first floor. Sure enough, when we reassembled the next morning, the ground floor was under water and destroyed, while the first floor was untouched. Tragically, sixteen people lost their lives in those floods, when 642 millimetres of rain fell in a thirty-six-hour period, and the damage was estimated at almost $1 billion.

The consequences of miscalculating the tides are not so severe here. I've only done it a handful times while I have been on Resto because I'm an old hand. I know that I can push the boat out in 1.2 metres of water at John Pritchard's beach, but only need 1.1 metres at my mate Chips's beach. Anything less than that and the boat will stick in the mud. When that did happen one time, I went down to Chilli Beach to kill a few hours beachcombing and was lucky enough to hear the powerful call of the rare trumpet manucode, a magnificent rifle bird, which sounds like the cracking of a whip.

There have been plenty of close calls when I have almost missed the tide. Often someone would persuade me to have one more cuppa or beer and then I'd have to drive too quickly on roads that are dangerous at the best of times. So, when I have to reach the mainland at a certain time, especially when a guest has to catch a plane, I try not to leave anything to chance. This was the case when two French wwoofers, a couple in their mid-twenties, were returning to the airport after spending just a few days on Resto. Their English was poor and my French was *comme ci comme ça.* But we didn't need words when my boat's motor cut out in the middle of the channel. They could see the panic in my eyes. I tried yanking the cord harder, and nearly pulled my shoulder out of its socket. I checked the fuel, and there was plenty. I tried the age-old remedy of bashing the motor. Nothing. There was a strong breeze, the water was rough and the current was powerful. My small anchor was not going to hold for long. And the French guy was nervously tapping his watch, making *mon dieu* eyes at me.

Reaching the airport on time was the last of their problems. I was more concerned about making it through the next hour, because we were drifting towards the rocks. To add to the peril, there were reports that a big croc had been patrolling precisely this section of the shore for the last few weeks. That made the alternative to risking the rocks – swimming for shore – considerably less appealing. Standing up in the boat, I made breaststroke motions with my arms. The French couple hugged each other more tightly. Neither was going to volunteer in a hurry.

The boat was now only about twenty metres from the rocks, but I would have to swim another fifty metres to a point where I could clamber ashore, near where Chips lived. The fastest swimmer in the world would have taken at least two minutes in the rough water. My swimming was strong, but I was no Ian Thorpe. Would the croc spot me flailing around in, say, four or five minutes? There was only one way to find out. I launched myself off the stern.

It took me two hours, thanks to a couple of wrong turns when the waves obstructed my view of the mainland. Or that's how long it felt like. It was actually closer to twenty minutes, which is way too long in muddy waters. Fortunately, Chips was home and he helped us tow the boat to safety. I even made it to the airport on time to wave a cheerful *bon voyage* to two extremely traumatised French youths.

***

The decision to swim had been an instinctive reaction. Unlike in the corporate world, where months of planning preceded every decision no matter how small, it was no longer possible to prevaricate. Living on the island had already taught me that in a crisis, you had to quickly weigh up the options, commit to your decision with a cool head and then execute it with precision. Soon after the French couple's departure, another life-or-death situation tested this new skill. I was back in my old routine of having no routine. On this particular day, I was clambering up the boulders at the southern end of the beach, looking for smaller rocks. When I stopped to draw breath, I was enjoying a Resto moment: the sun nipping at my shoulders as I gazed out over the swathe of shimmering green that separated the island from the mainland. Then I spotted a croc, thankfully heading away from the island.

It was strange that Quassi hadn't alerted me, though. Whenever a croc appeared on the beach or was on the prowl in the water, Quassi would run over to me and go crazy until I followed him back to the beach. He made Lassie look like a phoney. Most of these crocs disappeared back into the water when I shouted or flailed my arms about. But I'd still take along a few flat stones – or gibbers – in case the croc was feeling especially hungry and brave. The intention wasn't to hurt them, but I wanted them to know they weren't welcome here.

All of a sudden, this particular croc made an abrupt U-turn and headed straight for the beach. *Where the hell's Quassi?* I thought, and shimmied down the boulder on my bum, scraping the skin and jarring my ankle as I dropped down to the ground from a stupid height. As I limped towards the beach, I spotted Quassi's bum and tail sticking out of a deep hole right at the water's edge, where he was digging for crabs. Sand was flying out of the hole and his tail was wagging furiously. The croc was probably about fifty metres from the shore but making a beeline for Quassi at an incredible pace, but in a weird, ungainly way.

Shit, it's that bastard, Boxhead, again. 'Quassi! Quassi!' I screamed, as I ran down the beach. But it was a windy afternoon and my cries were blown away in the opposite direction. The poor dog couldn't see or hear a thing. Stooping down as I ran, I gathered as many gibbers as I could hold. Quassi still had no idea that Boxhead was now only about twenty metres from the shore. I would have just one shot at saving my dog. If I missed, Quassi was a goner. And if I threw too early, I was more likely to miss. I had to leave it to the last possible second and my aim had to be perfect. *Stay calm, stay calm.*

Having selected the best gibber – not too heavy but big enough to hurt – I dropped the rest and took aim. When Boxhead was about five metres from the shore, I hurled it and hit him right between the eyes. He twisted up out of the water like he had been shot in the paw again. Finally, Quassi heard the commotion in the water behind him, jumped out of the hole like a scalded cat, and came running into my arms as Boxhead disappeared underwater to nurse his sore snout. 'Shit, mate, you gave me a scare there,' I told him, rubbing his belly vigorously. 'You've gotta watch out for that bastard. Because you can be sure he'll be back.'

Chapter 10

Visiting time

Visitors are like fish – great when fresh, but they soon start to smell. Don't get me wrong – I welcome visitors: friends, family, neighbours, professionals, strangers. I hunger for different viewpoints and opinions, and feast on the variety of personalities and characters that this region washes up. I'm a recluse, not a hermit; but I also enjoy my own company and my own space – time to contemplate and cogitate. And to do that effectively, I need to have solitude. There's a time for everyone to visit, but also a time for them to leave.

One afternoon, I was exhausted after mowing the lawn and the beach shack beckoned, with Quassi and a cold one for company. This window of time is sacred to me; I don't even read. It's when I like to assimilate whatever has been fluttering about my brain all day; though there'd been plenty of activity out at sea to distract me that day.

Groups of black cormorants had been torpedoing into the water at one or two spots, confidently aiming and surfacing with supper. This usually meant big pelagic fish were in the area, which feed on smaller fish. It could be mackerel, trevally, coral trout, mangrove jack, gold spot cod or fingermark. It might even be Queensland grouper – a true monster of the sea. I have only ever seen two, a mother and baby, and I could have swum straight into the mouth of the young one. Some people consider them more dangerous than sharks and there are stories of them eating pearl divers whole.

My thoughts were turning to dinner when, from around the corner of the island, a yacht came into view. *Bugger,* I thought. Yachties could be a pain in the bum, especially the ones on the smaller, daggy boats. Grotty yachties, we call them around here. They tend to be notorious bleeders and bludgers, very keen to take what you have to offer but not so willing to contribute anything in return. We call any yacht with an engine a stink boat, because of the smell of petrol they carry about, and this superyacht was one large stinker. The owners of these boats are usually members of the gold-chain brigade – posers who were often just keen to see where Bligh had landed and didn't tend to intrude. Whether it was a fancy $5-million cruiser or a $5000 floating shed, I wasn't in the mood for company on this particular occasion. My heart sank when I saw the dinghy launch from the yacht and head for the beach. *Better pull on my lap-lap,* was my first thought. Fortunately, when David, the captain, and his girlfriend, Irene, hopped out of the dinghy, I realised that I knew them from a previous stop-off. 'G'day Dave, we have a couple of honeymooners on board who'd like to have dinner with you,' the captain said.

'Well, you could have called ahead. I've no fresh fish or cold beer,' I replied.

'No, no. We've plenty of food and drink on board, and a fulltime chef. We just want to bring it here and cook on the beach, if that's okay.' It transpired that David used to be the master of the replica *Bounty* ship in Sydney

Harbour. The original was of course Bligh's vessel, and the replica had been used in the film by the same name, starring Anthony Hopkins as Bligh and Mel Gibson as Fletcher Christian. David's party had stopped at many islands on their way up the Great Barrier Reef, but they were especially looking forward to seeing Restoration Island because of the Bligh connection. From here, the honeymooners were heading up to Thursday Island for the Anzac Day dawn service on 25 April.

A free feed sounded like a fair trade-off for the intrusion, so the captain and his wife headed back to the yacht, *M.V. Mustique,* while I lit the fire. They returned an hour later with the chef, a couple of deckies and the newlyweds, Russell and Danielle. Russell was an athletic, handsome bloke and looked like he could be a sportsman. Danielle was a beautiful blonde lady and equally lithe. Dinner was amazing, with as much fresh seafood as we could all eat. The wine was bloody nice, too, a Bowen Estate cabernet sauvignon – not the ideal match for seafood, but a real throat charmer. Much of their conversation was about showbiz, but chat between strangers can often revolve around movies and entertainment, so I didn't think any more of it. I had a niggling feeling that I recognised this bloke, though. 'I hope you don't mind me asking, but do you play tennis or golf?' I asked.

'No, I'm pretty shit at both,' Russell replied. And I left it at that. I'm not one to pry. If he was famous, he obviously valued his privacy. After dinner, Danielle excused herself and returned to the boat because she wanted to finish a good book.

'Mind if I stay on for a yarn?' Russell asked. 'The crew will bring a few more bottles from the boat.' A few more bottles? Jeez, my eyes were already meeting in the middle. But even through my blurred vision, this bloke still looked like he'd stepped straight off a movie set. He was good company, too, and very keen to know about the issues facing the Lockhart River community. He was also interested in my latest idea to build a healing retreat on the island as a way to create jobs for local young men and women.

'I'd love to have somewhere private like this to escape to,' he said. 'But I still reckon word would get out whenever I was here.' *So this bloke's a big name,* I thought. *Not a sportsman – talks about Hollywood ... I've got it.*

'You're Gladiator aren't you?'

'Yes, that's me,' he said, smirking. 'Russell Crowe, actually.' He told me he'd just finished filming *Master and Commander* and was appreciating time away from the public eye with his new bride.

'But we haven't even been for a swim or a dive yet – Danielle's too scared of what's in the water.'

'Don't go in the water off Resto with Danielle unless you want to start a family. It has magical fertility powers,' I said, and told him all about Kye's miraculous conception.

'That's fine by us – we want to get cracking straight away,' he said with a laugh.

The camp fire had performed its usual magic. Russell opened up like a giant clam and we talked long into the night. Whenever the Bowen Estate ran out, Russell was on the walkie-talkie for yet another bottle.

Something had been niggling at me throughout our chat. Even though I now knew that he was famous, Russell still reminded me of someone. And then I twigged. He was just like my dad's younger brother, Uncle Terry, my ultimate hero.

'This would make a good film,' I said. 'My own uncle – murdered by the CIA.'

'I'm all ears,' Russell said. And so I told him all about Terence Gilronan Glasheen, Rhodes Scholar at Oxford University, champion skier, brilliant cricketer, trained lawyer and talented career diplomat.

'He even rescued his pilot from the burning wreckage of their crashed plane towards end of World War II and was awarded an Order of the British Empire award for gallantry,' I continued. 'Then, as the Australian representative to the United Nations, he started to annoy the British and Americans. They called him the *enfant terrible.* Our prime minster, Ben Chiffley, had to defend him in parliament. Terry was even arrested for illegally entering Bulgaria in an attempt to rescue some children caught up in the Greek Civil War. Imagine that.'

'Sounds like your Uncle Terry was a real-life James Bond,' Russell said.

'You're not wrong. The last time I saw him was typical. His big chauffeur-driven black limo pulled up outside our house and, fresh off his flight from Washington DC, he breezed in with presents for us all but didn't have time to stay for dinner. And the next day he was dead, killed in a car crash on the Hume Highway on the way to an important meeting with the prime minister in Canberra. Doesn't that sound weird to you? It was broad daylight, on a busy road, and there were no witnesses. Terry never drove anywhere alone. And he'd only just written to my gran from Washington to warn her that he was making some powerful enemies. Nobody's telling me that the Yanks weren't involved somehow. Promise me one thing: when Terry's life is made into a movie, you'll play him.'

'Or I might end up playing you when they make a movie about Resto,' Russell said with a wry smile. It's rare to find someone, especially of his stature, who is just as happy to listen as to talk. He was fascinated by my family background, my business career and how I ended up on Resto. Most of all, he wanted to know how difficult the transition to life off the grid had been.

'It's challenging,' I admitted. 'Everyone has the romantic notion that this is paradise. And it can be glorious. It can be tough up here, too, though. Lots can go wrong. I found someone hanging from the end of a rope last year. That's disturbing, I can tell you, and suicide is a massive problem in the Aboriginal community. Everyone just gives up hope. But how could I ever leave this place? It's part of me, now. And I reckon you'll be back one day, too.'

'I like the sound of that. Do you reckon you could smuggle me here now and again without anyone knowing? Perhaps I could build a donga here as part of your retreat?' he suggested.

'Yeah, but how do you know we'll get on?' I slurred. 'You don't know me from a bar of soap. You need chemistry on an island this size. You might paint your donga pink and purple, and I might not like that, and you might lose your temper. I don't want to be donged by a drongo over a donga.'

In that hazy moment, this was the funniest sentence I had ever spoken and we both collapsed in tears of laughter.

'Nah, we won't fight. You're my mate,' Russell said once we'd finally composed ourselves. 'When the deckie brings some more wine, I'll ask him to take a photo of us.'

'Look, my daughters would love me to be in a picture with you. But that's exactly what you came up here to avoid. Next time, okay?' I said, chuckling. When we finally called it a night I stood up, tottered wildly and crashed face first into the sand, inches away from the fire, giggling like a piglet. Through my drunken haze I could just see Russell trying and trying again to clamber into the dinghy – and falling straight back into the water every time.

I woke up with a mouth like the bottom of a cockie's cage and a head like I'd just fought Maximus in the

Colosseum. I hadn't shifted an inch from where I had face-planted into the sand. The plan had been for David to pick me up and take me to the yacht for breakfast, but I knew the sight of food would make me chunder.

'Morning, Dave!' shouted the captain, as he strolled breezily up the beach. 'Oh dear...'

'Yeah, oh dear,' I groaned.

'You probably won't be too disappointed to hear that Russell's a bit worse for wear, too, and can't make breakfast. Is there a safe place for him and Danielle to have a swim, so he can clear his head? Then we'll be out of your hair.' The water was clear so I told the captain I would leave them in peace for a swim off the beach and that they should keep a lookout for crocs. Around nine months on their son, Charles, was born and Russell later spoke of an 'aquatic conception'. Had Resto worked her magic again? When the Crowes made it to Thursday Island there was a big party and Russell's band, 30 Odd Foot of Grunts, played the music. My invite must have been lost on the mail boat! Weeks later I sent his manager a limited-edition print of a famous Garry Shead painting of a man and woman sharing a mermaid tail, as a thank you for all the food and wine, but heard nothing back. It must have been lost in the airmail! Still, I reckon Russell's one of the good guys. His genuine concern for the plight of Indigenous youth, both here in Australia and in his home country of New Zealand, proved that. Sure, he might have a reputation for going off like a frog in a sock, but there are always two sides to the story. Like when he assaulted a concierge in a New York hotel with a telephone a couple of years after visiting here. He had been frustrated that a call couldn't be placed to his young boy. I know the pain of not being able to speak to my boy regularly, so I could sympathise, to a degree. And I was impressed when he banned pokies from his rugby league club, the Rabbitohs. Even if it hurt the club's profits, he recognised how toxic those things are and put the welfare of his supporters first.

Yeah, Russell's one of the good guys.

***

Well before my scheduled yearly Cairns trip, about ten years ago, my supplies of food essentials were low and I didn't really want to wait until Phil's trawler was heading back this way with my goods. So I contacted Scotty, who runs the road freight service. This meant a gruelling sixteen-hour trip in his truck and we didn't arrive at Lockhart until nearly midnight one Thursday. Returning to Resto was out of the question at that time of night. We had tried ringing ahead to find a room, but all the beds in town were taken by government people, so Scotty suggested we drive on to Portland Roads and crash in a house one of our mates was building. Scotty had a swag and was happy to stay indoors, even though the house was nothing much more than four walls and a concrete floor. Without a swag of my own, I told him that I was okay to lie down in the back of his truck for a few hours, but he persuaded me to sleep on a grotty old couch. There was a tarpaulin sheet in the corner of one room so I shook that off, covered myself and managed to grab some shut eye.

Quassi went berserk when I returned to Resto the following morning and squirted even more pee at me than usual. If there's one thing better than returning home to solitude, it's returning home to solitude plus a dog dancing on the beach. But, as the day went on, a pain developed in my foot. At first I thought that I was just stiff from the long journey the previous day. Then gradually it felt more like I'd broken my toe, but I was convinced I would be fine the next day.

On Friday the redness and soreness both increased and by Saturday I could hardly put my foot down. The next toe was also becoming inflamed; it felt like a fire was climbing up inside my leg. By Sunday my whole foot was bright purple and the fire had spread into my groin – and not in a good way. *Hmmm, time for action,* I eventually told myself, and rang the Poisons Helpline because there was obviously something nasty travelling in my blood. 'That sounds like a spider bite, Mr Glasheen,' the medic said. 'You need to get yourself to the nearest clinic first thing tomorrow.' *Shit!* The boat trip didn't worry me but how was I going to drive Colin's old truck all that way? I'd have to try and use my good foot for both the clutch and accelerator. Sitting upright was going to be painful in itself.

The tide was not in my favour in the morning and the trip into Lockhart took twice as long as normal. Whenever my foot slipped off the pedal, it jarred my body, sending a thousand volts down the other leg and I needed several stops just to take some deep breaths to cope with the pain.

When I dragged myself into the clinic on the Monday afternoon, David Manning, the duty nurse, took one look at my almost-black foot and grimaced. 'You need to see the Flying Doctor first thing tomorrow,' he said. A GP from the Royal Flying Doctor Service flies in two or three days every week, otherwise it's a fly-in/fly-out service for emergency cases. David put me up at his house for the night so that he could keep an eye on me. In the morning, the Flying Doctor assessed it was an emergency and called for a plane.

Before I knew what was happening, I was on a drip and the strongest antibiotics available were being pumped through my veins. 'This is the doctor at the clinic at Lockhart River,' said the Flying Doctor, radioing through to the hospital in Cairns. 'Please prepare for emergency surgery for a case of acute toxicity. Potential spider bite.' Surgery? Now I was as worried as these blokes seemed to be. The doc glanced anxiously over at me and then, still holding the phone, wandered away from my bed to carry on the conversation under his breath. Did I hear him mention *amputation?*

The flight to Cairns passed in a blur of panic. The Flying Doctor and his nurse wouldn't tell me more, and when we arrived at the hospital I was rushed straight to the surgical ward. 'What the hell's going on, doc?' I asked. 'Am I going to lose my leg? Promise me you'll do everything to save it. I live on an island on my own, I wouldn't survive on one leg. I'm Robinson Crusoe, not bloody Long John Silver.'

'Calm down, Mr Glasheen,' he said. 'It's likely this was a bite from a white-tailed spider. They like to live between sheets or towels.' *And, evidently, dodgy old tarpaulin,* I thought.

'Some people call them the "flesh-eating" spider – don't listen to that rubbish. But the bite has become infected and you should have been here three days ago. So our first job is to prevent gangrene, or we could have serious problems. You'll be with us for two weeks on industrial-strength antibiotics. Then you'll be able to walk out of here on two legs.'

I actually walked out after a week and checked myself into the Red Cross hostel nearby then attended hospital as an outpatient, because I can't bear to be around sick people.

The toe's still purple to this day.

***

The doctor recommended two weeks with my feet up once I returned home. Fat chance of that! But again I was fortunate that two German wwoofer girls were due to arrive. There wasn't a hope in hell of putting my feet up, but perhaps they would be able to share the load. Normally the rainy season wasn't the best time for wwoofers, but the two weeks around the end of February were special: it was when green turtles came in to nest. Just imagine the thrill when, just as the sun sets, a mother dawdles out of the ocean and starts to dig her hole around four or five metres beyond the high tide mark. Turtles are magnificent creatures – the ancient mariners of the sea for hundreds of millions of years. An adult female's migration to a nesting beach – often the place she was born – can be a 3000-kilometre journey.

The German girls were beside themselves and were up at first light to catch sight of the same turtle, totally buggered after laying about one hundred eggs overnight, flopping back into the sea at the next high tide. Occasionally, probably to try and hide the eggs from predators, some turtles ventured a little further inland. I had once spotted one trying to dig her nest right next to the beach shack, oblivious to Quassi's protests.

The spectacle repeated night after night until eight nests had been made.

The eggs wouldn't hatch for about two months. Then, if I was lucky on a full moon, I would see hundreds of baby turtles wobble down into the water together to begin their swimming frenzy to the safer outer waters. The girls would be long gone, but they were delighted to have seen even one full-sized turtle.

'Will there be any more?' one of them asked, as we finished dinner.

'No, I think that's it,' I replied, as we heard an almighty crash from the front door. *What the hell was that? Had some roofing fallen off?* I wondered. The girls looked at each other anxiously and I put my finger to my lips and tiptoed into the living area. There, as bold as brass, was mother turtle number nine. Perhaps she had sensed too many predators down by the beach and was looking for somewhere safer for her nest. Turtles may not be the scariest creature in this part of the world but, at about a metre long and weighing up to 160 kilograms, the adults are imposing. You need to take care around them, because one snap from those jaws could take your hand clean off. The girls initially freaked and ran out the back of the house. Once they realised this old girl wasn't about to launch an attack, we tried shooing her back out with a broom, but she was having none of it. She was determined to see whether the kitchen would make a good nesting place and nothing was going to get in her way. Then, with one girl at either side and me at the back of the turtle, we tried to lift her into a wheelbarrow, but she was way too heavy. It didn't help that all three of us were in hysterics by this point. 'Dude, you like totally need to move,' drawled one of the girls, imitating the Crush surfie turtle character from *Finding Nemo.* 'Coo coo ca choo back to the big old blue.'

Our last resort was to lay down an upright hand trolley, push her on and strap her down. This time she was more obliging and seemed to appreciate the lift back to the sand, flapping her fins in the air as though she was swimming. It was probably the fastest she had ever moved. After a couple more stubborn attempts to return to the house, which we blocked, she accepted defeat and started work on her nest at the beach.

There's not a happy ending to this story because, the following morning, we went to see if she was still hard at work but all that was left was a graveyard of turtle shells. One of the sand goannas that live here must have been watching her every move, and enjoyed the eggs for breakfast. Nevertheless, that year was probably our most prolific for nests on Resto and, sadly, there have been no turtles here for two or three years. Their numbers are dwindling, although Raine Island, a coral cay about one hundred kilometres north-east of Resto on the Outer Reef, is still one of the biggest rookeries in the world. Up to 18,000 females migrate there each year, depending on the water temperatures. Sometimes as few as one thousand arrive. Apparently, warmer waters result in a shortage of males and there are fears the species may soon face extinction. It's another symptom of the Great Barrier Reef's constant battle against man-made threats.

We all need to remember that this reef is Australia's greatest natural asset. Great Barrier Reef tourism brings in $6 billion each year to our economy and supports 70,000 Australian jobs. But in the past three decades, the Great Barrier Reef has lost half its coral cover. And tourists will soon stop paying to see dead coral with few colourful fish. The causes for the reef's ill health are numerous – with pollution right up there. It's incredible to think that more than five tonnes of marine debris are removed from Chilli Beach, opposite Resto, each year. This includes a staggering and shameful 4700 rubber thongs and 6500 plastic bottles. Sure, it means that I will nearly always find something useful when I clean the shore, but I would much prefer to find no rubbish. Lockhart River could do better, too. There's a mentality here of digging a hole, throwing the rubbish in and burning it, which is very bad for the environment. Local people should make more of an effort to put their rubbish on the mothership when it arrives with supplies for the commercial fishing fleets. It's *so* important to dispose of rubbish responsibly.

Toxic chemicals from rubbish dumped into the ocean accumulate in the water and penetrate food chains. I don't want to eat fish that have been feeding on microscopic bits of plastic that haven't degraded. Do you? These toxins can cause phytoplankton and algae to proliferate, which smothers food sources for the coral and allows the coral-eating crown of thorns starfish to attack. It's often down to volunteer divers to kill these starfish by injecting them with poison, but robots are now being developed to take over. Farm pollution is another factor, although obviously a lot further south than here. But marine-friendly pesticides and fertilisers are being developed, so why are they not more widely used? The expansion of several ports in Queensland, and the associated sea dredging, can also affect the delicate marine environment.

The preservation of the reef is an emotive issue in these parts, although the laws are pretty tough and diligently enforced. Overfishing is rigorously policed. The population of blacktip reef sharks has flourished thanks to strict measures from our local fisheries people, for example. This is success on a micro scale, though. Numbers of apex predators like great whites, hammerheads and tiger sharks are dwindling fast; it's the bigger picture that needs addressing. But how do you marry the profit objectives of industries like agriculture and mining with ecological sustainability? It's the big question that the human race must solve. And we are failing miserably. Australian politicians should be particularly ashamed of themselves. They are much more concerned with being puppets to the United States and China than protecting our true vested interests: our human and natural resources.

There, I feel better for that.

Chapter 11

Ricky

Though we were separated by thousands of kilometres, my daughter Ricky was never far from my thoughts. We spoke on the phone regularly and she often promised to come and visit me. Many of the conversations were vague, though. She was reticent about revealing too many details of her life, other than where she was working and when she last saw her mum and Samantha. Sam kept me informed that Ricky was still drinking heavily. Then I caught up with her briefly while I was in Sydney filming for *A Current Affair* in 2009. We laughed about the media attention – not many sixty-five-year-old dads were looking for love on the news. But Ricky had a faraway look in her eyes and I was paranoid that we were barely scratching the surface of her problems. 'Look, love, you always know where you can reach me and you know I'll come running,' I said. 'But the offer's still there for you to come and stay on Resto for as long as you like. Clear your head, give your body a break. Believe me, there's nowhere better.'

Several months later, Ricky was on the phone in tears. 'I'm not sure I can do it, Dad,' she said, sobbing. 'I've been in Concord Hospital in intensive rehab and now I have to attend AA sessions on a daily basis. But everyone around me is relapsing. I'm living in a shit apartment in Oxford Street – it's not a good place for someone trying to stay clean. Is it still okay for me to come and stay for a while?'

'Pack a bag now, don't go out tonight, and there will be a ticket waiting for you at the airport in the morning,' I said. 'I'm so glad you're coming.'

When I picked Ricky up from Lockhart River airport, I was careful not to say the wrong thing – at least until I had her on the island. I didn't want her to bolt at the last minute. When we arrived, it warmed my heart to watch her hop out of the boat, flick off her thongs and scrunch her toes into the cool sand as Quassi licked her ankles excitedly. I sensed the toxicity of city life, all its temptations and all its desperation, was being flushed out of her with the first few deep breaths of island air. Within minutes of being shown to the space shuttle, where Ricky would sleep, she was beavering away to make it clean and homey. It was clear she was determined to make a new start here. I left her to it, and headed back to the house to start dinner, expecting Ricky to wander over in her own time. An hour later there was no sign of her, and she wasn't at the space shuttle either. Then I spotted her doing shuttle sprints down on the beach, a highly excited dog in pursuit.

Ricky stayed for six months and the transformation was remarkable. I was probably expecting to nurse a baby chick with a broken wing, but within days she was more like a magnificent bird of prey. She was active from dawn till dusk and just watching her made me exhausted. Her room in the space shuttle was soon unrecognisable. She built shelves, draped curtains, hung ropes and buoys, and generally applied her woman's touch. Then she created a little garden behind the space shuttle, where she grew herbs, shallots, garlic and chillies from seeds she'd brought, and carved a sign into some driftwood: *Ricky's Patch – Keep Out.* I had no idea the garden was even there until I heard some strange grunting noises and discovered that she had fixed a metal bar between two trees for her chin-ups. It was as though the island had supercharged her.

The extra ingredients from her garden were essential for her culinary regime; I was not allowed in the kitchen for six months and I loved being fattened up. My role was clearly defined – to do the dishes and not interfere. Often we would take the boat out to fish, but our approaches were completely different. After catching two decent fish, I was happy to use one for dinner and put one in the freezer. Ricky loved fishing and wanted to stay out until the boat was full. We often took a box with as many as twenty surplus fish into town and handed them out to friends, which was a great way to gradually introduce her to everyone.

Although I didn't encourage her to drink, I didn't hide my grog away either. I wanted her to face and conquer her demons on her own. Around Ricky, I restricted myself to just one beer and let visitors, and especially the fishos, know not to drink to excess, without revealing any details except that she'd been unwell. There was the occasional lapse, naturally, and we had some terrible arguments – drunk and sober – especially when I noticed that my grog stocks were mysteriously low. Ricky was a firecracker likely to go off at any moment. The rows were always followed by lots of hugs, but I would rather have avoided the arguments in the first place. Often she would climb up to the Incredible Rocks for some space and spend a couple of hours up there pressing the reset button, and then return seemingly without a care in the world. 'I never had anywhere to escape to in the city, Dad,' she confided. 'Everything seemed to press in on me. It's the exact opposite here. This place is a natural release valve.'

The locals soon noticed Ricky's motivation and work ethic. One regular visitor, Rod Cordell, ran Jobfind, the community service for job seekers in Lockhart River. He offered Ricky a job there almost straight away, but she wanted to ease herself back into regular social interaction. 'I'll come to you when I'm ready,' she told him, and politely declined other job offers that came flooding in.

After six months of living on Resto, it was time for Ricky to take that next step. She moved to Lockhart River and lived in one of the bedrooms of the church house, which served as the Jobfind office. The room was tiny but she never once complained, even though she had to share a bathroom with every Tom, Dick and Harry who used the centre. For someone so fastidiously clean, it must have been a source of torment. Ricky was an instant hit and forged a fantastic partnership with Rod. He had two daughters her age and also loved to fish, so he often brought Ricky back to the island on weekends. He was her substitute father during the working week, and the rest of Lockhart River took Ricky to their hearts, too.

Her first community initiative was to cook breakfasts for the town's old ladies. They were her extended family, a substitute for the family she had left in New South Wales. She was often up at 6am, cooking away, in her element. But the service was not a handout; it was a nod to the old days of the mission, when the community provided their own food. Under Ricky's regime, the men had to go out and catch the fish with a new drag net, which Rod funded, and come back with it all nicely filleted and cleaned. The same went for any meat, which had to be hunted and butchered. The breakfast initiative soon morphed into another project, Healthy Affordable Meals for Lockhart. Ricky was appalled by people's diet in the local community and the amount of money they spent on processed food at the store, when so much fresh produce was right on everyone's doorstep. Again she persuaded Rod to find $68,000 from his meagre budget to buy a mobile kitchen that could be powered from the Jobfind office. She charged $5 for a beautiful dish of Thai curried fish or sweet chilli prawns, each meal with fresh vegetables from their small garden, a piece of fruit and a bottle of water. The meals were served on the church verandah, which became the town's social hub, and within months the investment on the van was repaid.

Then the younger girls started to pay attention and, as part of their work placement, Ricky showed them how to make tasty, fresh fish, chicken or meat stocks. She also taught food preparation and hygiene, in the hope that these girls would one day take over the venture. She made birthday cakes for $5 – previously people had flown them up from Cairns for more than $60. Then the local government people put their faith in her to cater for two big ceremonial events, the handing back of some land to the Kuuku Ya'u and a national parks event for upwards of 250 people. Ricky did all the planning, but insisted that the locals prepared the food on the day. The culinary standard was exceptional, and all of a sudden her flock had found purpose in their lives and hope for their futures. I could not have been prouder of my girl.

Not satisfied with just revolutionising the local nutritional landscape, Ricky then turned her attention to literacy and numeracy. She was appalled that kids were leaving high school unable to sign their own names, despite having supposedly passed their exams. 'Dad, these kids are just being processed by the educational system. Nobody cares whether they are actually learning anything. The education department just turns a blind eye. Nothing has moved forward in one hundred years,' she said.

Ricky realised that there was no point trying to thrust textbooks back on adults. That would have just intensified their shame at being illiterate. So she came up with a way to teach the same skills through practical projects that would benefit the community. She was even allowed into the Men's Shed to explain her plans – the only woman in town with that privilege. Her two prized projects, again funded from the Jobfind budget, were a play area in the middle of town and a new public barbecue area down on the beach. By ordering the materials and drawing up the plans, the participants were using new measurement, labelling and drawing skills. It was remarkable to watch and her reputation spread far and wide: she was soon invited onto a national community development advisory panel and regularly attended meetings in Alice Springs.

By then, Lockhart had become a dry area in a misguided attempt to tackle alcoholism and crime, but that didn't stop grog being sneaked in from Archer River, the nearest place to buy alcohol. Whenever that happened, her demons resurfaced, but it was manageable. Ricky was tireless and her dedication to making a difference was her medicine. She was helping herself by helping others.

***

Without knowing it, Ricky had also helped to bridge some of the gaps that lingered between me and one or two of the older men and women in the Aboriginal community. Most of the locals had warmed to me. Now that I had full control of my share in the island and had influential allies like Paul Piva, it was easier to state my case and convince the Kuuku Ya'u that my intentions were in their best interests. It had taken some time – ten years, in fact: the exact period that my brother Mick predicted it would take – to heal the wounds from our thoughtless early actions. It was only when I was invited to eat both dugong and turtle meat that I realised I had been truly accepted into this community.

For the Kuuku Ya'u people, both the dugong and sea turtle are highly prized and culturally significant animals that are consumed on special occasions. Although, there is an agreement in place to limit the size of the harvest because most of the world's dugong or sea cow population lives in northern Australian waters; the northern third of the Great Barrier Reef has the highest density of dugong on the planet. It's a beautiful animal, ponderous but graceful, with a large round head, tiny eyes and a large snout, and a flattened fluked tail like a whale. It looks like a cuddly, kind old uncle, and I occasionally see them in the shallow waters, hoovering seagrass off the sea bed. The dugong is one of those animals that looks too cute to eat. Even so, I wasn't about to waste a chance at formal reconciliation when a group of senior Kuuku Ya'u clan members pulled up onto the beach one afternoon and offered to share the dugong and turtle they'd caught. The group included some familiar faces from town: Albert Doctor, and the brothers Squeezie and Funny Face (Paul and Phillip Hobson).

'Got a present for you,' Albert said. 'Been meaning to bring it here for some time now.' I'd seen local men hunt turtles with a traditional harpoon, or *wop,* and butcher them on the island before. When they'd tossed the blood and guts into the sea, it had attracted every croc for miles around, so I politely asked them to stop. In those days, I was never invited to share the catch.

This time, the animals had been pre-butchered off shore. Once it was cut into thin steaks and lightly grilled on the barbecue at the beach shack, dugong meat was melt-in-the-mouth tender – better than the best fillet mignon. It would have fed the town for weeks, so I was careful not to take too much, out of respect for this revered animal. Then I was offered the soft, pink flesh from the turtle's belly, which looked like venison, not the darker meat from around the flippers. Again, it was – along with the dugong – the most delicious, juiciest meat I had ever tasted.

To this day, I don't know what prompted that invitation. Perhaps I was being accepted as part of the social fabric, or it may have been a seemingly innocuous good deed. Only a few weeks earlier, I had delivered some giddy giddy beads to Queenie Hobson, one of the town's female elders, to use for her jewellery making. The beads come from a vine that grows on Resto and are highly sought-after. Queenie was delighted. 'You are my new boyfriend!' she said, beaming.

'Queenie, if there were fifty men in Lockhart River, I would always be the fifty-first in line for you,' I joked. A few days later some really bad weather set in and stayed for more than a week. Queenie was worried that she hadn't seen me in town, and asked her grandchildren to ring and check that I was okay. It meant an awful lot to me. The difficulty with being ostracised by the community hadn't been the physical separation, it had been the social isolation. Queenie, the town's supergran, is still going strong – and so is our flirting.

***

By the time I tasted those special meats, I had also proven myself useful to the wider white fella community, but more through being a good friend and neighbour than through any grand gesture. My relationship with the fishos was symbiotic and I was always happy to lend a hand on their boats for a night or two when they were short of men. Admittedly, I was nervous when, the night before my first trip with Phil, he told me we would be heading over wonky hole country. 'What the hell's a wonky hole?' I asked.

'It's where an underwater springs exits the sea floor,' Phil explained. 'Soft coral and sea ferns grow there, which attracts bait fish and squid, as well as predators like large mouth nannygai or red emperor. They can be beaut fishing spots, but the spring can also spew up lots of shit and, without warning, the otter boards dig in and the boat's pulled over from the outriggers. It's only happened to me once, just south of Night Island. Normally you drive around in a circle to force the weight of the sand and dirt out of the net. But this time the weight was only on one side, the engine stalled and over she went, completely overturned. We were all tossed into the sea and managed to climb onto the hull. But the EPIRB was in the dinghy, which didn't automatically release like it should do. So we had to either sit there until a plane or ship spotted us, or one of us had to dive underneath to untie the dinghy. That was obviously the skipper's job!'

'And you're telling me we're actually trying to find a wonky hole tomorrow?' I said with an anxious laugh.

Once on board, wonky holes were far from my mind. I soon learned you had to be careful as hell when sorting through the catches, or you could find yourself in big trouble. It's now one of the few times I ever wear gloves for protection. The sorting trays are about two square metres, and it would not be uncommon for twenty snakes to be thrashing around in among the fish. The experienced fishos just pick them up and toss them overboard as second nature. Sea snakes are normally venomous, but their fangs are right at the backs of their mouths, so you would have to stick your finger down there deliberately to be bitten. Snakes were probably the least of our worries, though. All sorts of nasties could be dragged up in the trawler nets, like stonefish, potentially fatal cone shells, blue-ringed octopus, jellyfish, happy moment fish, routs, lion fish or catfish, which have a spike on the back of the head. I have seen men cry in agony in the foetal position for two hours after being stung by a catfish. All the fishos are stung at some point in their life while sorting their catch, and for that reason I'm very careful and hopelessly slow.

Then there are the bigger accidental catches. Turtles, for example, are exhausted after being dragged in the nets, and don't take too kindly to finding themselves on a tray. They can also bugger the prawns when they start flapping around. It can take three or four men and a winch to manhandle them overboard, although now turtle excluding devices (TEDs) mean we rarely have to. Sawsharks, commonly used for fish and chips, often come up in the nets, too. Their snout, with its razor sharp external teeth, must be cut off to prevent serious injury.

The teeth of some of the bigger fish can be just as dangerous, too, for professional trawler men and recreational fishermen alike. Early one afternoon, the sun was biting into my back as I was working to convert the old generator shed, where I survived the cyclones, into another sleeping area. Just by pulling down one wall, extending the roof and rebuilding the wall, I was creating the 'love shack', a little old place where visiting couples could stay with more privacy on a double mattress. Suddenly, from over near the beach, I heard a girl's voice. 'Hello, is anyone there?' she shouted, sounding really distressed. I emerged from the trees and probably startled her. 'Over there!'

she pointed. 'My boyfriend's hurt. He needs a bandaid.'

We ran to the beach where a young fella was slumped, holding a bloodied towel to his shoulder. 'What's happened? Can I see?' I foolishly asked. He peeled off the towel to reveal his shoulder, unzipped from top to bottom, tendons clearly on display. It was a miracle that I didn't faint again. 'Bandaid? You need more than a bandaid, mate, you need surgery,' I croaked. 'Come to the house so I can get you a clean towel.' The young fella told me that he was an electrician in Weipa and had wanted to take his girl somewhere special to impress her on their first date. Who said romance was dead? Round at Restoration Rock he hooked a beaut Spanish mackerel but, while skull-hauling it into the boat, the fish slipped off the hook and bit his shoulder. Mackerel have teeth like razors and their bite is far more dangerous than a shark's, because they slice rather than tear at skin. I poured some betadine onto the towel to prevent infection, then he insisted that his girl could manage the boat and drive him from Portland Roads to the clinic in Lockhart. He needed internal and external stitches just to close the wound.

***

The images of that gaping wound were fresh in my mind when a South Korean TV news crew arrived. The presenter was a famous comedian and actor, a big deal in South Korea, apparently. He taught me how to speak a few sentences in Korean to camera, but I could have been saying anything – 'Hello, this is Dave from Restoration Island. For all my friends in South Korea, I agree that North Korea stinks,' for example. I could have been advertising Samsung or Hyundai for all I knew. The six-man crew was way larger than normal, but these fellas were not too keen on paying the rate that I always request to cover my costs during their stay. The producers brought their own chef, too, and wouldn't eat anything I offered or prepared. The presenter was not the biggest comedian among them, it turned out. One of the tech guys also worked as a stuntman and showed me YouTube clips of him jumping into live volcanoes.

A few days in, we all went fishing from the boat together, with Quassi along for the ride. When the stuntman spotted a huge silver trevally gliding underneath the boat, he suddenly dived overboard headfirst, trying to catch it with his hands. What the hell was going on? I tried to warn him about sharks and crocs – and trevally – by making snapping motions with my arms when he came up for air. He thought this was hilarious and copied me, creating even more commotion to alert any lurking predators. His crew found it all very entertaining. I didn't.

Not too long after the South Koreans, a Dutch TV crew came to film. At first I couldn't understand what all the media fuss was about. I had calls from the *New York Times, The Sunday Times* in London, *Paris Match,* the *Toronto Sun,* all the Australian newspapers and an American literary magazine called *New Republic.* The attention wasn't something I had bargained for, or set out trying to attract. In my mind, I was just a simple bloke who dealt with the trauma in his life by removing the causes. I certainly didn't think I had done anything exceptional or noteworthy. But others obviously saw it differently. 'Dave, you're a curiosity,' *A Current Affair's* Margueritte had told me. 'People dream of this lifestyle. It's escapism for them. You bring it to reality. You'll never be short on media interest.'

The Dutch crew wanted to film me fishing, too, and were also keen for Quassi to come along. There's something about that shot – sitting in the stern, one hand on the tiller and the other around my handsome dog. But Quassi was unusually excitable on this occasion, constantly peering over one side of the boat then the next, probably looking for more crazy, trevally-hunting Koreans. Then he leapt overboard and straight onto the back of what, through all the thrashing, looked like a croc. The cameraman was on his feet in the boat, too, rocking us wildly from side to side. 'Sit down!' I bellowed, leaning right over to try and grab Quassi by the scruff of his neck. For a second it seemed like he was almost riding on the back of this creature like a canine surfer. After a couple of angry swishes of the tail, his opponent slipped away, but not before I realised that it was a wobbegong, a camouflaged bottom-feeding shark that looks a bit like a stingray. The name comes from an Aboriginal language and means 'shaggy beard', because of its growths around the mouth. They feed on octopus and crayfish, so their teeth are sharp and it could have given Quassi a nasty bite. The Dutch crew were delighted with their footage and Quassi seemed very pleased with himself when I hauled him back into the boat. But he was going to get himself in trouble if he didn't learn to pick his fights more judiciously.

***

Apart from the fishing footage, classic deserted island beach shots and interviews up at the Incredible Rocks, the media also consistently focused on Miranda. She was quickly becoming more famous than Wilson, the volleyball in the Tom Hanks film *Castaway*. Though now Miranda was sharing the limelight with her new companion, Phyllis. She arrived about a decade after Miranda and was a present from Denika, who had been working as a cosmetics consultant at the Myer store in Cairns. The store was throwing two mannequins out, so Denika kept one to hang her own clothes on and sent the other up on a trawler. I'm not entirely sure who came up with the name Phyllis, but I think it was one of the fishos. She probably reminded him of a woman who'd given him the clap.

Phyllis was more demure than Miranda – taller, skinnier but, if I'm honest, a bit aloof. Miranda was more willing to lark around with the boys. Whenever Bluey and I spotted the Coastwatch customs blokes flying over the island for a nosey, we'd race to the house, grab Miranda and then tie her to a palm tree on the beach so that, when the plane returned, the pilot spotted the damsel in distress. You can imagine him radioing back to base: 'Mayday, mayday. We have a bound female on Restoration Island. Potential kidnap and torture situation.' Their planes have circled back two or three times in the past. On other occasions I have invited Miranda, and lately Phyllis, to join us around the camp fire, often to provide some female company for the fishos. Miranda has a ball but Phyllis does not enjoy their bawdy tales, and one night she was visibly upset. Either that or I sat her too close to the flames and her eyeliner was melting.

I think I should make one thing perfectly clear here: I refer to Miranda and Phyllis as real women *as a joke.* I keep them here as a bit of fun, and they brighten the place up, like an artwork or a sculpture. They are a conversation piece, too. But the joke is lost on some people. I don't actually talk to them (unless I'm feeling really lonely) and I do *not* have sexual relations with them, as media reports have occasionally inferred. They are mannequins, not blow-up dolls, for goodness sake. Most reporters get the joke, but a few confuse my eccentricity with a few roos loose in the top paddock.

It's the same with mermaids. We all know that these beautiful creatures really do exist, right? But some narrow-minded twits have suggested that mermaids are mythical creatures made up by sailors who were too drunk to tell them from a dugong or a dolphin. Some even suggest that sailors would take their attraction to dugongs one step too far and so invented the concept of mermaids to hide their shame. These doubters obviously haven't lived on an island for more than two decades. Sometimes, like in the *Pirates of the Caribbean* films, mermaids are depicted as terrifying monsters who lure sailors to their deaths. I prefer the gorgeous, seductive Darryl Hannah-type mermaids from the film *Splash.* It's this type we find around Resto, especially around sunset after two or three bottles of home-brew. I haven't seen the human half too clearly yet – more often it's just the tail I glimpse before she vanishes back below the surface. So, until one plucks up the courage to come onto dry land and pay a visit – and maybe stay a while, because there's plenty of room in the water tank – I'll just have to keep reading about them and growing my collection of mermaid pictures and artefacts to display around the house. But I won't obsess over them – I definitely won't do that!

***

The media attention became a necessary evil, although at times I felt like it was spiralling out of control. It was fun to have visitors breezing in and out for a few days, but I was always thankful to have the place to myself again. However, I was starting to feel vulnerable. It had become obvious that no development was going to materialise through Longboat, and Colin Lindsay wasn't going to sit back and let the grass grow under my feet. Soon enough, he would want new buyers. And, armed with his seven-eighths of the head lease to sell, my dream of being the long-term custodian of Resto and building an inspirational healing retreat was precarious.

Early on, Colin had been delighted with all the building improvements I'd carried out like the tiki bar, the extension to the house and kitchen area, the shower area, the beach shack, the love shack and a new, bigger generator shed – not to mention the rubbish clean-up. Building value-adding infrastructure was an obligation of his head lease and my company assumed that obligation as part of our sublease. But I couldn't pay for all this work and continue to pay the rent on my own, so Colin agreed to pay the rent and rates. Or so I thought, until I was informed in 2004 that Colin had lodged a court claim against Longboat for rent that he claimed I owed for the period when I was carrying out the improvements. It was like a punch to the guts from out of nowhere.

The surprising part was that the claim was lodged at Victorian Civil and Administrative Tribunal, or VCAT. This was an action against a New South Wales–based company and involved a dispute in Queensland. So why Victoria? Colin lived in Victoria and probably didn't expect me to turn up, but there was no way I was going to let this go ahead uncontested. I planned to take along a mate, Chris Purdie, who wasn't legally qualified but was legally savvy and knew the ins and outs of my situation. He was a dapper sort of bloke and certainly looked like a lawyer.

On the morning of the hearing, Chris took me to meet a solicitor mate of his, John McMullan, at his plush Melbourne office in the Rialto Towers. It was obvious from the sculptures in the foyer that this guy was successful. He would also have been way out of my price range, but Chris managed to pull a favour on the condition that we only took up fifteen minutes of John's time. So I launched straight into the background of the case and was about three sentences into the story when John stopped me. 'You talk too much,' he said.

'Oh, okay. That's probably been said before,' I replied.

'Remember these three things, and do not say a word more, and the judge will throw it out. First, tell them that this is the wrong jurisdiction. Secondly, tell them that Colin's company owes money to Longboat, and not the other way round. And thirdly, tell them that the local Aboriginal people should be here as witnesses. Not a word more, not a word less. Then sit down,' John said.

I did as I was told but Colin, who was not represented and arrived with a tonne of paperwork, rabbited on and on. The magistrate was like a nodding dog in the back of a car window, trying to keep awake. At the end of Colin's submission, the magistrate told us to retire to separate rooms and came to see us moments later to say that Colin had made me a financial offer to leave the island. I told the magistrate that I did not want to leave and so the offer was pointless. Moments later the magistrate came back with an increased offer from Colin. 'Thank Mr Lindsay for his kind offer, but no thanks,' I said, and the magistrate took us back into the courtroom to dismiss the claim. Colin met me outside the court and offered to take me for lunch.

'Colin, if I had lunch with you now I would throw up,' I said, but Chris grabbed my arm and suggested we all go back to John's office.

'How about we approach this differently?' Chris said to Colin. 'Let's see how much it will take for us to buy you out.' Colin's eyes lit up and my jaw hit the floor. I hadn't been expecting that. When we arrived at John's office I could see that Colin was impressed by the decor, and a little daunted. John was typically straight to the point.

'Look, Glash is a mate and we are happy to help him out,' Johnny said, pulling out his chequebook. 'Will you sell for $1 million?'

'B-b-but John Travolta has shown an interest in the island,' Colin stammered. 'Other Hollywood stars are interested, too. I've been offered much more.'

'I'm a busy man, Mr Lindsay. One million is more than a fair price and I can pay you here and now. Take it or leave it.' He left it – but I had a smile like a split watermelon. To this day I'm not sure whether John and Chris were bluffing, or whether they would have bought Colin's shares for a million. But their support was enough to see off the immediate threat, although I knew that this was only the eye of the storm.

Chapter 12

Kinship

It's always something of a shock when the phone rings. Not only can it shatter the tranquillity, but it also often signals bad news. I had an immediate sinking feeling on one occasion, about six years after moving to the island, when the caller was Kath, the wife of my younger brother, Phil. Kath was calling from Leeds, England.

'Dave, I'm sorry to tell you that Phil suffered a heart attack last night and passed away,' she said. For the first time for a long time, a familiar tightness gripped my chest and I struggled for breath. It was too much to take in that my kid brother was dead.

Phil was another maverick Glasheen. Two years younger than me, he was a conscientious objector to the Vietnam War and dodged conscription by fleeing to Papua New Guinea on a cargo boat with his girlfriend. From there, the pair made their way to the Indian subcontinent, where they worked for the Red Cross for a year. Word on their whereabouts was sketchy, until he called home to beg Mum to buy them two plane tickets to England because their camp was under attack. Penniless, he found a place to squat in Hackney, a run-down borough of East London that probably resembled Sydney's Redfern at that time. When faced with the threat of eviction, Phil's legal training came in handy. He discovered a 500-year-old law that could be exploited to allow the squatters to stay, as long as they were actively involved in refurbishing the properties and paid a nominal rent. So Phil lived for a good number of years paying £1 rent a week in a beautiful house.

Along with his new girlfriend, Kath, another activist, he worked for a community law centre called Up Against the Law, which campaigned against police corruption. The organisation was contacted by the aunt of Anne Maguire. Anne was the matriarch of the Maguire Seven, a family that received sentences totalling seventy-three years for their alleged role in the 'bomb factory' the

IRA used in the October 1974 Guildford Bombings. The Maguire Seven served their full sentences, but their convictions were declared 'unsafe and unsatisfactory' when new evidence emerged and were quashed in 1991. Phil and Kath were involved in the early stages of that battle to clear the names of Anne Maguire and her family, writing articles for small publications and attending the trial daily. Phil used his legal training to take meticulous notes, which differed greatly from the official court version and shed light on the feverish anti-Irish mood of the time. He donated the notes to the Irish in Britain Representation Group (IBRG) archives at London Metropolitan University, where they remain a valuable resource for researchers, scholars and historians studying this landmark case. What an amazing legacy.

The last time I saw Phil was in London more than twenty-five years earlier. I was still trying desperately to establish Tetra Toys, the business I started with my brother, Mick. The initial growth of the company was funded from savings I had accumulated from trading uranium shares, but the only way to scale up was to take Tetra Toys global. A two-month whistle-stop global tour took in the Middle East, Europe and the States and was my first introduction to the world beyond Australia's shores.

This trip also allowed me to visit Phil in London, who was still living in his first squat, a hovel. There were junkies' needles in the parks and burnt-out cars on the street. The girl who kept a ten-foot python as a pet in the flat upstairs wasn't even the most shocking thing about this place; it was the fact that there was no bathroom in the house. 'This is hopeless,' I told him. 'You've got to come back to Australia.'

'It's fine,' Phil said, laughing. 'We go to the bathhouse once a week. It's cold here, Dave. We don't need to shower every day.' I visited Phil twice more over the next few years, when he was living in one of the houses he helped renovate, which put my mind at ease. Shortly after, Tetra, which had been my first real chance to prove myself out in the big bad world, flopped when cash-flow and supply issues combined to unravel the great progress we had been making, especially in the States. I was devastated, and equally upset for Mick. While he hadn't lost money in the venture as I had, he'd invested his talent, time, energy and hope. I felt I'd let him and his family down, not to mention my own family. For me there was no option but to return to consultancy projects, hoping another chance would come my way for me to prove myself as an entrepreneur.

***

Over the next few days, painful memories surfaced as the news of Phil's death sunk in. It conjured past griefs and traumas, like when we lost Dad. I first realised that Dad was ill when Mum rang to say that he had not gone to play bowls on the weekend. Dad never missed bowls. When I cycled over from Church Point to visit, he was grey, life already disappearing from his body. He died of bowel cancer just six weeks later, at the age of sixty-eight. 'Your father is a very spiritual man,' the doctor told me. 'Most people are afraid of death, but not him.' Following his burial, we held a three-day wake at home and it was clear how highly everyone regarded this kind, intelligent and caring man, my consummate role model. Mum also died of cancer at seventy-four, and was fiercely independent to the end. A carpenter installed rails around the house, and Mick moved back in with Mum so she could stay at home for nearly two years and use her skills as a dietitian to manage the disease. Mum was also highly esteemed in the community, and she used her last years to spend quality time with her many friends. 'Don't bury me,' Mum, who was not religious, had told us. 'It will be a waste of land.' To scatter her ashes and say farewell, we held a second wake where some younger fellas from her side of the family performed a Maori ritual to celebrate her New Zealand ancestry.

When Phil died, he was younger than both my parents had been when they died, which made it all the more difficult to accept. Although he never made it to Resto, my brother had always been so supportive of my life choices. When Kath and I discussed funeral arrangements, the island seemed like a fitting final resting place. 'Maybe have a ceremony in England, then when you're all ready, come over to Australia,' I suggested to Kath. 'Talk to Mick about scattering some of Phil's ashes in Sydney, then please come up to Resto for a couple of weeks.'

In the days leading up to Kath's arrival with Cian and Eavan, two of their three children, I worked hard to make the island look her best. I mowed the grass, picked up any rubbish on the beach and took it to the skip in Lockhart, and packed away all the equipment in the shed.

Phil's small and private remembrance service was to be on the day after his family's arrival, a Sunday, but on that morning a couple of respectable yachties turned up on the beach unexpectedly. I explained to them what was happening and, after talking to Kath, invited them to stay for the ceremony and dinner. We all wandered down to the sandspit, where each family member took a handful of ashes from the urn to sprinkle into the sea, and said a few words about Phil. It was one of the rare times of the year when the weather and currents combine to turn the sandspit into a golden crescent that almost doubles back on itself to form a lake. It was a gentle, cathartic process, which I could not have imagined happening anywhere else. The two yachties were visibly moved, too.

Kath, Cian and Eavan stayed for two weeks. We strolled, climbed, swam and fished, and most of all, we yarned about love and loss. It was poignant for me to witness how the island could have such a profound effect on others in their time of need.

'Dave, you and Phil were similar in many ways,' Kath told me one night by the camp fire. 'You shared a sense of justice and were not scared to crack a few eggs to make an omelette. It's a shame he didn't see the shelter you've found here.'

Having Phil's family celebrate his life here on Resto meant a lot to me. People do need time and space to come to terms with the death of a loved one; the last thing you need is your boss breathing down your neck, timing your compassionate leave to the hour. It had been like a good old-fashioned Irish wake, but a holiday instead of the wild party that can last for days.

Just months earlier, I had discovered how certain elements of white fella traditions had been absorbed into the Aboriginal cultural practice 'sorry business' – the mourning of a death – when I was invited to the funeral of Donnie Hobson. Donnie was one of the elders who had initially opposed our development, so the invitation alone was humbling and another giant stride forward in my relations with the Aboriginal community. After the male family members added earth on top of the casket, Paul Piva tapped me on the shoulder. No words were necessary. It was time to accept responsibility and show my respect through participation. After the casket was covered, the wooden cross, which everyone kissed, was put in place. Gorgeous flowers were laid on the mound as soothing guitar sounds drifted across the gathering. Then the women began to ululate. It made my hairs stand on end, and it was every bit as intense a gesture as the symbolic sprinkling of ashes. The funeral was followed by a small, private family gathering.

Many aspects of this ceremony had their roots in Christian burial traditions but the real difference in Aboriginal customs is the 'tombstone opening', which can take place many years after the death. Firstly, the wooden cross is replaced with a marble tombstone. Then a social celebration begins, which can last for two days, to honour the person's life on a grand scale. When it came time for Donnie's tombstone opening, I was one of only three white people invited, along with Lynn from the clinic, who was well respected in the community, and her husband, Stewy. The old canteen, which had not been used for years, was spotless for the occasion and every dignitary from miles around was there, along with about twenty dance groups from neighbouring communities. The food was incredible, but nobody was allowed to eat until midnight, as per custom – not even the young kids, who were unbelievably well behaved. And all I was allowed to contribute were two five-kilogram boxes of prawns. It was an incredible display of kinship, of the complex, non-static relationships – professional, personal and familial – that make up the Aboriginal social order. It made me even more determined to honour my place within that kinship.

***

It was a breathless June afternoon, and reflected clouds resembled stalactites in the glass-like sea. Shafts of dusty golden light sporadically pierced the stifling cloud cover. Kye and I were playing chess down at the beach shack. He was probably winning.

'Dad, I just saw a dolphin! It was huge!' he shouted. We waited for it to surface again where he was pointing, about thirty metres off the edge of the reef. Then the surface rippled and a bulbous head emerged, and emerged, and emerged, before the tell-tale white belly became visible. The creature pirouetted and crashed back into the water. 'That's no dolphin,' I said. It was about four metres long and the body was too bulky, the head too flat. 'I think it's a short-finned pilot whale, and it's way too close to the reef. It's going to beach itself. Quick, jump in the tinny, we might be able to steer it towards deeper water.' And off we went on our rescue mission.

Whales – mainly dwarf minke and humpback – come to Resto between May and September to calve and build up strength over the winter before returning to the cold Southern Ocean in summer. As we approached, I saw it was a baby humpback. Before whaling was banned in the 1960s, the eastern Australian humpback whale population was thought to have dropped to about 500 from a previously estimated 25,000. As a protected species in these waters, the population recovered to about 10,000 a decade ago. I'd seen them from bigger boats before, but only their top side, which looked like a submarine. The way this one was rolling and flapping around, I thought it might have been in distress.

'If we can throw a rope around it, we might be able to tow it out into deeper water,' I told Kye, who was mesmerised. Then the water around the tinny started to bubble and rise ominously. Out of the depths rose a huge adult, maybe more than ten metres long.

'Ohhhhh shiiiiit!' I practically squealed, which was probably not what a ten year old wanted to hear. When I cut the throttle, we drifted further towards the baby. Then the water bubbled again, and an even bigger adult surfaced. These magnificent creatures can grow to weigh thirty tonnes – and this male would have broken the scales. We'd obviously disturbed a family Sunday afternoon jaunt around the reef, and I wasn't at all sure how mum and dad would react to finding us so close to their pride and joy. The baby wasn't in distress, though – it was just having fun. As if to prove it, it soared out of the water and thumped back down, close enough to half fill the boat with water. *Had Kye read* Moby Dick?*I wondered. Would he mind having a dad with a leg made out of whalebone like Captain Ahab?* 'Quick, Kye! Grab this bucket and bail out the water and I'll start the motor!' I yelled. 'If I can turn around tightly enough, we might not disturb the family.'

'But, Dad, this is amazing. Let's stay and watch – please!' he shouted back over the noise of the motor. The little fella was right. It was a once-in-a-lifetime opportunity to view one of nature's most magnificent creations at close quarters, so we cautiously followed them at a safe distance around the headland and phoned ahead to the people at Portland Roads so they could witness the spectacle through their telescopes. Kye would have followed them all the way down to the Southern Ocean. It was the kind of fatherson moment that's hard to surpass.

***

The *Kokkinou* claims pride of place on Restoration Island's north-facing esplanade, the flat stretch of sand at the high water mark of the beach. The forty-foot double-masted timber ketch, built to classical yacht lines, broke down north of here and a big hole was punched in the side when she lifted up onto the reef in stormy weather. It was one more job for our salvage guy, Jason, who for another $1 coin or the price of a cuppa sold the *Kokkinou* on to me again, rather than towing her to Cairns. This was an expensive boat – the three tonnes of lead on the keel alone was worth a lot of money – but it was never my intention to sail her again. *Kokkinou* would become my retirement pad. A touch of paint, a new mattress in the three-quarter berth, a renovated bar and food prep area with a stove, and maybe some new shade sails, and I could make a cosy nest there to enjoy my sundowners on the deck, as Willie Nelson or Miles Davis lulled me to sleep under the stars.

Jason used dangerous underwater welding equipment to repair the hole with a temporary patch of timber, Visqueen and epoxy sealant, but lost his rollers to the depths of the sea while dragging *Kokkinou* off the reef. This made the job of hauling this beast up off my beach even more daunting. It was easy enough to bring her part way out of the water by digging a trench and pushing her up the beach when the tide came in. The tough part was the final ten metres up onto the flat ground above the soft sand. We used smaller pipes for rollers, logs for levers, roofing iron for a hard surface and a come-along hand winch tied to one of the bigger palm trees for traction. The first galvanised steel chain stretched like chewing gum and snapped. Thankfully nobody was standing nearby because the flying chain could have sliced someone in half. We then found some thicker ship's chain and built a shield out of roofing iron to protect us in case it snapped again, but this time the tension started to uproot the tree. The *Kokkinou* refused to budge and I called in the cavalry, Paul Piva and his mob. This was the ultimate tug-of-war team: twelve strapping blokes with Paul as the immovable anchor man. People power – and the all-important new-found sense of kinship – did the trick, and we collectively slumped around the beach shack to enjoy our reward: a huge side of wild beef that Paul had brought for me to marinate in olive oil and garlic and cook on the rotisserie. Over the following few weeks, I cemented four big timber poles into the ground to hold *Kokkinou* in place, using a come-along again to make sure the boat was level. With a final coating of tar on the keel, to prevent termites but also to add a cosmetic flourish, and the *Kokkinou* was transformed into an imperious sentry.

It will take another four or five years to restore the *Kokkinou* to her former glory, another project for the back burner, but even in her current condition she's the sleeping place of choice for visiting television royalty. Nobody, not even Rolf Harris, created a bigger splash in the Lockhart community than English actor Martin Clunes. In Australia his most famous show is *Doc Martin,* which has run for eight seasons. Having never seen the program, I had no real idea of Martin's popularity before he visited for a few days to film a segment for his show *Islands of Australia.* But everyone wanted his autograph when he went to buy me some coffee, jellybeans and salami in town, where I picked him up.

On Resto, we explored the bushes near the love shack and they filmed me showing Martin the kapok tree and the cotton-like fluff from its seed pods, which can be used for stuffing duvets. Perhaps he opted to sleep in the

Kokkinou after seeing one of our bigger spiders, the golden silk orb-weaver, because guests are out of the way of most creepy-crawlies – and crocs – up in the boat.

The presenter most in tune with my brand of escapism was another Englishman, Ben Fogle. His career was launched on a BBC show called *Castaway 2000,* in which he and thirty-five other participants lived on the remote island of Taransay in Scotland's Outer Hebrides. Ben is now a major star in the United Kingdom and has presented many TV shows. His first visit here was for the first series of a show called *New Lives in the Wild,* which featured people all over the world who have turned their backs on the daily grind. As a former castaway himself, I didn't have to do anything for Ben during his stay, and he also chose self-sufficiency at the *Kokkinou*. Women presenters usually appreciate the fact I have a mirror in the shower area, although you'd be lucky to recognise yourself in it because it has seen better days. Ben didn't care how he looked on camera – a few days without a shave just meant that he blended in with his host. He has always been inspired by escapism, especially to islands, and wrote a book many years ago called *Offshore: In search of an island of my own,* about his own attempts to buy an offshore retreat.

'I envy you, Dave,' he told me at the camp fire. 'I might easily find myself doing this one day. I often dream of this type of solitude. I may be knocking on your door for some tips, one day. I'm just not so sure I would have a couple of mannequins in my front room!'

Ben was fascinated by my possessions and took his crew on a guided tour of the house. My assorted odds and ends could have starred in their own series. Edited highlights included: a bosun's chair; a sawshark snout; a stingray barb; a spear and bow and arrow from Papua New Guinea; a polished turtle shell; salt-curled books; ancient Chinese pottery; faded framed maps and posters of the Great Barrier Reef; an obligatory didgeridoo; a cassowary tail; a sextant; hand-carved chairs from Mali; a barometer from one of the wrecks; the shell of a giant spider crab; valuable glass fishing floats and a sporran – what home would be complete without a sporran? At the entrance to the house, a sunbird has built a cocoon-shaped nest with detritus trailing from the bottom that visitors often mistake for a spider's web when it brushes against them. All I had to do to attract the bird was hang some string from the rafters and she is now a cherished custodian of my ever-growing collection of paraphernalia. There is surely no comparable living space on Earth, and Ben relished its uniqueness.

I was pleased that Ben's first visit coincided with one of Kye's occasional trips to Resto, and that Ben wanted to interview him. 'What should I say about you, Dad?' Kye asked.

'Just tell the truth,' I told him. 'It would be nice if it wasn't all negative, I guess, but don't feel that you need to tell lies.'

When the show aired, Ben described Kye as a mini version of me and brimming with confidence. 'It's clear Dave's son loves this place,' Ben told the viewers. 'I thought he would be a stroppy teenager and wouldn't want to be here – but he's morphed into an islander himself.' The camera panned to Kye.

'What would your dad be like if he ever had to live anywhere else?' Ben asked.

'It would be pretty sad,' Kye replied. 'It would be like a fish on land, or a turtle without a shell.' That was a pretty smart answer for a fourteen year old. And then Ben asked him for one word to describe me. 'Eccentric,' he answered with a wry grin, after only the briefest pause for thought. The broadcasters were so happy with the response to the show that Ben returned a few years later to film an update for their Christmas special.

Kye and I have a strong relationship, but an unusual one. That's a natural consequence of him growing up so far away from me. When I was young, my dad would be at his most open around the camp fire on holiday in Huskisson, and that's usually where Kye and I find the closest connection, too. We try to catch up whenever I am in Cairns and, though he's a good kid, I often feel I have to offer some fatherly words of wisdom because he worries the hell out of me. He's extremely creative, great with technology and a very talented musician – one of the youngest DJs on the Cairns nightclub circuit, and I wonder about the influences that he might be exposed to in that scene. 'The dumb kids who play on the rail tracks edge further and further away from the platform until they are hit by a train,' I once told him. 'You're not dumb, Kye, so please be careful out there.'

In fact, he's the opposite of dumb and I would love to see him work in computers – perhaps as a hacker for the good guys, whoever they are. When he does come to the island he looks perfectly at home and we are very relaxed in each other's company. If I should drift off for an afternoon nap, I might wake up and see his silhouette on the beach in the distance, fishing for his supper – another independent Glasheen soul.

Chapter 13

The slap

Grace was amazing. Her father was an English SAS officer and her Hong Kong–born mother practised ancient healing, and Grace was looking to set up a healing retreat of her own. When she tracked me down on Resto, she was honest from the start that Australia was not her preferred country for the retreat but, after several telephone conversations, she agreed to spend two weeks here to see the potential of the island for herself. When she stepped off the plane, wearing bright red lipstick and designer fashion, I was shocked. 'Grace? Is that you?' I asked. 'I had a mental image of you wearing hippy clothes.' She was shocked that I was shocked, but over the course of the first week we developed a deep connection. For someone in her mid-thirties, Grace was incredibly mature and an astute, profound thinker.

'How much do you know about crystal healing?' she asked on her first night here.

'Well, I've seen the film *Ghos* t with Whoopi Goldberg,' I replied, and Grace rolled her eyes. Then she scanned from the bottom of the hill to the very top. 'I can tell you where there is water, for example,' she said. *That's not difficult, I thought, I can easily divine water by snapping an old stainless steel coat hanger in half.* So, to put Grace's crystals to the test, I set her the challenge to find underground water in the paddock. She pulled out a diamond-like crystal from a satin pouch and dangled it from a string as we walked around. As we crossed the underground pipes leading from the tank on the hill, the crystal began to spin like a merry-go-round.

'The crystals can also identify places of enormous power,' she said, pulling out a few more and cupping them in her hands. Grace seemed to deliberate, then turned towards the mainland. 'That group of rocks over on the mainland, there. Have any of the local Aboriginal folk ever mentioned their powers before?' She was pointing to a cluster of granite boulders on the headland between Cape Weymouth and the next small beach along, where Chips lives.

'No, but I have always felt this island has incredible energy. My hair stands on end when people with an aura, like you, visit,' I replied. 'It would not surprise me at all to find that Resto has healing powers.'

As the first week progressed, Grace realised that Resto might be the perfect place for her retreat after all. Phil the trawler captain was also staying for a few days over the full moon and took us to Curd Reef on his boat. Stripped of make-up and the designer threads of her Melbourne self, Grace blended seamlessly into this natural sanctuary. 'Curd would be the perfect spot for my one-on-one sessions with clients,' Grace mused. Later that night, she proposed a deal: she would provide capital to upgrade the living arrangements and fund marketing to attracting groups of ten to the island for ten days at a time, while I would stay on, with Quassi, and curate the island in return for a third of the profits. 'No phones, no booze, no cameras,' she insisted. 'We catch and grow as much as we can to sustain ourselves. These people must be out of their comfort zones, to an extent. And we should involve the local Aboriginal community, especially their healers.'

Grace had pretty much articulated my dream for the future here, and I didn't need any crystals to recognise a fair deal. We talked incessantly over the ensuing days until her partner arrived for the second week and put a dampener on everything. Their relationship issues quickly surfaced; for every positive that Grace put forward, this bloke would slap it down with his negativity. Nevertheless, when I dropped them both off at the airport, we agreed to continue to explore the idea when she returned to Melbourne. My hopes were not too high, given her partner's disapproval.

Meanwhile, I had some detective work to pursue. What magical powers did the rocks on the mainland hold? I knew the land across the water from Resto had cultural significance. On weekends local families gathered there, back on their traditional lands. The area is the setting for their turtle and stingray stories from Dreamtime, the Aboriginal understanding of the world. These stories teach emerging generations of local Aboriginal people how to hunt these animals in the summer months when winds are down and the water is clear. But I had never heard anyone talk of those rocks. The best person to ask was Silas Hobson. Silas is one of the most prominent members of Lockhart River's talented group of local artists, the Art Gang, which has exhibited all over the world. He's the type of bloke who would make the Queen wait for an appointment rather than decline a clan obligation. 'Hey, Silas,' I said, as I wandered into the arts centre where the Art Gang is based. 'What do you know about the rocks directly opposite Restoration Island?'

Silas smiled.

'...Do they have any spiritual significance?'

Silas smiled.

'A white woman told me to ask ... An ancient healer woman?'

Silas smiled.

'Can you just nod your head if something happened there?'

Silas smiled.

His reluctance to give anything away reminded me of a local piece of folklore. Narcisse Pelletier was a cabin boy on a ship called the *Saint-Paul,* which left France in 1857 loaded up with wine bound for Bombay. It then carried on to Hong Kong to pick up 300 Chinese labourers who were going to work in the Australian goldfields. The ship hit a reef near Rossel Island, southeast of New Guinea, and twelve men, including Narcisse, sailed across the Coral Sea in a longboat, surviving by eating seabirds and drinking their own urine. After a 1200-kilometre journey they landed at Cape Direction, about thirty kilometres due south of Restoration Island. Somehow, Narcisse was left behind and discovered by three women of the Uutaalnganu people, who nursed him back to health and gave him the name Amglo. He was raised in the ways of the Aboriginal people and adopted their distinctive body markings, or cicatrices, across his chest and arms. He was discovered nearly two decades later by crewmen of an English pearling boat, and taken to the small outpost of Somerset at the tip of Cape York. Narcisse eventually made it back to his home town in France, and was greeted as a hero.

It's a fascinating story that was featured in a recent novel called *What Became of the White Savage.* There's also talk of a movie, but more than just a ripper story, Narcisse's account of his time living with the direct ancestors of some of today's Lockhart River families, provided a unique anthropological insight into Aboriginal customs and social order of that time. Interestingly, Narcisse refused to talk about spirituality and sacred knowledge, which was consistent with the belief system that this information should stay within the clan groups.

And that's why Silas was smiling, not talking. Grace's theory about those rocks would have to remain a theory.

***

The void Grace left was soon filled when a pair of Italian women, both in their early forties – much older than my usual wwoofers, arrived for three weeks. Anna was a curvaceous, blonde Gina Lollobrigida type, and a bundle of fun. Roberta was more petite with the dark and mysterious looks of Sophia Loren, and much more my physical and intellectual type. Finally, a woman I could fall for. And I did. Head over heels. There was just one nagging doubt, though. I wasn't sure whether or not they were gay. Maybe the constant hugging was just a typically Italian show of emotion...?

This question was eating away at me one afternoon as the girls strolled along the beach and I enjoyed a quiet cuppa in the house. Suddenly, a blur of scales, claws, teeth, tongue and tail flashed across my lap and vanished into the bedroom, knocking over the coffee table and my cuppa on the way. There wasn't even enough time for me to squeal. *It must be a sand goanna,* I thought. But it was smaller than the one I had occasionally seen before, which was about two metres long. My new visitor was about a metre long, and lightning quick. I grabbed a broom for protection, because I guessed all monitor lizards have a nasty nip, and I edged into the bedroom. I couldn't see him anywhere. Cautiously, I sank to my knees and looked under the bed. The little bugger was nestled between two boxes, cheekily flicking his tongue in and out at me. My pokes with the brush only pushed him further under.

The girls returned to find me on the bedroom floor and, when I explained what had happened, they ran for the hills. 'You cannot sleep there tonight, Dave!' said Anna, when I caught up to them. 'There is space in the love shack with us.' And so, that night, I found myself snuggled between two gorgeous Italian women on a double mattress. It was the stuff of dreams, but I didn't sleep a wink. *Was that a slight nuzzle from Anna? Would Roberta mind a gentle cuddle? Did one of them just accidentally fart? Did Roberta just whisper something passionate in her sleep?* Every day for the next two weeks, I checked whether the goanna had left the bedroom and, even though he was probably long gone, I thought it best to play it safe for the time being and stay in the love shack.

Several days later, we climbed up to the Incredible Rocks. The track was relatively clear but I did notice that a network of vines had grown over the path. Near the top, one of the girls accidentally disturbed an ant nest in the low branches of a tree. Within seconds, thousands of green ants had covered them both from top to toe. I could barely see their skin beneath this living blanket. Both girls freaked out and screamed, slapping themselves wildly. 'Stop!' I yelled. 'If you panic they will bite you! I've been bitten on the balls and it's *not* pleasant.' That grabbed their attention, and they paused to listen.

'It's too far to run to the water and too dangerous. Trip over one of those vines and you could break your neck. But if you stay calm and slowly take off all your clothes, then pick the ants off each other and out of your hair like monkeys, you will be fine. I'm not going to stand here and perv – I'll be round the corner. When you're finished, sing out.'

Safely back at the house, Roberta was interested to discover that green ants were edible and tasted of peppermint, and that local Aboriginal people used them in a special tea thought to have soothing properties. I discovered she came from a humble background, but followed a calling to medicine to seek a cure for her mother's long-term illness. Roberta quickly reached the top of the tree in her speciality, but was disillusioned with the profession's male dominance. During her stay on Resto, she asked me to help write a letter to her father telling him that she was no longer going to practise western medicine. Instead she was heading to Nepal and Peru to explore alternative healing methods.

'You should stay in Australia,' I suggested. 'Learn from the Aboriginal people. They kept themselves healthy for tens of thousands of years, before the white fella arrived and ruined everything ... and besides, I think we could really have something here. I like you, Roberta.'

'Australia is not the place for me, Dave. It is not a spiritual country,' she said. The words were like a spear to my heart.

'So is this the last I'll see of you?'

'Maybe. But perhaps we could have an open relationship? I like you, but you are ruled by your head, not your heart. I do not think this kind of relationship would work for you.' It was true – I have never rushed into physical relationships. Maybe my strict Catholic upbringing held me back. Even as a teenager, I wanted to meet girls who were saving themselves for the right bloke, not the girls who were throwing themselves at any boy whose parents had a lot of dough.

'Jeez, Roberta, my head's telling me right now that I'm going to really miss you.'

There were tears, from all three of us, when I waved them off at the airport. And again when I returned to Resto to find Roberta's message in my guestbook: 'I'm breathing slowly so that you, David, Restoration Island and Quassi can sink and melt down in my heart. I feel you are an amazing companion along life's journey. You have a big, big heart, man! I'm sure we will meet again and at the same time I know we already met in a place where we cannot miss each other anymore...'

***

For weeks I moped. The upsides of solitude were being overruled by the downsides of loneliness. And I didn't want those lines to become blurred. The answer was to throw myself into activities that uplifted me. Fishing! That would take my mind off the bloody gorgeous, potentially once-in-a-lifetime soulmate who had just slipped through my fingers. Louis and Fiona over in Portland Roads were always up for an afternoon's fishing. So what if the clouds were building on the horizon like the black mushrooms of consecutive nuclear explosions? According to forecasts, the storm would hit us in the evening. *We'll be fine,* I told myself, as I rang Louis and Fiona to say I was on my way to pick them up.

At the time, I had a fibreglass Southwind longboat with a much more powerful – but also more temperamental – fourstroke Yamaha motor capable of doing thirty knots, which meant I could venture further away from the island

and be confident of returning home before the weather turned. As long as the motor kept running.

It had cut out on one previous occasion when a French TV crew was here filming a popular documentary series, *Thalassa.* The show was an adaptation of the Jules Verne novel *L'Île Mystérieuse* or The Mysterious Island, a sequel to his book *In Search of Castaways.* I had dropped the crew off on Restoration Rock so they could film me catching fish with a lure from the boat. And I was just far enough away – probably one hundred metres – for them to be oblivious to the fact that the motor had stopped. I threw out the reef anchor and assessed my options. I was between a rock and a hard place – literally. Perhaps I could wait until the tide went out, but that would mean scrambling over coral in bare feet, which was never fun. There were oars in the boat, but I realised I hadn't fixed the loose rollicks to hold the oars in place. I could carry on yanking the ripcord, but both my arm and the cord felt like they were going to come loose. Maybe I could swim to the rock or back to the island, but that sure would test my stamina and nerve. The final option was to bash the bloody thing with a spanner. With one good dong, and one more tug of the cord, the motor spluttered miraculously back to life. The crew had no idea how lucky they had been not to spend a long, cold night stranded on Restoration Rock.

That day when the motor stopped with Louis and Fiona on board, there were fewer options. The weather system had arrived much earlier than we'd thought and the seas had transformed from placid to wild in an instant. Swimming would have been impossible, plus there was nowhere to climb ashore. The boat was rocking violently and I could see that Fiona was beginning to lose her nerve; she gripped Louis with one hand and her seat with the other. Louis, normally an unflappable bloke, was also looking concerned. He knew even less about motors than I did, which was bugger-all. No matter how many times I pulled the ripcord, nothing happened inside the motor – not even after several good wallops. To make matters worse, the reef anchor was not holding in the sand or mud, and we were drifting towards the rocks. Hitting them was the worst-case scenario. The boat would be smashed like an eggshell, and its passengers scrambled.

Although I could barely see to the end of my arm as salt water lashed my eyes, I concluded our only option was to take apart the motor to try and spot the problem. With every passing minute, the rocks loomed nearer. It was a classic race against time, and I needed calm and a clear mind. But that was impossible, because Fiona became hysterical. 'We're going to die! We're going to die!' she wailed.

'We're not going to die!' I shouted. 'But if you don't stay quiet I can't think clearly, and we will be in serious trouble. Louis, can you keep her quiet please?' Louis tried to soothe her but it didn't work.

'Do something, Dave!' she yelled. 'Save us, please!'

'I'm trying to save us but I can't function with you screaming in my ear!' I replied.

'We're near the rocks, we're all going to...'

That's when I slapped her. Not a jaw-breaking punch – a firm slap across the cheek. And it worked. Fiona was stunned into silence and sobbed gently as Louis wrapped her in his arms. At last I could concentrate, and instinct told me to detach the fuel line and suck in case there was an airlock. A mouthful of petrol fumes was a small sacrifice. Working quickly but methodically, I reattached the hose, screwed the motor back together and put all my might into that first pull of the ripcord. The motor purred like a pussycat. I dragged up the anchor and cut through the waves as quickly as possible without capsizing to reach the shelter of Portland Roads.

Not a word was spoken as Fiona and Louis climbed out of the boat, and we haven't spoken about it to this day, although we remain friends. The slap was an instinctive way of making sure her panic didn't have disastrous consequences. I'm not proud of raising my hand to a lady. I wouldn't have been proud if it had been a bloke, but I would have done the same thing. And I would do the same thing again.

Because we are all here to tell the tale, which didn't look likely at one point.

Chapter 14

The battle of Resto

There had been an uneasy truce between me and Colin Lindsay ever since the VCAT hearing, including a few more attempts at mediation. But there was no escaping the fact that Colin wanted to sell, and wouldn't be able to unless I wanted to leave. There was even more incentive for him to sell when the head lease was confirmed until 2039, thanks to all the improvements I had carried out, which had effectively secured the value of the island. But he knew that I had no intention of leaving and I first got wind of his change of tactics through the bush telegraph, which is a very effective means of communication, if you know the right people. On this occasion it worked something like this: Colin asked a guy in Weipa if he knew anyone in the demolition business for some work on Restoration Island. This guy approached another fella, whose apprentice overheard the conversation.

The apprentice told his dad, who knows me. The dad called his mate in Mission Beach – one Dave Nissen. Nothing escapes Dave.

'What's all this about you demolishing everything on the island?' he asked.

'What?' I asked, astounded. 'I'm not demolishing anything. I'm building, not demolishing.'

'Well, your mate Colin has just bought a new car and a boat in Weipa, and is heading your way with two other blokes,' said Dave. 'One of them has been pricing up a job to pull everything down and clear it off the island.' Stunned, I put the phone down, wondering what the hell was happening. Then the phone rang again.

'Davo, it's the clinic in Lockhart River. I have three months' worth of medication for someone, care of Restoration Island. Do you know anything about it?' Now this was worrying – why would anyone have ordered that much medicine for this address? The phone went again.

'Hi Dave. It's the cabins at the airport. I just wanted to check that

Colin and those other two blokes are using their bookings tonight. I couldn't understand why they wouldn't be staying with you.'

The penny was starting to drop. Colin was fed up with trying to manoeuvre me off the island; he was going to ask me to leave point blank. The bloke with the medicine was probably going to be his new caretaker. But they'd lost their element of surprise – and I had to move quickly. *This might be illegal,* I thought. *The police are sure to help.*

'Look, Davo,' the copper said. 'This is a civil matter – it's nothing to do with us.'

'Just remember that I'm a legal tenant and own a share in the island. I'm not going peacefully and I'll chain myself to the house if I have to.'

The copper rang back a few hours later. 'We've just been over to speak to Mr Lindsay at the cabins, and we're going to come over tomorrow to make sure nothing gets out of hand,' he said. 'Come and pick us up at Cape Weymouth at 9am, and Mr Lindsay will be there at 9.30am.'

I didn't sleep a wink that night. Every rattle of the windows in the wind felt like someone was breaking in. In the morning, the copper and his sergeant arrived at the island as planned at 9am in full uniform. An hour passed but there was no sign of Colin and his mates. Another hour went by, and then another. The coppers were becoming frustrated because it was a Saturday and they wanted to return to their families. My mate Chips rang to tell me that Colin and his two mates would be late because he missed the tide at Portland Roads and was driving round to Cape Weymouth. Finally, at midday there was a sighting – a very comical sighting. The tide was out at Cape Weymouth, too, so as a last resort he had rushed round to Casuarina Beach, directly opposite us. It was like something out of the *Keystone Cops,* but this time the cops were the amused audience.

The wind was blowing around forty knots and it's never a good idea to launch in that weather. Regardless, they backed the trailer down the beach and struggled to put the boat into the water. Then the car became bogged in the sand. Through binoculars, we could see all the huffing and puffing as they pushed the car back up the beach. Then it looked like someone dropped the car keys in the sand – that added another half-hour. Once they were finally in the water, they ran the boat directly onto the reef and almost smashed the outboard motor. I took the coppers over to Resto and, eventually, Colin and his men sheepishly dragged the boat ashore and staggered up to the beach shack.

'G'day, Colin,' I said, offering to shake his hand. 'What brings you here?' Then I introduced myself, very politely, to his two companions. Colin virtually ignored me.

'Here, you take these two bags over to the house there and you carry this stuff over to the shuttle,' he ordered his lackeys.

'Err, just hang on a minute,' I stopped him. 'You can't bring anything further than the high water mark. That's where public access ends. You can't just barge your way into someone's home. Even if you think you're the landlord, you need my permission to come beyond that mark. And you don't have that permission. However, if you agree to talk this through like gentlemen, I have prepared some food and I would happily invite you all to share lunch, but only after we speak to the police and resolve everything amicably.'

At the tiki bar, Colin handed me an eviction notice and told the police that he wanted me off the island the next day because I was trespassing, and he was concerned I would do damage to his property. That's when I lost it. 'Why would I want to do that?' I said. 'I love this island – why would I want to damage it? I built most of this!'

Colin just asked if the police had anything to say.

'Mr Lindsay, we have conducted a thorough search of the island and we have found no weapons.' I was smiling inwardly. The cops had not searched anywhere. Colin's mates knew the score and started to load up the boat. Even so, I invited Colin and his friends to stay the night. I wanted to keep this civil. But he climbed back into the boat and left, his pride clearly wounded.

***

My colourful family background should have stood me in good stead for a protracted legal fight. Granddad Denis was a practising solicitor in West Maitland, in the Hunter Valley, at the turn of the twentieth century, and an active member of the local debating society. He once defended an American itinerant worker called George Clark who, while working for the travelling Marconi's Circus, was charged with attempting to commit a 'serious offence with a Saint Bernard bitch dog'. Clark had previous convictions for drunkenness, so perhaps granddad's defence was that he was just trying to get at the brandy in the barrel around the dog's neck? I can only imagine the discussion at the next meeting of the local debating society!

Then Granddad made his own headlines, for being on the wrong side of the law. In 1918 he was sentenced to eighteen months' hard labour for swindling £20,000 from a lady called Cecilia Pierce, but he didn't turn up for his trial. Stories surfaced within our family that Denis also robbed the Maitland branch of the Commercial

Banking Company of Sydney – with the help of the bank manager. My Welsh grandma, Marie, was one of nine children. Several of her sisters were nuns in the local order of the Sisters of the Little Company of Mary. Granny's sisters were apparently fed up with Denis, the black sheep of the family, and wanted him out of Marie's life. So they conspired to help smuggle him out of West Maitland and down the Hunter River on a boat – dressed as a nun.

'Sister' Glasheen made it out of Australia and all the way back to England, leaving his wife and four children destitute and dependent on the charity of the local Catholic Church. But Granny Marie was a survivor; she moved to Sydney, where she brought up four successful, strong-minded children. My dad, Max, was intelligent, principled and opinionated – a real leftie – although a pronounced stutter meant that he often kept his opinions to himself. Like his younger brother, my Uncle Terry, he also received a scholarship to study law, but Dad was less ambitious and happy to build a small but successful family practice. My mum Valda was the daughter of a prominent doctor – the Grand Poobah of the Freemasons in New Zealand – whose tyrannical behaviour led her to flee to Australia with her sister, closely followed by their mother. Their dad cut the girls off when he discovered that both his daughters had taken up with Catholics, who were openly opposed to the Masons. Like Dad, Mum was also very left-wing in her politics and supported various women's rights movements. This was a partnership of intellectual equals, although Mum was content in the role of homemaker.

When Mum and Dad moved to Sydney's Upper North Shore, a middle-class, white-collar area populated by lawyers and accountants, they started to move in connected circles. My godfather was Supreme Court Judge Jock McClemens, a convert to the Catholic Church who, in his early days on the bench, would walk straight from the court to St Mary's Cathedral to pray for men he had just sentenced to death. He and Dad once travelled to Rome to meet the Pope to try and persuade the Catholic Church to approve birth control.

You can bet mum would have had a hand in that mission.

Jock was a regular guest at the frequent weekend parties at our house, along with a pompous barrister I detested from a young age, John Kerr. I have never understood why Dad insisted that Kerr should be the Master of Ceremonies when Sylvi and I were married. My suspicions about the prick were confirmed a few years later when, as Governor-General, he sacked a former associate of my Uncle Terry and the greatest Prime Minister that Australia has ever had, Gough Whitlam, over the notorious 'loans affair'. Kerr was despised throughout Australia after that and escaped to London, apparently seeing out his final years sozzled in various gentlemen's clubs with other born-to-rule types. When Dad died, Kerr rang mum to offer his condolences and it was the only time I ever heard Mum swear. 'You're a bloody idiot, John Kerr. I've wanted to tell you that for a long time. We don't need sympathy from you,' she said.

Although he wasn't as much of a high-flyer as some of his peers, Dad was pretty shrewd. He was happy to help friends and acquaintances out for next to nothing in those early days, in the hope that it would pay off when they were rich and famous and needed help with family matters. Take Frank Lowy, for example, whose future wife lived across the street in Turramurra. Dad put together the lease agreement for Frank's first ever delicatessen free of charge. Now Lowy, the owner of Westfield shopping centres, is worth something like $8 billion. I wonder whether Frank still remembers the bloke who helped him way back – I bet he does!

Dad was also in his element tackling the establishment and championing the underdog. In one famous case during World War II, Glasheen & Co demanded that the police release the body of a murder victim dubbed the 'Pyjama Girl'. Dad's client claimed the body was her missing daughter, but the police claimed it was another missing woman's corpse and charged her husband with murder, although recent evidence suggests that police corruption forced the man's confession. Dad would have loved those David and Goliath battles.

When Mick, the number one son, chose to study architecture, Dad hoped I would carry on the family tradition in law. I wanted to be a vet but, without financial support from Dad, the course was too expensive. So I opted for a commerce degree at University of New South Wales, before moving to a management degree at University of Technology Sydney. All the while, I worked part-time at Consolidated Milk Industries as a commercial trainee, where I learned the ins and outs of the business: which refrigeration plant manager turned up late every morning and was straight on the grog; which salesman was fudging his expense account or which member of the buying team was rooting his secretary behind the back of the filing cabinets every Friday afternoon.

When Colin Lindsay launched proceedings in the Queensland Supreme Court to evict me from the island, a good knowledge of the law would have come in handy for my own David–Goliath battle. Colin's argument relied on the fact that a resort development was part of our original deal, but I maintained that we were *jointly* committed to raise funds for the development, and that my company's only obligation was to secure development approval, which we did. All the attempts to mediate were unsuccessful but I managed, somehow, to stay on civil terms with him. Colin even brought friends up to holiday on the island while I was preparing my defence, with the help of a Cairns-based lawyer. Initially, I had no money to pay a lawyer, but my business instincts kicked in. I'd buy bars of silver on eBay for a good price then sell them on at a decent profit, or trade pieces of local Aboriginal art to scrimp and save just enough for legal representation.

For months I lived like a hermit – and not in a desirable way – trapped in a cave of paperwork. Although I was convinced I had an airtight defence, I wasn't going to leave anything to chance. So I collected affidavits from anyone who I thought could vouch for my character or recollect those early agreements, and I delved through all the minutes of the company's annual general meetings.

Crucially, the Aboriginal community was firmly in my corner. Paul Piva recognised that I wanted to use my share in the island to benefit the local community. I also had the support of Greg Pascoe and Wayne Butcher, who were influential Lockhart figures: Greg was another respected Aboriginal elder and chairman of the Kuuku Ya'u Aboriginal Corporation, which represents the traditional owners, and Wayne was the local mayor. They wanted to work with me towards a solution that respected the rights of the local community, no matter what judgements might be made against me and my company.

To make their involvement official, I granted the local community one share in Longboat, which meant they could never be thrown out of any court case involving my company. As the court battle loomed, I also reached a written agreement with the Kuuku Ya'u Aboriginal Corporation to protect both our interests. The local people already owned the wild and rugged two-thirds of the island not covered by the lease, which Colin had given back in 1989. So wasn't it logical for them to have rights over the remaining third? Under my new agreement with the community, if I brought in a new investor to buy Colin Lindsay out, and they accepted such an investor, one share in the new head lease company would be theirs for $1. Then, we would transfer Colin's other seven shares to the Kuuka Ya'u for a nominal $1 each. They would therefore own the head lease, and could grant a new sublease to the new investors. This would have been a winwin-win arrangement for me, the Kuuku Ya'u and for Colin. But, without a new investor in sight to buy Colin out, it was imperative I won the court battle and remained on the island to safeguard my own interests, and those of the Kuuku Ya'u.

There were times in the build-up to the court case when I questioned my sanity. Not for contesting the case; it was a matter of principle, and a legitimate fight to secure my own future and to build a future for others. But I had always considered myself a good judge of character. Perhaps I was too trusting and took people at face value. It certainly appeared that way when I tried to track down the two police officers who had witnessed Lindsay's cack-handed attempts to remove me from the island.

Both officers had moved on from their Lockhart River posts, and it took countless calls, knock-backs, red herrings and dead ends to locate just one officer. He did finally respond, but told me that he was working undercover in a Brisbane jail on a murder case, and there was no chance that he would be able to appear in court on my behalf. And, in any case, he had probably breached protocol too many times that day to be able to put anything in writing. *Fair enough,* I thought. *There's always his partner.* The second officer was now stationed in Cairns, but didn't return any of my calls. So, while visiting my lawyer in town, I found out when the cop was on night duty, and sat outside the station for half the night until he showed up. 'Hey, remember me?' I asked, blocking his way into the station. 'You were on

Restoration Island that day when I thought that I was going to be thrown off.'

'Nah, no idea what you're talking about, mate,' he said.

'What? You rang me a couple of months later asking if you could bring your girlfriend for a holiday.'

'Nah, not me, mate. You've got the wrong fella,' he said with a snarl, and the bastard barged past me into the station.

The case was finally scheduled to be heard in Cairns nearly four years after it was first lodged in 2008. It's really hard to live any kind of normal life with that hanging over you for so long. Nevertheless, I was ready for a battle and, on the day before the trial, I went to see my lawyer for a final briefing.

'Right, Dave, I've prepared everything in these files,' he said, pointing to a huge folder on his desk. 'I just need a down payment on my fee for the trial.'

'But that was covered in the money I paid up front, wasn't it? I've literally got no money left. You know we're going to win, and then Colin will have to pay your costs.'

'...Well, as a gesture of goodwill, I'll hand over the files and wish you luck. I reckon the judge will take pity on you when you represent yourself,' he said, only a little apologetically. Was this how lawyers operated? Where was any client loyalty? Where was the honour in this profession? My dad would have turned in his grave. My brother Phil would have been horrified. Even my rogue of a granddad might have been mildly perturbed. A last-ditch attempt to secure Legal Aid failed because this was a civil dispute. *Would it help if I went out onto the street and donged someone?* I wondered. My mind was in a tailspin.

Frazzled and furious, I stayed up into the wee hours, trying to make sense of the legal depositions. It was hardly the best preparation for the three-day hearing, and I turned up bleary-eyed to court the next day. Inside the courtroom, I was nervous and I could see that Colin was, too. There was one major difference: on his side of the court was a legal army in full court regalia. On my side was Dave Glasheen, in a moderately clean shirt.

'And who will be representing you, Mr Glasheen?' asked the judge.

'I'm representing myself, your honour,' I replied, and the judge rolled his eyes. 'But there's no need for all of this if Mr Lindsay will just...'

'Silence, please, Mr Glasheen. You must adhere to court procedure at all times. We will hear from the plaintiff first.'

And so it went on. I was blocked at every turn. I couldn't even hear what their QC was saying because he spoke so quietly. Whenever I wanted to interrupt, I was told to be quiet. Whenever I was asked for input, I was confused. Whenever I asked a question, I used incorrect terminology. Like my dad, and granddad before him, I'd been a member of the debating society at school. Surely it shouldn't have been this difficult. Then, when it came to my turn, none of my affidavits were deemed admissible. This was hopeless. I was right, royally screwed. Over those three days, I didn't score one single legal point against Colin, despite the witnesses who testified on my behalf, including Paul Piva, Greg Pascoe, my friend Chris Purdie and Tom Goode, the son of one of Colin's original partners. But I wasn't stupid. It's just the odds are so heavily stacked against the little guy in these instances. Invariably the side with the most money and access to the best legal team wins these battles, not the guy with justice on his side. By the third day, I was a gibbering wreck and about to throw in the towel, when there was a glimmer of hope. The three-day session was nearly over, but it was estimated the case would need another three days. Happily, there were no available slots for another two months. Had I been thrown a lifeline? Would this give me enough time to regroup and pull victory from the jaws of defeat?

'You need a lawyer, mate,' said Dave Nissen, who'd sat through the proceedings, along with a few others including Paul Piva, my brother Mick and Cheyenne.

'I know that, Dave, but I've no money left to pay for one,' I said.

'Look, let me talk to a few people. Go back to the island, catch your breath and try to relax. You can't give up – we all need somewhere to fish,' he reassured me with a laugh.

***

Relaxation was, of course, impossible. My blood pressure was through the roof and I was probably clinically depressed. My psychiatrist friend, Ernest Hunter, had written a letter to the court stating that he was worried about the effects of the stress on my mental health. Back on the island, there was no sign of a posse coming to the rescue. It was disappointing, but I couldn't go cap in hand to anyone. I just tried to expel all thoughts of the court case by playing with Quassi and immersing myself in the island chores I'd neglected. The rubbish had been building up before I left for Cairns, so I jumped into the boat with four or five bagfuls and headed to Portland Roads. The sea was as flat as a pancake. The breeze parted my beard down the centre and my legal trials and tribulations were suddenly of another world. Then the motor stopped. Two strong tugs on the ripcord. Nothing. A few good bashes with a spanner. Nothing. Check the petrol. Nothing, as in no petrol. Zilch.

My mind had been so scrambled that I had committed the cardinal sin of island life: forgetting to check the fuel. I was way too far out to swim for the shore, so my only option was to drop anchor and sit tight in hope that other boats would spot me. But the water was too deep and my anchors didn't reach the bottom. All the while, I had been drifting out to sea on the strong currents. Thankfully, I could see a trawler in the distance heading my way. Soon I could tell that it was the *Elizabeth J* and I knew the skipper. But it was heading directly for me and not slowing down. *Shit, the captain's got her on autopilot,* I realised. It's something skippers often do while they see to some job at the back of the boat. This bloke had no idea I was there.

I clambered over to the bow and pulled out a V-sheet – a PVC sheet with a large black 'V', which internationally symbolises a boat in distress – and held it with outstretched arms like a matador. Still the trawler tore through the water, oblivious. I couldn't bring myself to abandon ship so, cringing behind the V-sheet with my eyes firmly closed, I braced for impact.

The noise of its engines increased, then my boat was rocking violently in the trawler's wake. Peeping through one eye, I watched it pass just ten metres away. The danger wasn't over, though. I was drifting perilously close to the shipping channel on the Inner Reef. If someone didn't rescue me soon, then I didn't stand a chance of being spotted by one of the tankers. Luckily, John Pritchard was at home and looking out to sea through his telescope, as he often does. He radioed to Portland Roads to tell them I was in trouble, and a local came out to tow me back to shore within thirty minutes. I didn't know whether to laugh at my own stupidity or cry with relief.

***

The incident seemed to sum up how I felt at that crisis point in my life –

all at sea. Still, while there was a chance of staying on Resto, I wasn't going to give up without a fight, even though I didn't even have enough money for the airfare down to Cairns. Thankfully, a good friend, Bruce Davey, took pity and offered me a lift in his beautiful multi-million-dollar cruiser and charter mackerel boat, *Wild Card.* He also loaned me enough cash to provide a roof over my head during the proceedings. I hoped the two-day trip down might take my mind off things, and Bruce did everything he could to distract me.

The final three days of the trial were a carbon copy of the first three. I was hoping that some more key members of the Aboriginal community would turn up but, apart from Paul Piva, they were hesitant to become too involved. They did send a letter to the court expressing their support for me and my intentions for the island. And I could understand their reluctance to participate in a fight between two white fellas in a white fella court.

I was soon back to being bewildered by the technicalities, and the judge was losing patience. At one point Colin's lawyers felt so sorry for me they tried to tell me which rulings and landmark cases to look up. But it didn't prevent a slow, humiliating death by legal jargon. Nobody, least of all me, was surprised when the judge ruled categorically against me, although it was nothing to do with justice or fairness, in my opinion. Sole possession of the lease was awarded to Colin, and all subleases were cancelled. Half of Colin's legal costs – about $60,000 – were awarded against me, but the most his lawyers could ever have hoped for was $5 a week from my state pension.

As I staggered out into the blinding light and suffocating heat of a Cairns afternoon, the maelstrom of emotions was bewildering. On one hand, there was pure relief that it was all over. But then I was paralysed with fear at the implications. Although I still owned one-eighth of the head lease, I had lost my tenancy rights when the sublease was cancelled. Effectively, Colin could – and still can – evict me at any time. I was a squatter in my own home. Paul

Piva could sense my desolation and put his giant arm around my shoulder.

'Come on, Davo, let's get you a beer,' he said.

'Do you mind if I have some time on my own, Paul?' I asked.

'Yes, I do mind,' he said. 'That's the last thing you need. You need people around you right now, and also when you get back to the island. We're all worried about you, mate.'

We probably did go for a beer – I honestly can't remember. Over the next few days, I retreated to the island, my one-time sanctuary, and into a fog of despondency. Living anywhere but here was unthinkable. Resto and I were inseparable, symbiotic. Being home, the bliss of intimacy with nature, made the imminent separation all the more unbearable. The mind can be a cruel companion in those situations. Yes, there were probably times – awful, fleeting moments – when I wondered whether life held enough promise for me to continue.

The only advice that my dad ever gave me rattled around my head as I headed to my reliable refuge, the beach shack, as the afternoon sun slowly sunk behind the mountains. 'Son, just remember these three things in life,' he had told me. 'Always let your woman think that she's the boss; never go to court to dispute something, only go to resolve a legal matter and enjoy yourself.'

Jeez, Dad, if you could see me right now, you'd think I hadn't done a very good job with any of that, I thought, as a solitary tear rolled off my cheek and dropped onto the sand. I reached over the arm of the deckchair and ran my fingers through the soft granules, obliterating the droplet. I let a handful of sand, cool to the touch, trickle slowly between my fingers, then wandered down to the water's edge and waded out to my waist. *There are two ways this can go, Glasheen.* I sank my knees onto the seabed and silently supplicated. Then I leapt onto my feet again and burst out of the water like Poseidon, shaking the sea out of my hair and beard.

Right, you bastards, there's life in the old dog yet.

Chapter 15

Sorrow

Initially, I'd considered an appeal against the court's ruling. Another reporter who had written about me, Susan Chenery from the *Sydney Morning Herald,* said the newspaper's legal department would help. But, even with their expertise, I couldn't manage to fill in the preliminary forms. It was mind-bogglingly complicated, probably designed to prevent appeals in the first place, and I just didn't have the resources – mental or financial – for another long, drawn-out legal battle. Instead, I set up a GoFundMe campaign with a target of $200,000 in case I ever needed to go back to court to prevent eviction. It was featured prominently in the media and a trickle of money arrived from all around the world – about $4000 in total.

The coverage of my predicament also generated genuine interest in the potential of the island. Iconic Australian entrepreneur, aviator, philanthropist and political activist Dick Smith had lived near us in the North Shore when I was in Sydney, and he'd always had a soft spot for Cape York. I'm told that the Cape York edition of his *Australian Geographic* magazine is still their number one seller. Dick had visited Lockhart River in 2005, shortly after one of the town's darkest days; a Fairchild Swearingen Metroliner, operated by the now defunct Aero-Tropics airline, crashed in the highlands near the airport, killing all fifteen people on board. The weather had been atrocious but the pilot, unaware that conditions were clear to the east, took the normal north-west route over Mount Tozer and hit a cloud-covered ridge. The first I heard of the disaster was when a mate who worked as a coastguard at Airlie Beach in the Whitsundays rang to ask if I'd seen a plane land in the water off Resto, because it took them almost a day to locate the wreckage. The plane was coming from Bamaga and no Lockhart River locals were on board, but my German wwoofer had been booked on the outbound flight from Lockhart. She cancelled at the last minute, so that she could stay a few extra days, although the crash freaked her out and she looked for other ways out of the region.

It was one of the worst crashes in Australian aviation history and, in my view, not totally unexpected. On my very first flight up to Lockhart River from Cairns, I had been amazed at how close we were to the mountains when we emerged from low cloud. And there were many hairy moments after that, in much worse weather. Ever since that disaster, larger planes take a safer, wider approach path across the water. Smaller, nimbler planes are still allowed to duck through an opening in the clouds, though. Aviation safety was one of Dick Smith's many crusades and his visit to the airport confirmed his theory that each remote and rural airport should have a local, trained to operate the radio and give information to the pilot on the safest approach path.

Dick had visited Resto once before, probably to tick Bligh's historic site off his adventure checklist, arriving unannounced in his blue helicopter and wearing his trademark khaki outfit.

Then, when Dick heard about my predicament on Resto, he returned to explore potential solutions and we discussed using the island as a marine research base, because ecology was another of his passions. In return I offered to lend my food marketing expertise to his range of iconic Australian Dick Smith foods. The range was trying to replicate the success of Paul Newman's sauces by featuring Dick's face in the marketing of their brands, which I thought was too restrictive. I believe Dick approached the Australian Institute of Marine Science, based in Townsville, about the marine research idea, but without success. Nevertheless, it was heartening to know that well-connected business contacts were showing an active interest in my plight.

***

It was encouraging that Ricky's health appeared to have stabilised. Rod, her boss at Jobfind in Lockhart River, had been worried that she was burning herself out with all her commitments. He almost forced her to take an extended long weekend every third or fourth week with an all-expenses-paid break in Cairns. And, once every couple of months, Ricky would come over to the island for the weekend, bubbling over with news of the success of one project or another. On one of these visits, around 2011, she was staring wistfully into the fire as we cooked dinner down at the beach shack. 'Anything the matter?' I asked.

'No, just the opposite actually,' she smiled. 'I've met someone in Cairns, Dad. She's lovely. We have so much in common. She's super smart and has a real social conscience. In fact, she talks about this stuff more than me and you! It's early days, but I really think we want the same things in life. I can see a real future together.'

'That's great. Bring her up here soon, I'd love to meet her.'

For a while, Ricky had that infectious spring in her step again. But then I started to notice that, when she stayed here, grog was going walkabout again. There were a few random incidents, too. One time Ricky was donged on the street in Cairns by someone who asked her for a cigarette. Then Rod told me she had missed a couple of planes home. It was obvious to me that she was hitting the bottle again.

Sadly, over the course of a few years, Ricky had become more and more estranged from her mum and her sister, to the point that she wasn't invited back home for a couple of Christmases or her sister Samantha's wedding to a great guy called Myles. We all agreed that it was too great a risk to put her in those family situations where old issues could resurface when the booze started to flow. At least she now had an alternative, and Ricky spent the 2012 Christmas with her girlfriend in Cairns. But the holiday period mustn't have gone to plan ... With her partner's encouragement, Ricky accepted that she was back on the slippery slope and booked herself in for two weeks of intensive Alcoholics Anonymous therapy in Cairns. Her previous spell in rehab, in Sydney, had produced an immediate, if not lasting, effect. It shocked her to see people who were in a far worse position, and I was very proud that she was again facing her demons at this Cairns course.

Towards the end of the second week of the course, Ricky's timetable meant that she had a free lunchtime at home. Her partner worked nearby and came home to share a lunch that Ricky had prepared. Later that afternoon Ricky spoke to Peter, a former colleague in Lockhart, and made plans to visit him that weekend.

Then, when her partner returned home from work, she found Ricky hanging from a tree in the garden.

Ricky's partner rang me as soon as the police had been alerted. There can be nothing quite so devastating for a parent than to hear their daughter has taken her own life. I collapsed into a chair, stunned, and asked her to repeat what she had told me. I simply couldn't believe what I was hearing. I can still barely believe it. There had been so many positive signs that Ricky was getting her life back on track. Why would she throw that all away? Her partner told me there was an empty bottle of spirits in the house, but Peter said she didn't seem drunk when he spoke to her, which could only have been a couple of hours before her final act.

The Thursday plane from Lockhart River to Cairns had already left, so the next flight was first thing in the morning. Skytrans told me it was booked up. I would have begged someone on my knees to give up their seat, but luckily there was a cancellation. There wasn't much more I could do except to try and tell Sylvi and Samantha. There was no answer from their mobiles or home phone, so I asked their local police to go round. Sylvi called later but we were both almost struck dumb with grief.

'We should think about where to scatter her ashes,' I blurted out. In hindsight, it was way too early to be discussing that kind of detail, but I wasn't thinking straight.

There wasn't too much I could do when I arrived in Cairns, except talk to the police and meet her partner. She was as shocked as anyone and obviously devastated, so her family was trying to limit her time with visitors, including me. But the subject of Ricky's ashes had been playing on my mind, and I wanted her partner's opinion.

'Where do you think Ricky would like to be laid to rest?'

'Restoration Island,' she replied instantly.

Back at Cheyenne's home, where I was staying, I was starting to wonder why Sylvi and Samantha weren't due to arrive until Monday, four days after Ricky's death. Something seemed strange and, when we did eventually meet at a quiet restaurant in Cairns, it didn't stay quiet for long. As soon as the subject of her resting place was raised again, Sam let rip.

'Forget this idea of cremation, Dad! Erika wanted to be buried. We'll take you to court if we have to! We've been collecting affidavits.'

Burial? It was the first I'd heard of it and, although it's not the kind of thing that children discuss with their parents, I reckoned I would have known about her wishes, if she had ever expressed any. I was surprised that she'd raised the subject with her mum and sister. I didn't want Ricky to be buried. I believe the spirit is separate to the physical body, and departs at the moment of death. For that reason, a lasting connection forms when ashes are scattered on land that has been significant to the deceased, rather than the confinement of a coffin. I wanted Ricky's ashes to be shared between Restoration Island, Lockhart River and Berridale, where Sylvi and Sam lived, like we'd done with my brother Phil's ashes. And why the hell were courts and affidavits being mentioned?

'This is ridiculous,' I spluttered. 'Why are we talking about legal action? Do my feelings not count? And what about the people of Lockhart, and her partner? They loved her like she was family, too.'

It was already clear that we were in desperate need of mediation, and we hadn't even viewed the body yet. Tensions were running understandably high. I felt like I was being somehow blamed for her death. It was a tense taxi ride to the morgue in the hospital, where I asked to see her first, alone. The moment the mortuary technician pulled back the white sheet was the worst in my life. This couldn't be my Ricky – my spirited, loving, caring, tortured girl. 'What secrets were you keeping from your dad, darling?' I whispered through floods of tears.

That image will haunt me forever, and I really wish I hadn't seen her like that. Dazed, I had to leave the building for fresh air while the others took their turn. We were all handed leaflets by a counsellor about dealing with grief. I was pleased to read that there was no rush to make a decision about the fate of the body, but there was little left to say to my family at that point. Mediation was the only solution, in my opinion.

The following day I received a call from Wayne Butcher, the Mayor of Lockhart River, to tell me that Sylvi, Sam and Myles were arriving on a chartered private flight from Cairns to go to Ricky's place. He couldn't understand why I wasn't booked on the flight with them. By the time I had flown back to Lockhart River later that afternoon on the Skytrans flight, nearly all Ricky's possessions had been removed from her digs. It felt like I was being denied the chance to mourn her properly. The others flew straight back to Cairns, and I cleaned her room in Lockhart River over the next two days. All that was left of hers was a diary and some small personal effects. A set of small salt and pepper pots, shaped as teddy bears, will always be my most cherished possession.

Eventually, the coroner ruled that Ricky's body should be buried in Berridale, in accordance with the majority of the family's wishes. It was made perfectly clear that I wasn't welcome and I'm still distraught that I didn't attend my own daughter's funeral. But what happened can't be changed. Just as distressing is the fact that I have not spoken to Sylvi or Samantha since. I now have a grandson, Connor, who I have never seen.

It's time to forgive each other, if not to forget the hurt and the anger. And I do sincerely hope that we can one day put these differences aside, in honour of Ricky's memory. My memories of my daughter will never fade. I think about my gorgeous girl every single day.

Every. Single. Day.

***

The following few months were the hardest of my life. There was no respite from the torment of Ricky's death. When I was on my own, the silence was deafening. It was impossible to escape the constant internal dialogue. When well-meaning visitors did come to check on my wellbeing, they were treading on eggshells, which didn't help. Only Paul Piva, whose own brother took his life, could recognise when I needed to talk and when to give me space. Resto tried her best, bless her. I don't like to think about what may have happened had I not had daily chores and duties here to distract myself with. But sometimes the island could be suffocating. It was as though the hurt could not escape, and was intensifying like a pressure cooker. I was in deep trouble and needed repair, not restoration. Ernest, my psychiatrist friend, was very concerned and regularly checked to make sure that I wasn't going to do anything drastic. He was also concerned about the effect that Ricky's death would have on Kye. I eventually made an appointment to see the Flying Doctor, who recommended biweekly sessions with a psychologist, but I just wasn't convinced that western methods were going to work. Who knows what abnormalities a mind-doctor might unearth when rummaging around my head? Pills and potions were not going to fix my broken spirit. I needed healing at a deeper, more fundamental level. And there was only one person who really understood me at that level: Grace.

Our plans for a healing retreat had predictably fizzled out after Grace's partner's intervention, but we remained in contact over email and social media. She even sent Phil and his deckies a mankini each, claiming the boys had been too uptight during her visit. The last time I'd heard from her, she was based in Phuket in Thailand, and people were travelling from all over the world for her services.

Christmas 2013 was approaching, and I desperately wanted to avoid being alone for it. I felt like I needed some respite from Australia. Jake, my old mining business partner, was living in Laos, where he still worked on various exploration projects. He insisted that I join his family for the holiday period and it was the perfect chance to catch up with Grace, too. She was so tricky to contact that, as Christmas approached, I decided to travel to Pa Tong Beach to track her down, and left Cheyenne and his daughter to look after Quassi and the island.

For four days I was like a private detective. I left messages at her last forwarding addresses until finally she called my guest house, the Little Buddha. 'Dave, so lovely to hear from you and I'm so sorry it's taken me so long,' she said. 'I've taken a leaf out of your book and gone off grid. But I can come to you in a couple of days, if that helps.'

'Grace, you've no idea how much that will help,' I said, already feeling relieved just to hear her gentle voice. It meant I had a couple of days to kill in Pa Tong, although the hustle and bustle of South-East Asia proved a jarring contrast to Resto's calm.

Meeting Grace again was one of the most intense experiences of my life. We found a quiet cafe overlooking the ocean, away from all the tourists. There was so much to catch up on but without any need to go into detail about Ricky's death. Grace instinctively knew how much I was suffering. When we were on Resto, she never once tried to convert me to the ancient healing she practised, because she knew I didn't believe in mysticism. But here, when she finally took my hands in hers and stared silently into my eyes, I felt a power from a different dimension. All my pain, accumulated over many years, seemed to drain from my body. Then she let go of my hands, stood slowly and leant over to kiss me tenderly on the forehead. There was no need to linger and she left without another word, bearing my emotional burden. Her job was done.

Chapter 16

Survival

The story of Bligh's stay on Resto continues to capture the imagination. After Russell Crowe's visit I learned that another Hollywood superstar, Errol Flynn, also visited the island in 1932, the year before he starred as Fletcher Christian in the film *In the Wake of the Bounty.* Flynn and three friends sailed a leaking yacht called *Sirocco* from Sydney up to Papua New Guinea, gambling, womanising and fighting in each port. Sounds like a few of my mates! In his book, *Beam Ends,* Flynn wrote of swimming in the Restoration Island 'lagoon' then lying on the beach, trying to imagine what was going through the minds of Bligh and his men when they were confronted by Aboriginal people in war paint, waving spears, over on the mainland. I wonder whether, by lagoon, he meant the water that's almost enclosed by the crescent of sand that forms once or twice a year at the spit. It's something I find myself thinking about frequently – how attached I am to history here, yet so detached from the present.

There had been two previous attempts to recreate Bligh's journey from the Tongan island of Tofua to Timor, but they were before my time on the island. Neither voyage was very authentic, apparently; they'd used almanacs and charts for navigation, torches and modern time pieces, and they'd made unscheduled stopovers. Then in 2010, famous Australian adventurer and round-the-world yachtsman, Don McIntyre, stepped up to attempt a more realistic re-enactment. His journey was sponsored by the whisky company Talisker to raise funds for motor neurone disease research in Sheffield, England. His team initially struggled to find a crew, so I volunteered on the dual condition that I could finish at Resto and that my friend Kate Yeomans, a capable kayaker, would also be invited. I didn't fancy that amount of time in a boat with complete strangers! Kate got cold feet when she discovered the level of media interest and, by then,

I was reluctant to sign their mountains of waivers and disclaimers. Even though I was sixty-seven years old at the time, I was confident I would have handled the physical challenge – I just didn't want to sign my life away.

McIntyre's journey to Resto sounded horrendous. One guy, a Pom, was carrying on like a pork chop about the standard of the meat rations and lack of toilet paper. Bligh's crew had to eat a whole sea bird between them: head, beak, feathers, the lot. McIntyre was in agony for much of the voyage, until he passed six kidney stones in twenty-four hours. Still, the boat made it to Resto, where famous Aussie television presenter Charles Wooley and a crew from *60 Minutes* was waiting, before it set off again for East Timor.

While McIntyre's re-enactment raised the bar, a British reality television series called *Mutiny* took it to the next level. The series was fronted by former special forces soldier Ant Middleton, who had found fame on the British survival show *SAS: Who Dares Wins*. The producers paid attention to every detail – including the near-exact replica of the boat and accurate allocation of provisions – although a few shortcuts were inevitably taken. The *Mutiny* boat arrived in September 2016 and the island was as dry as a dead dog's donger, but Bligh arrived in late May just after the wet season. It would have been easy for Bligh and his men to find running water, just by scraping away at the surface of the slopes. The producers considered going to elaborate lengths to pump water uphill so that it would appear that the men found it on their own, but the plan was abandoned and the scene was cut.

The eight crew members were then free to forage for food, and I tried to provide a few tips. I felt sorry for the poor bastards. Some were begging to chew on the leftover chop bones from the dog bowl. But, if you know what to look for, it's not difficult to survive on Resto. When Major Les Hiddins visited the island a few years ago for his TV show *The Bush Tucker Man,* he found thirty-five different foods on the island. But you also have to be careful. When Kye was small, he was playing near the bushes while one of the elderly Kuuku

Ya'u women, Lorraine Claremont, was visiting. 'Old fella, stop your son right now!' she said to me. 'He will die if he eats that berry.'

'Jeez! Thanks, Lorraine,' I said, grabbing Kye away from the bush. 'What other things should we avoid?'

'I will tell you when you need to know,' she said. By then I'd learned not to push too hard for detail.

I warned the British participants about this poisonous bush, and then pointed out the edible plants, like the acidic beach almonds, edible pigface, bush cherry, native capers and the wongai trees. They could mash up wongai plums with fresh water to produce a jam that would make their mouldy biscuits half-palatable. They could also add water to their empty rum barrels to make rum water. The lemongrass in the paddock might add a little flavour to their stew. And, with a few rocks, they could bash a few oysters loose, just like Bligh's men had done on their first day. In reality, I took a screwdriver and hammer down to the rocks and helped the men fill a few jars.

There were coconuts galore, too; the challenge was breaking into them. I already suspected Ant's survival instincts were responsible for the disappearance of a bag of bugs and a few bottles of grog from the fridge in the out-of-bounds area. So perhaps he felt obliged to show some true leadership by demonstrating how to drink from a coconut. Normally, I would use a spike to break into the husk and then clumsily crack the shell with a machete. Unless Paul Piva was around; he can tear off the husk with his bare hands and then slice the top off the nut like a knife through butter. Ant was only allowed to use the blunt machete from the boat but, even so, his technique left a lot to be desired. I was also surprised to find a survival expert gripping the coconut between his shins while he hacked away.

'Shouldn't you be a bit more...' I started to say, as Ant looked up mid-slash, just when the machete bounced off the husk and straight into his calf. It wasn't caught on camera and I'm pretty sure his reaction couldn't have been broadcast anyway. The

Queen's English has never been so abused. My reaction was equally predictable – general whimpering and wooziness. It was a clean cut and the production team's medic stitched him up without problem. If he had been using a *parang,* a sharp machete from Indonesia, he would have taken his foot clean off. Ant later described the voyage as the hardest mental challenge he'd ever undertaken. It was obvious to me these men were nearly broken when they set off to sail the enormous distance to Timor.

***

This interlude, among others, gradually helped to moderate the intensity of the pain Ricky's death caused. She had been a real animal lover and often took in local pups that needed help. For her, money was no object when it came to nursing them back to health. So when she died, there was never any question that I would adopt her dog, named Locky for obvious reasons. He was another handsome dog, smaller than Quassi, with more of a slender dingo shape and, at eighteen months, a good few years younger. He and Quassi hit it off whenever Ricky brought him over to visit and the two dogs became a real double act around the camp fire when we asked them to sing for their supper. Their finest performances were around full moon. Lots of pet owners will tell you that their animals' behaviour changes during this period. Something odd happens, for sure, but there was another good explanation for Quassi and Locky's showmanship on full moons: the trawler boys were a captive audience and the dogs probably received more titbits than usual. Quassi once had a beautiful, deep baritone voice but, when Locky arrived with an even deeper howl, he lost confidence and changed into a yappy tenor. It wasn't unusual for Quassi and Locky to swim in the water together, but I tried to stop them. It was impossible to keep an eye on them all day every day, though.

One day, several months after taking Locky in, another regular solo kayaking mate, Anthony Malloch, came to stay with me for a few days. Anthony loved adventure, and wrote about his travels in a popular blog called Sea Mongrels. He was showing me his new reverse osmosis desalination water pump, which forced salt water through very fine membranes at very high pressure to produce drinking water while at sea. Although it fitted in the space at his feet in the kayak, it looked heavy and complicated. But if the alternative was running out of fresh water, I could see the appeal. Then a shrill yelp from further down the beach interrupted our chat.

We looked up to see Quassi race over, then skid into a U-turn, in his highly agitated I-can-see-a-croc state. Anthony and I ran after him towards the water but there was nothing to see, until two sneaky eyes broke the surface. Two sneaky eyes and a squashed snout. Boxhead. The bastard had returned, after all these years, wanting revenge for the time I hit him between the eyes with the rock.

'Where's Locky?' I yelled. 'Quassi, where's Locky?' That made him even more anxious and I thought he might charge into the water. 'Grab some gibbers!' I shouted to Anthony. 'The prick must've dragged Locky under and left him on the bottom. But he's not getting Quassi. We have to put a stop to this right now!'

Then Quassi *did* charge into the water. He was ready to take on Boxhead for killing his best mate. I screamed at him to come back, while Anthony hurled a few gibbers at the croc. There could only be one outcome if Quassi went any further in, and I wasn't about to do a Crocodile Winky and dive on Boxhead's back. I knew that the muscles that opened the croc jaws are really weak, but I didn't have any rope handy to tie his mouth shut. So I could only watch on in horror and howl for Quassi to come back. Then, luckily, one of Anthony's rocks landed just close enough to remind Boxhead of our last confrontation, and he reluctantly disappeared back below the surface, to retrieve Locky as his prize. I was devastated, especially because Locky had been Ricky's cherished dog. Quassi was inconsolable and hung around that spot for weeks, heart-achingly waiting for his mate to return. I'll never be convinced that

Boxhead has gone for good until I see the evidence, because these bastards can live for more than seventy years.

The attack naturally freaked Quassi out, and he became very insecure whenever I left the island. He started to follow the boat out, swimming after it for about fifty metres, and he probably would have tried to follow me all the way over to the mainland if I'd let him. So I either had to tie him up, which I didn't want to do, or drive the boat up and down the beach in the shallow water six or seven times until Quassi was too exhausted and gave up trying to follow. He had become warier of crocs and would rigidly stand guard behind a tree and grow under his breath whenever one appeared.

While I was spending Christmas with Jake in Laos, I learned from Cheyenne that Quassi had been ambushed again in the shallows. I'll never know whether it was our old foe on a crazed revenge mission, or just a case of wrong place, wrong time. Either way Quassi received a nasty bite, much deeper than his first wound. When Quassi came limping back to the house and Cheyenne saw how deep his wound was, he took him to the nurses in Lockhart immediately. It was too deep and wide to stitch, so the nurses had to sedate Quassi and follow a YouTube video on how to staple the wound from the inside, then close the outside. He was a tough cookie, though, and was soon back on his feet, looking for more trouble.

***

Humans can be taught how to avoid the dangerous creatures up here. Animals can only learn by trial and error. Fortunately, Quassi was used to seeing snakes and had never chased one. But one Friday afternoon, when I was washing the dishes after lunch, I spotted him fussing around some building materials that had been piled up for a few days. He was pawing at the planks of wood, when all of a sudden there was an almighty commotion. Quassi sprinted away with a beautiful, long snake dead in his mouth. When I caught up with him I could see a big hole in the snake's belly, but no sign of any bite on Quassi.

'Jeez, that was a lucky escape, you crazy mutt! Leave those bloody snakes alone in future, okay?' I scolded, while rubbing his belly.

As the evening wore on, Quassi started to show signs of discomfort. There was an occasional whimper and he was a bit slower than normal. *This isn't right,* I thought. *Perhaps the snake did get a bite in first.* I wasn't an expert on snakes, but I did know that some of the deadliest in the world lived on Cape York. The region's home to the coastal taipan, northern death adder, western brown and king brown snake. It wouldn't have taken much venom from any of these species to floor a human, never mind a dog.

For humans, the first-aid advice is to keep pressure on the bite wound with a bandage, and not to wrap a tourniquet above the wound or try and suck out the poison. But I still couldn't see any bite marks under his fur, so I didn't know where to apply any pressure. In the morning he was much worse and I rang Lockhart. The visiting vet, who comes around once a month, wasn't due until after the weekend.

'Never mind the vet,' I said to Lynn. 'Can one of you help?'

'Afraid not, Dave, the nearest antivenene is stored in Cairns. There's nothing in Lockhart,' she said.

'What do you mean there's no antivenene here? This is tropical Australia! There are poisonous snakes everywhere. What happens when a human is bitten?' I was astounded to hear that antivenene was no longer stocked, just because it was perishable and too costly. These medicines are quite specific to the species of snake, and it's unusual for people to be able to identify the culprit species. But I still had the snake as evidence and, after speaking to a few locals on the phone, I was more and more convinced that it was a taipan. If a human had been bitten, the Flying Doctor would have been here straight away – as a general rule you need to be in hospital within four hours. But there was no equivalent service for pets.

There was no way I could afford a private helicopter, even if I could find one at short notice. So there was nothing I could do until the vet returned on Monday. I was going out of my mind with worry, because Quassi's health was rapidly going downhill. And he knew he was in trouble. I tried to make him eat and drink, but he was having none of it. I tried walking him – which I now know isn't helpful, because it boosts circulation and spreads the poison around the body – but he could barely walk. I wasn't sure he would make it through the night and I let him sleep on my bed for comfort. By morning he was barely conscious and could scarcely manage a whimper. Nothing can compare with seeing your own daughter on a mortuary slab; but seeing Quassi like this was another wound to an already fragile heart. There was nothing more I could do apart from hold him in arms, let him know I was there for him and watch the life drain from his eyes. My big, handsome, mighty Quassi – the best friend any man could have – was gone. Safe travels to doggy heaven, mate.

***

Tom, a German mental health nurse who worked in the Lockhart clinic, heard about Quassi's death and realised that I needed a new companion. His own pet was a pure dingo called Toya, who had just had a litter with a dingo with a bit of kelpie in his genes. Dingoes get a bad rap, but it's unfair. It's largely due to the famous case of the death of two-month-old baby girl, Azaria Chamberlain, on a family camping trip to Uluru in 1980. The phrase 'a dingo ate my baby' became famous around the world and the story was made into the film *A Cry in the Dark,* starring Meryl Streep.

The dingo is actually a beautiful dog, which usually lives in feral packs and is notoriously difficult to domesticate. Although it lives in the wild all around Australia, it's now a listed threatened species, partly due to cross-breeding with domestic dogs. As soon as I set eyes on this puppy, I could see why someone would want a dingo as a pet. She was a stunner, as bright as a button, and needed a name to match. A few weeks earlier, a competitive catamaran racer called Polly Fitzgerald had turned up on the beach. She was young, adventurous, energetic and red-haired – much like this pup. So Polly it was.

My pet name for her was Wild Dog, but Polly loved human company and was at her happiest when all the humans were in one spot, either in the house or down at the beach shack, where she could keep an eye on us from a respectful distance. One night, when Polly was about a year old and Kye was visiting, Phil and I prepared a lamb roast for the spit and we were enjoying a few beers before dinner. The sky was cloudless and the sea as calm as black marble, mottled with streaks of sliver moonlight.

We were just about to tuck in when I saw a three-metre wall of white water hurtle towards the beach. 'Phil, have you ever heard of a tsunami on the Great Barrier Reef?' I asked.

'Nah, mate. How much have you had?' he replied.

'Look, there! It's a bloody tidal wave.'

The wave smashed onto the reef, lifted the tinny up like it was made of tinfoil and dumped it down onto the beach headfirst with an almighty crash.

Water surged up the beach way further than the king tide mark, almost up to the beach shack.

'What the hell was that?' I asked.

The three of us stood gazing out into the darkness, wondering whether Kim Jong-un had detonated his nuclear weapons. The big waves continued for ten minutes before a lull and silence – apart from the sound of Polly wolfing down the whole roast lamb, having seized the opportunity when our backs were turned.

'We'd better check if there's any damage to the tinny,' Phil suggested.

'Are you mad?' I asked. 'Until we know what's happening, I'm going nowhere near the boat. What if the same thing happens again? You'd be killed if that thing landed on top of you! Let's wait until morning.'

At first light I discovered that the motor was smashed and I'd lost the fibreglass box I stored all my equipment in, as well as the spare fuel tank. The boat was practically useless. I rang round to see if anyone else had been affected, and a few people were also assessing damage to their boats.

One bloke was fixing the windsock at the airport on Hicks Island at the time, and had seen the whole thing. The USS *Ronald Reagan,* the $4-billion US Navy nuclear flagship, had thundered down the coast at about fifty knots, just less than a kilometre from the island in the shipping channel – way closer than it should have been. It was heading to a field-training exercise called Talisman Sabre near Rockhampton. The ship was effectively a giant speed boat, and it created giant ripples.

As a good citizen of Cape York, I alert the customs or quarantine people whenever I suspect something non-kosher is happening – particularly if a small plane is flying at night. Lots of dodgy stuff goes on in these parts. Crocs are still hunted illegally for their skins and there's also a lot of wildlife smuggling. Green pythons are very expensive on the black market, and fines for selling them can run into the hundreds of thousands. Birds, especially rare species like the eclectus parrot and palm cockatoo, are also trapped and either smuggled onto yachts, or spirited away on light aircraft that use remote landing strips. It's probably way more profitable than drug trafficking, but I care about the rare species more than the drug smuggling. In fact, I was once awarded a Top Watch certificate by Australian Quarantine and Inspection Service (AQIS) Far North for 'looking after everyone's interests'. It was another way of saying that I'm a conscientious dobber.

This time, when I contacted the usual officials to discuss the US vessel's dangerous coastal jaunt, nobody wanted to know about it.

'What do you mean you have no knowledge of this ship?' I asked, incredulous. 'It's about 300 metres long! It carries about ninety planes! Did it slip under your radar? My mate saw it with his own eyes.'

'I'm afraid we cannot comment on classified information,' the uncivil servant replied, brusquely.

'Well, who's going to pay for my boat? I'm buggered without that tinny.'

'Your observations will be passed on to our American counterparts,' came the reply. I'm still waiting for their response. Trump, if you're reading this, you still owe me a couple of grand for a new outboard motor.

Chapter 17

Solo

Sea kayakers are a fascinating breed, especially the solo adventurers. What motivates these people to push their mental and physical endurance to such extremes? Is their quest similar to my own – to redefine success by learning to conquer the challenges of solitude? I have certainly found kindred spirits in regular visitors like Anthony Malloch, the Sea Mongrel, and Crocodile Winky, and I look forward to their company. Their perspectives seem to mature like fine wines during those endless hours at sea and, when uncorked and allowed to breathe around the camp fire, they pack a delicious complexity. These people are in tune with the failings of the modern world, but choose to tune out and use their kayaks as an escape, in much the same way that the island is my protection from reality.

Solo extreme female kayakers command an even greater degree of respect. Their adventures seem to take feats of endurance beyond the boundaries of their male counterparts. Freya Hoffmeister was the first to arrive, totally unannounced, during a record-breaking attempt. *Have I been in the sun too long today?* I asked myself, when this strapping brunette German woman strode confidently across the paddock at dusk. She certainly didn't look like a classical mermaid. 'Freya Hoffmeister, pleased to meet you,' she announced, offering her hand and then crushing mine like plasticine. 'You have probably heard of me. People call me the Goddess of Love to the Seas. I'm a big deal in kayaking circles.'

'Pleased to meet you, Freya,' I said. 'My name is Dave. I had no idea you were coming – it's a big deal for me because I like to prepare.'

'Don't worry, I will only stop tonight. I will be the first woman to kayak solo and unsupported all the way around Australia. I must finish within 350 days to beat the male record. I will do this easily. Did I tell you I was a former Miss Germany contestant?'

Freya was unlike any kayaker I had met. There was a significant ego inhabiting this significant frame. She had already been attacked by a shark and, when I told Crocodile Winky about her visit a few weeks later, he was seriously worried that she would not survive the eight-day crossing of the Gulf of Carpentaria. But Freya completed the 14,000-kilometre trip in 322 days – twenty-eight days faster than the only previous successful attempt. She's since kayaked 27,000 kilometres around South America, which took her thirty months, and is now preparing for North America. There was one chink in her mental armour, though. She succumbed to accepting one glass of wine under persistent pressure.

***

Sandy Robson, a young Western Australian woman, was also attempting to kayak solo around Australia. She emailed me in advance to ask if she could forward some food parcels and collect them on her way past Resto. Even from her emails, I could tell there was a different humility to Sandy and

I looked forward to her visit. It was hard to gauge exactly when she would turn up but, a few days after her expected arrival date, the phone rang just as last light was fading. 'Dave? It's Sandy Robson,' she said, breathlessly. 'I think I'm quite close to Restoration Island but I have a bit of a situation here. A bloody big croc just attacked the back of the kayak. I gave him a slap with my paddle and I made it to shore. But now he's patrolling the beach and won't let me get back in the water. Any chance you could come and pick me up? Please.'

'Righto, Sandy, don't panic,' I told her, trying to hide my own panic. 'There's nothing anyone can do tonight, because the light's fading and the tide's going out. Give me your satellite phone number and an exact lat. and long., and I'll be with you at first light. All you can do tonight is find some high ground and light a fire. He'll not bother you.'

Sandy provided her coordinates and I worked out that she was near Orchid Point, near the old mission site and the mouth of Lockhart River.

It was blowing over forty knots in the morning. The police didn't have anyone licensed to drive a boat in those conditions so I had to go for her myself, although I shouldn't really have been taking my boat out in that kind of weather. I persuaded Phil to be in the area in case I found myself in trouble. But when I turned up at the coordinates Sandy had provided, she was nowhere to be seen. *That's okay,* I thought, *I'll call her satellite phone and check the coordinates.* There was a digit missing in her phone number! *Jeez, now we're stuffed.*

I had to think on my feet and I called the police again to tell them this was an emergency and they needed to track down Sandy's family in Western Australia for the correct phone number. As more and more time elapsed, I became increasingly worried about her safety. There was no way the croc would have left her alone. He'd sooner sit there for days than pass up a tasty meal. I had no idea how much fuel she had for a fire, and the mouth of any river around here is prime croc country.

Sandy was in real danger – and I was out of my comfort zone.

When Sandy's mum eventually called with the correct number, I discovered that she was probably only half a kilometre away, a couple of beaches further up the coast. I had just enough tide to work with to land, tie her kayak to my boat and then fight our way back out into the waves. Amazingly, she told me she would usually carry on kayaking in those conditions, but she hadn't slept and decided to stay the night on Resto. When the weather system blew over, Sandy didn't need as much persuading as Freya had to join me for a glass of champagne at the beach bar to celebrate the successful rescue operation, and for her to tell me about the plans for her next adventure.

'Have you heard of Oskar Speck?' she asked. I hadn't. 'Oskar was twenty-five when his business went bust in 1932, and he decided there must be more to life. Come to think of it, he sounds a bit like you. Anyway, he originally set off in his kayak for Cyprus from his home on the River Danube, but then carried on through Syria and

Iraq, past India and Sri Lanka and, seven years and 23,000 kilometres later, he arrived at Saibai Island in the Torres Strait. Unfortunately, he had no idea that the war had just started and, after all that unadulterated freedom, he was locked up for six years for being a German. Now that's tough luck, isn't it?'

Midway through Sandy's story, without warning, we heard a man shouting my name from the direction of the other beach behind us. I jumped up and raced over to find Anthony Malloch, running along the sand, having dragged his own kayak onto the southern end of the beach. 'Dave, you've ... got to ... help,' he said, gasping for breath. 'There's a woman kayaker ... called Sandy Robson ... in real trouble. She sent out ... a mayday ... and I can't locate her.'

'Anthony, slow down, come this way and let me introduce you to someone.'

'We don't have time for bloody tea and scones,' he barked. 'This is a matter of life or death.'

'Anthony, meet Sandy,' I announced as we rounded the corner to find Sandy with her feet up on the concrete table, draining another glass of bubbles.

'What the...?!' shouted Anthony. 'I've just kayaked for two days solid from Night Island to try and answer your distress call. I've been worried sick! And you've been living it up with Dave all this time?' He was seriously pissed off, but saw the funny side after I'd opened another bottle. Sandy's attempt to kayak around Australia failed, but she did manage to recreate the Oscar Speck's journey from Germany to Australia, earning her the title of Australian Adventurer of the Year.

***

Polly was also beginning to demonstrate an adventurous streak. She loved to sit patiently on the beach when birds appeared around a bait ball. The birds wait for the big fish or dolphins to do the hard work, then swoop for the smaller fish that have been wounded or killed. Polly was after the same spoils, and saw the birds as competitors. Once, she decided to skip the bait fish and instead grabbed the tail of a blacktip reef shark, which was well over a metre long. It snapped back at her in retaliation. Polly raced out of the water like a whippet. The wound wasn't deep enough to require stitches, and I was careful to regularly apply Betadine to prevent infection. From that day on, she had a permanent smiley-face scar on her back.

Polly seemed to have been born with a smile on her face, too. Whenever I returned to the island, unlike Quassi, who would go crazy, Polly sat waiting demurely on the beach until I was out of the boat to welcome me home. She'd jump up on her hind legs so we could waltz along the beach like a couple of dainty ballroom dancers. She was a real flirt with visitors, too, and would pester anyone who didn't show her affection. Then, just when she'd earned their trust by protectively sleeping at their feet, she might steal their toothbrush from a washbag or their laundry from the line.

Polly was a real favourite with the trawler boys. Whenever a boat appeared, she waited patiently for her 'Polly bag' of leftover scraps and old bones. One night she must have swallowed a chop bone without chewing it and began to make a horrible rasping sound, trying to cough it up. I couldn't see the bone but could tell there was a small piece lodged at the back of her jaw, preventing her from opening or closing her mouth properly. It was like she had lockjaw. She could drink, but over the course of the next few days she couldn't eat a thing and was going downhill rapidly. I couldn't cope with the thought of losing another dog.

The vet, Joanne Squires, was not due back at Lockhart for a few days, so my only option was to put Polly in a cage and onto the plane for a nurse from Joanne's mobile clinic to meet her at Cairns airport. It was easier said than done. It was hard enough trying to cut her claws, let alone cage her. When we reached the airport, I lifted Polly up towards the cage and she went bananas. It was understandable – she was virtually a wild animal, after all.

'Is that a dingo?' one of the airport staff then asked. Thank goodness I had my wits about me. You can't officially keep dingoes as pets. On the island it would have been easy for me to argue that she lived in the wild because she did roam free most of the time.

'No mate, she's a kelpie,' I quickly answered. 'See that little black streak there? You'd never get that on a dingo.' It was enough to throw him off the scent and save myself from spending the next few days filling in forms before she would be allowed on a plane. I finally wrestled Polly into the cage and listened as she howled her way onto the plane. The wait for the call from the vet was agony. Would they need to operate? Had she even survived the flight?

'Mr Glasheen, I have Polly the ... *ahem* ... 'kelpie' here. What seems to be the problem?' Joanne asked.

'What's the problem?' I spluttered in exasperation. 'She can't open her mouth, that's the bloody problem. Call yourself a vet? There's a piece of bone stuck there.'

'She can open her mouth just fine, and there's no bone in her mouth or throat,' she said. 'In fact, she'll be on the next plane home.' The bone must have either dislodged or dissolved in her saliva. It was one expensive lamb chop, make no mistake. When the return flight landed and I collected Polly, she was as cool as a cucumber. As I opened the cage door, she hopped out and looked at me as if to say 'what the hell was all that about?'

***

In Far North Queensland, the intense heat and humidity can suck the energy from your bones, especially during the hot, damp summer months. It can make people irritable, sleepless and anxious – signs of 'going troppo', or losing your mind in the tropics. For me, it's the opposite. I love the warmth. It relaxes and invigorates me – but I do take precautions, like staying in the shade, especially when the sun is directly overhead, to avoid sunstroke and sunburn. Melanoma rates continue to soar in these parts. Other people, especially English wwoofers, ignore my warnings and prefer to play games with the sun rather than return home without a tan. The sun always wins. One girl could barely blink when I dropped her off at the airport, because her eyelids were burnt to a crisp and the rest of her body was one big blister.

It's also crucial to stay hydrated, too. Perhaps on this occasion, I had been working too long on the new boat garden in direct sunshine, or perhaps I hadn't been drinking enough water, but as I wandered over to the generator shed to turn off the power converter for the night, I fell without warning. I may have fainted, or maybe I just tripped, but I knew instantly that I was in serious trouble. The pain in my hip and leg was excruciating. I could feel, almost hear, the broken bones grinding together when I tried to move.

Flat on my back on the concrete floor, I needed a plan. I had to make it back to the house to try and contact someone, otherwise I could've been lying there for days without food or water. Screaming in agony as only men can, I managed to sit up slightly, grab the bench and pull myself upright. It took me several minutes just to compose myself. For some reason, I was still intent on switching off the converter, probably thinking that to leave it running all night might cause lasting damage. Then, I shuffled around to look for something that would help me to reach the house. I found a small stepladder and used it as a kind of Zimmer frame to make my way slowly across the paddock. For every two steps forward, I needed a two-minute break. I was sweating like a racehorse and gasping for a drink. Polly knew I was in trouble and slowly guided me back to the house, whimpering all the way and lying at my feet whenever I stopped. That sixty-metre stretch of ground took me almost an hour to cover.

First, I needed water. Putting my weight on the work surfaces, I shimmied along to the kitchen and grabbed two bottles, which I had luckily pre-filled from the tank, and two paracetamols. The bed and chair were tempting, but I decided to stay on my feet because I worried I might not be able to stand up again if I sat down. Then I reached for the wireless landline and called the clinic at Lockhart. My mate Dave Manning was on duty. 'Dave, it's Davo,' I croaked. 'I'm in serious shit here. I reckon I've busted my hip. I've taken two paracetamols, but can you get someone out here with any of the good stuff?'

'Sorry, Davo, I'm on my own here. Look, I'll call the Flying Doctor and they will organise the air ambulance. Deep breathing, mate, and plenty of ice.' Ice? I wasn't about to drag myself back to the bloody freezer. The Flying Doctor told me that because the injury wasn't life threatening, I would have to wait until morning for the heli-ambulance. Next I tried my mate Jimbo at Portland Roads. I remembered that he had a pair of crutches, which I had borrowed when I tore a ligament in my knee climbing into my tinny at Portland Roads a few years back. On that occasion, I couldn't put any weight on my knee by the time I reached the island, so I'd flopped overboard headfirst into the shallow water and dragged myself up the beach.

Jimbo no longer had the crutches but he did arrange for a friend of his, who was out on his fishing boat with some mates, to come over even though it was already nearly dark. The tides prevented these blokes from going back into Lockhart that night for any medicine, so there was little they could do other than make me comfortable in a chair and check I had lots of water, because the temperature wouldn't drop below thirty degrees all night. 'Could one of you fellas stay the night?' I pleaded. 'It would make me feel much better.'

'Sorry mate, we need to get back to the boat,' said the fisho. 'But chew on this ganja. That will help you sleep.' He handed me a big lump of dope. It was ten times more effective than the pills I'd taken and I did manage a few minutes' sleep, maybe even a few giggles with Miranda and Phyllis, who were used to broken limbs and looked on dispassionately. It was the longest night of my life and I genuinely felt I was going to have a heart attack whenever I accidentally shifted in the chair.

At 9am the helicopter arrived with one doctor and one paramedic. The doc told me that my femur was probably broken, and then there was a whirlwind of activity. A morphine drip was inserted into my arm and I was soon on a stretcher being lifted into the helicopter to fly to Lockhart River where the Flying Doctor was waiting to take me to Cairns. The morphine started to wear off a few minutes into the flight so when we hit some pockets of turbulence, I asked the nurse for more medication. Suddenly, I wasn't flying above the Great Barrier Reef; I was soaring through space like Superman, but disintegrating because I was travelling at warp factor seven.

'Stop! I want to get off!' I screamed.

'We're nearly there, Mr Glasheen. You can't get off the helicopter,' the nursed said soothingly.

'Not the bloody helicopter, the Starship Enterprise! Or whatever I'm on. What the hell's happening? There'll be nothing left of me in a minute. Hit the brake thrusters, please.'

The nurse had injected me with ketamine – horse tranquiliser. And I reckon the dose she used would have flattened a thoroughbred. How some people can use ketamine recreationally, I will never know. The classic adverse side effect of ketamine is severe hallucinations. I was aware of where I was, but I was also on another plane of consciousness. It completely freaked me out and my heart was going like the clappers. Since then I have been advised to take antiarrhythmic drugs to control irregular heartbeats, but I swear it wasn't a problem before that ketamine injection.

At the hospital, X-rays showed that the head of the femur, the ball that fits in the hip socket, was badly fractured. My bones had become brittle through osteoporosis, a common condition older people experience when bones fail to absorb calcium. When the doctor told me that one in four people may have some form of brittle bones it sounded like an epidemic. In my case, an overactive thyroid was also a factor. An operation to insert two steel pins was the only option to repair the break. The surgeon looked like he had come straight from his Year 8 biology lesson to show me the operating table contraption. My head would be strapped down at one end and my feet at the other so they could rotate me like a pig on a spit. It was not reassuring, especially for someone who had never been under the knife before. Then I was presented with a consent form to sign.

'What are the chances of something going wrong, doc?' I asked.

'That's very rare – we only lose patients in about five per cent of cases.' Five per cent? Jeez, I was hoping for better odds than that!

Thankfully, I was one of the 95 per cent to survive, and I was up and about the very next day after the operation, with the help of a proper Zimmer frame. All the nurses fussed over me, which I enjoyed, but I stubbornly refused their help. When you are so used to your independence, it's hard to suddenly accept assistance. I progressed to a frame with wheels within a week and then graduated to a walking stick by the time I left hospital. The doctors wanted me close by, so I stayed in Cairns for three more weeks, bored out of my brains.

There was general reluctance among the medicos to allow me to return straight to the island on my own, so Phil found a 'carer' through a friend. This bloke was out of work and, in becoming my official carer, he would be entitled to more benefit. We all travelled back to Resto on Phil's trawler, which was fine except for when I had to climb up and down the ladder from the wheelhouse. Back on the island, the boys loaded up my tinny with supplies and helped me into my boat. From that moment on, I essentially had to look after the carer, although he disappeared into the bush camp and I hardly saw him again. In any case, I didn't actually need any help, I just had to take things slowly for a while.

***

One year on and the hip still isn't as mobile as it once was. Climbing into the boat in deeper water can be a bit of a struggle, or it may take me an extra day to mow the paddock, and it's been a while since I bush-bashed the tracks up to the Incredible Rocks. Sure, I'm never going to beat Usain Bolt in a race along the beach, but the hip doesn't actually prevent me from doing anything. I plod along just fine. The fall was an eye-opener, though, and a call from a Spanish friend reminded me to think about the bigger picture. This mate, Alvaro Cerezo, runs a company called Docastaway, which sells unique castaway experiences to travellers.

Alvaro told me I had become the longest-surviving castaway in the world. The 'claim' was previously held by a Japanese guy called Masafumi Nagasaki, better known as 'the naked hermit'. For nearly thirty years, he had lived on the island of Sotobanari, in the Yaeyama Islands, an archipelago in the south-west of Okinawa Prefecture, Japan. Nagasaki actively shunned company and chalked off his days on the island on a rock. That seemed a bit weird to me, as though he was trying to punish himself for something by forgoing company and basic needs. He didn't like to talk about his backstory, but there were suggestions that he used to run a hostess club in the port of Niigata, and something inside him snapped when he learned how much the seas were being polluted. So we share some similarities, in that we both distanced ourselves from what is happening to our planet. We'd both had our fill of the consequences of consumerism. I take my hat off to him, because he apparently survived solely off food from the land and the sea – although he did look really skinny and unwell. He was always naked, too, even on the rare occasions he was being filmed. I may not live a normal life, but I do cover up for company.

All castaways are inevitably compared to Robinson Crusoe. Daniel Defoe's classic story is about a man who ran away from home to join the navy and found himself washed up on a remote desert island where he spent more than two decades in solitude before discovering Man Friday's footprint. (I would be extremely surprised if I discovered that someone else had been living on Resto for the last twenty years without my knowledge!) Until then, Robinson Crusoe had no option but to fend for himself: he built a little fortress, glazed pots, baked bread and stitched clothes from animal skins. There's no need for me to do any of that. So Nagasaki was perhaps more like Robinson Crusoe. Once he chose the castaway life, Nagasaki wanted nothing to do with the world he left behind. He opted for the extreme existence that was forced upon Crusoe. I choose the best of both worlds – isolation with occasional company.

In 2018, the authorities moved eighty-two-year-old Nagasaki to the nearest city because his health was failing. In a rare interview he once spoke of his desire to die on the island, surrounded by nature. Now he is locked away in a nursing home or hospital. That's my worst nightmare. I'd be climbing the walls within a day. How could I swap a daily bath in these salubrious seas for the confinement of a shower? What could replace the breeze in my hair? Not a bedside fan in a stifling box-room, that's for sure. Here, I can gaze in awe for hours at the huge brahminy kite, which nests at the top of Resto and floats on air like a stingray glides along the seabed. In a nursing home I'd be lucky to see a magpie land on my windowsill. Imagine sacrificing a daily sundowner at the beach shack for a weekly bridge tournament. It's not going to happen.

I'm not eighteen anymore, though, and I act accordingly. I don't jump off rocks or try to climb palm trees. I try to limit myself to one beer a day, and only recently went a whole month without a drop of alcohol. I didn't miss it at all – although the next one didn't touch the sides. There was another small scare a few months back, when tests on my thyroid discovered a small lump. A biopsy found it's benign and doctors aren't worried. I also need a small procedure on my right hand's little finger, which has Dupuytren's contracture, a stiffening of the tissue in the palm which causes the finger to bend inwards. Apparently ninety-five per cent of sufferers can trace some Viking bloodline. It must be the Celt in me. It's slightly uncomfortable but doesn't stop me doing anything except pick my nose, and an injection to soften the tissue will straighten the finger.

So, for a seventy-six year old, I reckon I'm in pretty good shape. I keep myself strong pushing a mower, hauling logs off the beach, carrying rocks to Hadrian's Wall or dragging nets filled with coconuts, and the warmth and ozone here are very therapeutic. I'm probably much fitter than most people my age. Earlier this year, I shared three weeks on Resto with my brother, Matthew, a fitness freak who's eighteen years younger than me. He couldn't believe how well I looked – and that means something coming from a real action man: a surf nut, expert skier and very good triathlete. Pablo, as Mick calls him because he was born on Pablo Picasso's birthday, still has a home in Bondi but spends most of his time in the Mexican city of Huatalco – yet another Glasheen who's unafraid to do things differently. Initially he worked with street kids, but now he teaches English at the university. Pab loves to talk, just like our mum and me, and on Resto we talked ourselves into submission whenever he wasn't jogging along the beach, training for his latest marathon. It's the only quality time we have ever spent together and his parting words really touched me. 'You were a fat cat city type when I last saw you, all those years ago,' he said. 'It didn't suit you. This suits you.'

The four surviving Glasheen siblings were able to meet up when we all attended the wedding of Josh, my sister Kate's son. Kate has had a successful career running her own events management company. We call her Mother Theresa because of her selfless generosity of spirit. It was great to be around younger members of my extended family at the wedding, and I like to think that I still have a youthful outlook.

In any case, I often read about strong and healthy people who are aged over one hundred. I just haven't quite figured out what would happen if there was an emergency and the phone wasn't working, as can often happen, especially in the wet season. But I don't want to dwell on what might happen if something goes wrong. I'm too busy planning for what can still go right.

Epilogue

Almost two years after Polly joined me on the island, a visiting English writer woke one morning to find a dead snake just a few metres away from the bed – clearly the dingo's handiwork. Just a few days later, when I banged Polly's bowl at lunchtime for her to come and lick out a can of tuna, there was no sign of her. Polly had acute hearing, so I knew something was up and set off to look for her. My heart sank when I saw a lifeless brown shape on the beach. There was no doubt it was Polly, and the poor girl was dead. On examining her body, I noticed foam around the mouth and a bite mark on a rear leg. Then I spotted the distinctive tracks of a death adder in the sand; perhaps Polly thought snakes were an easy target after that first incident. I buried Polly next to Quassi and I will make a joint headstone one day where they rest side by side. When I posted about Polly's death on social media, the story was picked up by news outlets around the world – an incredible response. Polly's memory will live long, near and far.

It wasn't long before I welcomed a new furry mate to the island, Zeddi. He had been a birthday present from a zoologist friend, Christina Zdenek – hence 'Zeddi'. Christina had heard about Polly's death, and when she was making a film in Cape York about the palm cockatoo she found a small dingo pup all alone in the wild. He was obviously struggling to survive on his own, so she managed to catch him. The rule of thumb is that if you haven't tamed a dingo within ten weeks, it's a lost cause. Zeddi was probably about ten weeks old when I released him on the island, and he ran straight for the hills. The food I left out every night, when dingos are most active, was always gone by morning so I tried the old Native American horse-breaking trick of separating his water from his food to try to starve him out of hiding. But Zeddi was too smart and just found his food elsewhere. At one point, his bowl was untouched for about ten days and I thought he must have died, too, but dingos are savvy survivors and I soon discovered his tracks on the beach. He must have found a soak on the other side of the island for fresh water and would probably have been feeding on lizards.

Mystery Dog, as I called him, wasn't much company, so Tom, the German mental health nurse at the Lockhart clinic, planned to give me a pup from Polly's mother Toya's latest litter with a Siberian husky. The puppy earmarked for me was the cutest little thing you can imagine and I planned to call her Xena, after the Warrior Princess. But then Tom told me that she'd quickly become fond of the water and might put herself in too much danger on Resto until she developed some island instincts. 'Take Toya instead,' he said. 'She's seven years old and great around people. She's basically a lap dog and she already has the smarts to adapt to island life.' Tom thought she would be a perfect companion on the island, just like her daughter, Polly, who had been overprotective of her human friends.

I was just starting to make progress with Toya when Cyclone Trevor struck in March 2019. Toya had been living on

Resto for about two months but I had barely seen her. The second I opened the cage door she bolted off into the bushes, like Zeddi, and, although she almost always came for her food at night, she was invisible by day. John Pritchard even rigged up an infrared camera system while I was in Cairns seeing the doctor. While the footage clearly identified her, the picture was not clear enough to tell whether or not she was thriving on her return to the wild.

Lap dog? Great around people? I began to suspect this dingo was an imposter. But, ever so slowly, I started to gain Toya's trust. If I left food out during the day, always a good few metres from the house so as not to spook her, I'd spot her creeping towards it whenever I wandered off on an errand. Once it had happened on a few consecutive days, next she needed to trust that I wasn't going to catch her. So, when I filled her bowl, I placed a deckchair about twenty metres away and remained there while she ate. Then fifteen metres away, then ten metres. Eventually, she was happy to lie down after her feed and we coexisted in the afternoon sunshine for a half-hour before she moseyed off. *Surely it wouldn't be long before she was eating out of the palm of my hand,* I thought.

Then came the news that Cyclone Trevor was approaching. Even though he was only a Category 2 – less intense than Ingrid and Monica – I still had to prepare, and there was no more time to coax Toya into submission. Although it had been more than a decade since Monica, I was well versed in the routine. I tied the boat to the largest palm, fixed five anchors in the ground, removed the motor, and half-filled her with sand. She was going nowhere. Then I waterproofed the loose items in the house under the tarpaulin, and took a chair over to the shelter in the bushes, along with some bread and soft cheese, water and a couple of beers. As both night-time and the cyclone approached, one thing struck me as different from previous years: the frigate birds and seagulls were still here. Normally all the birds except the plovers disappear long before a front arrives. *If these fellas think it's going to be okay, there's no need for me to worry,* I thought. *Perhaps I'll see this one out in the house.*

The other cyclones I'd experienced had built up gradually, but Trevor just bashed the bloody door in. It was like someone flicked a switch into terrifying overdrive. Ingrid had howled, Monica had screeched, but Trevor roared. I was hunkered down in my bedroom, trying to distract myself with one of my favourite books, *Shantaram,* when I heard an almighty tear. It sounded like an oil tanker scraping down a harbour wall. As I poked my head tentatively out the bedroom door, I saw the kitchen roof was gone. Just then, there was another terrible metallic ripping noise and three sheets of the main roof were wrenched off into the night. It would be a miracle if the tarpaulin held now. I had no option but to try to scramble across to the shed for shelter. Walking was impossible. Crawling was agony, but it was the only way I would survive and, miraculously, I made it to the shed, blinded by a mixture of rain, salt and dirt, and bloody from the knees down.

Trevor's fury did not subside until the morning when, without a wink of sleep, I emerged into a post-apocalyptic landscape. I had to blink several times to make sure I wasn't seeing things. This wasn't my Resto. Half the vegetation had disappeared. My home was unrecognisable. The solar panels had disappeared along with the roof. No power, no internet, no satellite phone. The dining table looked naked without the surrounding kitchen. Miranda and Phyllis were bedraggled and miserable; Miranda had lost an arm. Sodden books and precious photos were strewn around, ruined, the loose tarpaulin flapping apologetically. I almost couldn't face going to the beach, because it would inevitably confirm my worst fear: the boat was lost. On the way there, I discovered holes where some of my cherished frangipanis had once clung to life, and the trailer I used to store spare sheeting had been flicked thirty metres up onto the rocks. The tiki bar was flattened, the barbecue obliterated. And my beautiful beach shack had finally buckled. I felt like a painter whose life's work had been destroyed by vandals. A house that Colin had started to build appeared to be covered in a sprinkling of soft snow. The tidal surge must have been more than a metre, and right at high tide. Quassi and Polly's graves were completely buried but, amazingly, there were already footprints in the fresh sand. Toya had survived and had been on an early reconnaissance mission.

The palm that the boat had been tied to was one of about forty trees to have blown over. About half the tree line of the esplanade was down. The boat had been dragged about thirty metres out and was virtually under the sand. The motor was gone, along with the five anchors. If I wanted to rescue it, I had to work fast and dig out the sand before the tide came back in. Someone could lend me a motor, but sturdy boats were harder to come by. In the calm the sunshine was hot, which would have seemed impossible hours earlier, and I summoned every ounce of energy I had to try and rescue the tinny. As I worked feverishly knee-deep in the water, I could see and feel blacktip sharks, which had been stirred by the cyclone, nibbling around my ankles. When the incoming tide prevented further digging, I turned back for some food, water and a rest.

This time, when I fainted, I landed on the soft sand, not concrete. Groggy and confused, I staggered to the house, drank some water and ate some cold baked beans from a can because the gas lighter and matches were too wet. Then I laid down in the one dry area, my bedroom. But I couldn't sleep. My mind, active as ever, wanted answers. The question I asked myself fourteen years ago during Cyclone Ingrid was: 'How the hell did you end up here?' Now I was asking myself: 'Why the hell are you *still* here?'

It's not the first time I've asked myself that question during my twenty-two years on Resto, but never before with such sincerity. Living on Restoration Island has meant many sacrifices: respect, companionship, love, family. It has also been heartbreaking at times. It was devastating enough to cope with the death of a daughter, but even harder to deal with that grief alone. Suddenly, everything seemed so futile and fragile here, including my own health. After I fainted I realised that, in the chaos of the cyclone, I had forgotten to take my heart medication, which had probably caused my blood pressure to drop dangerously low when I was so tired. Did that mean I was now totally dependent on these pills? What would happen if I ran out and was unable to contact anyone? Had I not fallen on sand, I could have fractured my hip again. With all communications down, it could have been days before I was found. Who knows how long I would've lain unconscious on the beach? Certainly long enough for Boxhead or one of his mates to smell supper. Then there was the clean-up operation, and its cost, to consider. It would take a year to restore the island to any semblance of the radiant haven I had worked so hard at. Why should I bother? After all, I only owned a small share, and could theoretically be evicted at any moment.

'Is it not time to call it a day?'

It was as though the words were spoken by a separate entity. *Snap out of it, man,* I told myself. Where had all this self-pity come from? Had I forgotten what brought me here in the first place? Had all the hardship been for nothing? Had I lost sight of my new purpose, to use my remaining time on the island to create change for the traditional owners?

Having earned the trust of the Lockhart River community the hard way, I could see how much trouble they're in. There's a stifling hopelessness and despair about the place. White fella ways aren't working on so many levels: health, education, housing and employment. A recent Kuuku Ya'u vision statement included these words: 'We will drive our vehicle with our outside friends as the passengers'. That's simply not the case at the moment – it's more like the people of Lockhart River have been run over, scooped off the side of the road and dumped in the back of a vehicle that's running on empty. Non-Aboriginal Australians – 'outside friends' – should hang their heads in shame over the treatment of Indigenous people. That's not an original sentiment, and I'm not just talking about historical abuse, because our approach has actually not changed much. Continually throwing money at the issues that face our Indigenous communities does not work. Don't they say the definition of insanity is repeating the same thing and expecting a different outcome? This money only masks our feelings of guilt and, unless it is targeted to address specific outcomes, it might as well be thrown into the sea. All too often, it's just another box ticked on a sheet of paper. How about we try some practical initiatives: a movie night for the kids; an outdoor swimming pool; more Indigenous teachers; nutritional initiatives at the community farm; a coin-operated launderette or allowing grog at certain times at the old canteen? If I could help in any way to carry on Ricky's legacy with schemes like this, then I would be a very happy man.

More than anything, these proud people don't want handouts. They want to pay their own way with meaningful jobs. That's why a healing eco-retreat, for rich and poor alike, would be perfect for Restoration Island. I could contribute as much or as little as the owners of the retreat see fit. I would love to train as a drug and alcohol counsellor, and serve guests and the local community under the banner of the Erika Ruby Glasheen Foundation. It could be a place to treat any type of addiction. There's not enough awareness about money addiction, for example. The venture would create sustainable jobs for local people, with any surplus revenue going towards specific community programs in Lockhart River – a true social enterprise. Such a retreat might provide just one struggling person enough hope to save them from taking their life. What price could be placed on that outcome? It's my obligation to these proud people, the Kuuku Ya'u, who have allowed me to be a guest on their land for so long, to make it happen.

  First someone will have to come out of the woodwork and buy Colin out, so that ownership of the whole of Restoration Island can effectively be handed to the Kuuku Ya'u. Despite our differences over the years, I'm always civil when Colin spends a few weeks on the island each year. One thing I have learned, throughout my life and especially here, is the importance of forgiveness. That's not to say others are to blame for my troubles, or that I've been purely a victim of circumstances. Far from it. I've made many mistakes, on both personal and professional levels. The lure of wealth was powerful and I was selfish with my time, especially with those who mattered most. And I paid the price, as many do. But now I'm tired of all the negativity that goes with conflict and confrontation – I want to channel those energies into positive outcomes. So I hope beyond hope that a reconciliation with my family is possible. I would gladly meet them anywhere, but imagine the potential for repair if we could all spend a few days here to work through our differences.

There is so much island life can teach us all about living in harmony with nature. There are limited resources here, and there is no option but to make the most efficient use of them. The same goes for our planet – our resources are finite. So, do we really need that bigger car, or the holiday home? Too many of us chase our tails in the exhausting effort to earn more and more money to maintain such extravagances. I learned what is and what isn't important in this life the hard way. The answer isn't for everyone to run off and live on an island, of course. You need a rare kind of resilience to pull this off. But I've found a home where I am so truly content, no amount of money could tempt me away. What would I do with $1 million, $5 million or $50 million now? Where would I go? Cruise around Fiji for the rest of my days? Buy a one-bedroom apartment on Sydney Harbour? I can't think of anything worse.

The grass could – literally – not be any greener anywhere else on Earth, and I'd give my last breath fighting to stay on this piece of land. Where else could I have turned such a desperate situation into such a success? Years ago, I would have judged success on my bank balance or the number of shares I owned. Now I view success as being happy in my own skin. And, while I may not leave Kye with an inheritance that the rest of society deems adequate,

I do hope that he will one day recognise a much richer legacy. Son, have the courage of your own convictions. Never be afraid to take the road less travelled – it's a Glasheen family trait. When I die, I also hope the people of Lockhart River will think of me as someone who made a difference in their lives – for their island has restored me in every way possible. Restoration Island put the pieces back together when I was broken, and added a few of its own to help me become a much better version of myself. No man is an island? That's bullshit.

To answer your question, David Glasheen, it is definitely not time to call it a bloody day.

***

Sleep finally catches up with my thoughts, and I drift away on currents of subconsciousness to my happy place. Here, I climb aboard an inclinator, powered by a wind turbine at the top of the island. It traverses slowly upwards, passing the two walking tracks which lead to sheltered treehouse dwellings and the Incredible Rocks, and stops at a communal meditation platform on the summit with panoramic views over the reef and the hinterland. On the way down, I proudly admire another clam-shaped meditation pavilion nestled into the natural contours of the rocks. A communal barbecue area slots neatly into a clearing with natural ventilation. Beachside units with flowing shade sails blend in seamlessly with the island's natural architecture. At the eastern edge of the north beach, there's an entry point for a tinny, creating a small private beach linked only by a wooden bridge. The paddock lawn is irrigated and jungle-green. The old lime tree bears fruit again and the pumpkin patch is flourishing in the shared garden area. The generator shed showcases stylish pieces of furniture, crafted from wood washed up on the beach. The *Kokkinou* is my resplendent home on the foreshore. Floating around the island like this makes the hairs on the back of my neck stand on end. Then the sound of the phone pierces the dream.

'Davo, it's Paul Piva. Are you okay over there?' he asks. 'It hit us bad here. Nobody hurt, but lots of damage.

The bastard was joined by another low pressure front. Double whammy. Category 4 when it hit land at Cape Direction. That's bloody close to you, eh?'

'Yeah, I'm okay, I suppose,' I tell him. 'Category 4? That explains a lot. I was expecting Category 2. The island's a mess, mate. And my boat's buried. Shit! What time is it? I fell asleep. I need to try and drag her out on the high tide.'

'Leave it until I can come over. The road down to the beach should be cleared soon. At least the phones are working now. Let me know if you need anything,' he says, and hangs up. The light is fading fast but I reckon there's just enough time for me to dig out some more sand and drag the tinny up onto the beach with a new stern line. With my torch to light the way I head for the shore, thankful to have friends like Paul Piva watching my back. *This whole place would fall apart without him,* I tell myself. *No real harm's going to come to me with people of his calibre around.*

For nearly two hours I dig the sand out with a bucket. I almost give up several times and by the end my left hand is one big blister. Maybe Paul's right, it's too much on my own. It's a losing battle. There's no sign that she's going to float and the water is rising quickly. One last try. And then I feel a thud at the back of my knee, powerful enough to knock me onto my back in the water. What the hell was that? I scramble to my feet, grab the torch and, ready to jump into the boat, shine the light into the inky water. Whatever it was, it's circling back this way. I can see a pointy snout. Croc? Then a dorsal fin. Shark? No, gliding gently by is a two metre giant shovelnose ray, the biggest I have ever seen, but as harmless as it is clumsy. It takes me a minute to catch my breath. I'm bushed. But I continue to dig.

Acknowledgements

Dave Glasheen

I would like to thank my old and new friends, particularly in the Far North and especially in the Lockhart River region, who have always been there for me in moments of need throughout my life. And I would like to thank my family, who have also been supportive during the tough times. Last, but not least, I would like to thank Neil Bramwell, who convinced me to write this book, and Affirm Press – Martin, Kieran, Grace and all the team – who helped shape my story.

Neil Bramwell

Big thanks to Martine and Teddy – this book was a team effort. Thanks to Martin, Keiran, Grace and Freya at Affirm, for their support and guidance. And, most of all, thanks to Dave, for placing your amazing story in my hands, your enthusiastic cooperation and generosity of spirit, and for becoming a valued friend. (Not forgetting Polly, for protecting me from that bloody snake.)

What a serious baby! In the arms of my mum, Valda, soon after I was born in August 1943.

My dad, Max, was a giant of a man in many ways.

My hair's still as unruly as it was when I was five years old. My nickname at school was 'Spiky'.

Captain of the rugby team at St Aloysius' Primary School in Kirribilli (front, middle).

My first girlfriend, Brit, was from Norway.

An early date with my wife-to-be, Sylvi, at a wedding reception.

Money talks. Representing my company, Tetra Toys, and Australia at an international trade fair in Kuwait.

Regular family ski holidays were some of the trappings of success – until it all went downhill...

The stock market crash of 1987 wiped more than $10 million off my fortune.

This was the first picture I ever saw of Restoration Island. It was love at first sight and I knew straight away that I wanted to make the island my home.

Total isolation. The sand spit has curved around, as it does in the wet season.

What a view! At the top of the island in my lap-lap. Restoration Rock is in the background.

The lap-lap wasn't always on hand! Unlike the rat-race in Sydney, there's often no need for clothes on the island.

My son, Kye, was conceived on Restoration Island and I flew to Sydney to be at the birth.

Water baby. Kye was in his element playing in the water off Resto. How healthy he looks!

A lovely shot of my elder daughter, Samantha, taken in Sydney soon after I split with her mum, Sylvi.

My mate Phil's trawler, the Blue Riband, hit the reef off the beach and sank when he miscalculated his position one night, six or seven years after I moved to the island. There's always some drama around the corner.

My beautiful daughter Erika, busy as ever. Here she is working alongside the local Aboriginal community of Lockhart River and doing what she did best: nourishing people.

Outside the eating area of the house that Hippy Richard helped me build. This image was used in a Cape York calendar. I was Miss October!

Man's best friend. Bath time with the magnificent Quassi, who became my constant companion for more than a decade after I lost my first dog to a spider bite. Brian Cassey Photographer.

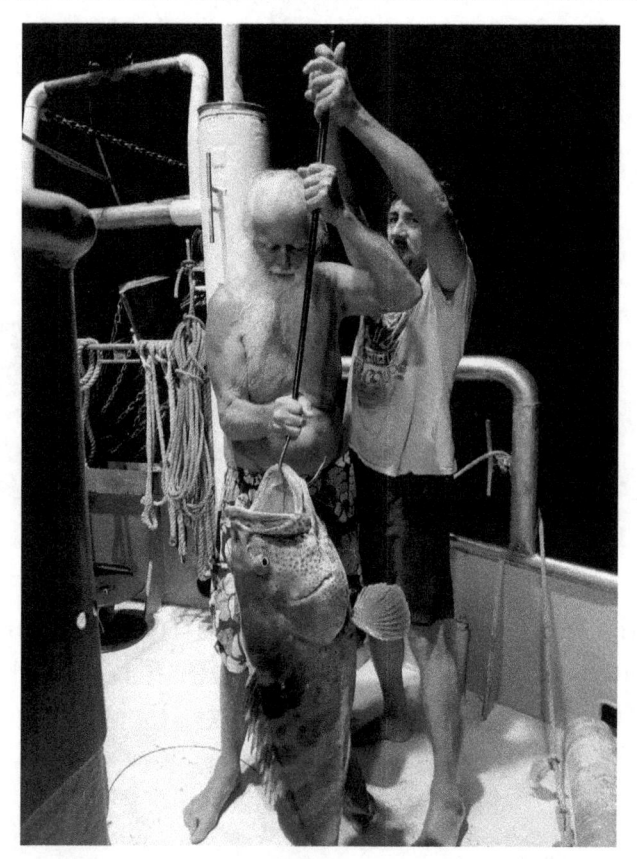

Hooked. One of my fisho mates helps me land a spotted cod. The trawler boys often take me out fishing when there's a full moon.

Heading back to the mainland in my tinny, which is my lifeline whenever I need essentials from Lockhart River.

A rare catch-up with my brothers, Mick (left) and Matthew, for a family wedding in 2018 when Matthew was visiting from Mexico.

Polly, the beautiful dingo who replaced Quassi, was always ready to greet me on the beach for a dance.

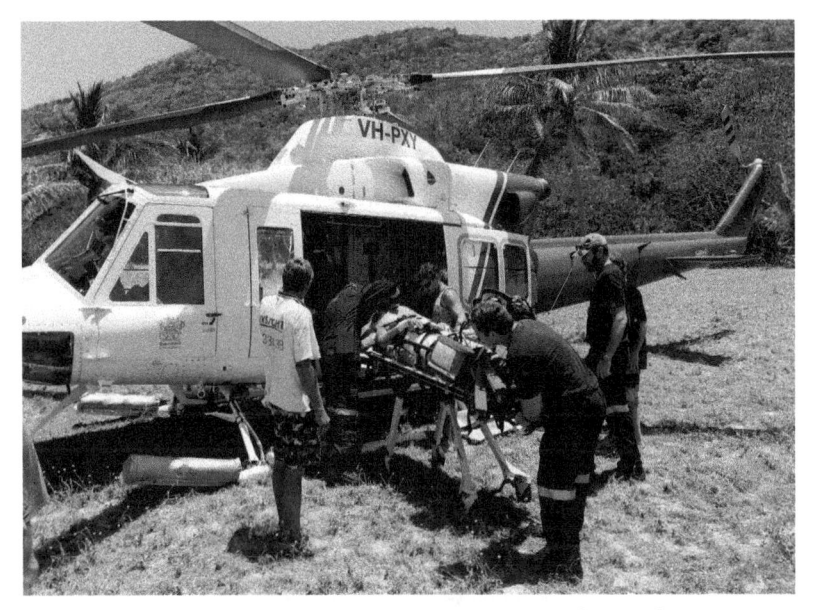

Being airlifted from the island after fracturing my hip.

A breath of fresh air. Looking out over the Coral Sea and Great Barrier Reef from the southern tip of the island's spine.

My pride and joy: the beach shack. With Polly, and a cold beer for company, it's the best way to end another hot day – total relaxation.

The sign says it all. There's always a warm welcome on Resto. You never know who will drop by – from the chairman of McDonald's to Hollywood superstar, Russell Crowe.

Miranda, the first of the two mannequins to live with me on Resto, does not like to be left out, so I often wheel her down to the beach to share a sunset. Brian Cassey Photographer.

Devastated. The beach shack was reduced to rubble by Cyclone Trevor in 2019. The clean-up operations are ongoing.

Pure isolation. Clear blue waters for as far as the eye can see.

Sun, sand and sea. This is the life...

Back Cover Material

'Dave Glasheen is a 21st-century Robinson Crusoe ... his story is wild, eccentric, romantic and sad. Dave changed my life and maybe, just maybe, his story will also change yours.' – Ben Fogle

Dave Glasheen's life began spiralling out of control after he lost his family's vast fortune in the stock market crash of 1987. After a series of catastrophes, he needed to take drastic measures to restore himself. Opting out of the rat race, he cast himself away to a deserted island off the north-east tip of Australia, as far off the grid as was humanly possible. He has lived there ever since.

One annual supermarket shop, a sketchy internet connection and enough ingredients for a home-brew satisfy Dave's material needs. He catches fish, traps rainwater and cooks on an open fire. For company he tames dingoes, meets with friends from the Aboriginal community 40 kilometres away and entertains drop-ins such as Russell Crowe sailing past on his honeymoon. Then there's Dave's running feud with Boxhead, an antisocial saltwater crocodile who just won't leave him in peace.

BETWEEN HEARTBREAK AND HAIR-RAISING ADVENTURES, DAVE HAS FOUND HAPPINESS ON RESTORATION ISLAND. BRIMMING WITH HUMOUR, ECCENTRICITY AND HARD-EARNED WISDOM, *THE MILLIONAIRE CASTAWAY* WILL GIVE YOU A WHOLE NEW VIEW ON LIFE.

Lightning Source UK Ltd.
Milton Keynes UK
UKHW020611100722
405623UK00004B/452

9 780369 356710